OECD PROCEEDINGS

THE LOCAL DIMENSION
OF WELFARE-TO-WORK
An International Survey

ORGANISATION FOR ECONOMIC CO-OPERATION AND DEVELOPMENT

ORGANISATION FOR ECONOMIC CO-OPERATION AND DEVELOPMENT

Pursuant to Article 1 of the Convention signed in Paris on 14th December 1960, and which came into force on 30th September 1961, the Organisation for Economic Co-operation and Development (OECD) shall promote policies designed:

- to achieve the highest sustainable economic growth and employment and a rising standard of living in Member countries, while maintaining financial stability, and thus to contribute to the development of the world economy;
- to contribute to sound economic expansion in Member as well as non-member countries in the process of economic development; and
- to contribute to the expansion of world trade on a multilateral, non-discriminatory basis in accordance with international obligations.

The original Member countries of the OECD are Austria, Belgium, Canada, Denmark, France, Germany, Greece, Iceland, Ireland, Italy, Luxembourg, the Netherlands, Norway, Portugal, Spain, Sweden, Switzerland, Turkey, the United Kingdom and the United States. The following countries became Members subsequently through accession at the dates indicated hereafter: Japan (28th April 1964), Finland (28th January 1969), Australia (7th June 1971), New Zealand (29th May 1973), Mexico (18th May 1994), the Czech Republic (21st December 1995), Hungary (7th May 1996), Poland (22nd November 1996) and Korea (12th December 1996). The Commission of the European Communities takes part in the work of the OECD (Article 13 of the OECD Convention).

FOREWORD

The papers and much of the material for this book were originally presented to a conference on 'The Local Dimension of Welfare-to-Work' held in Sheffield, United Kingdom (UK) on 18-19 November 1998. The conference was organised by the OECD Local Economic and Employment Development (LEED) Programme in collaboration with the Department for Education and Employment (DfEE) in England. It was held at the invitation of the UK Minister for Employment, Andrew Smith, with the participation of the Secretary of State for Education and Employment, David Blunkett, and drew together more than 100 delegates from 23 countries, including OECD analysts, national policy-makers, local practitioners and other experts. The aim was to debate the design and implementation of welfare-to-work solutions to unemployment and labour market exclusion and to examine the role that local approaches should play in these policies. The United Kingdom's flagship New Deal programme for tackling unemployment and integrating disadvantaged youth and excluded groups was presented to international delegates. It is a programme that builds heavily on the provision of 'local solutions for local needs', an emphasis that is shared with welfare-to-work initiatives in a number of other OECD countries. There were further presentations of welfare-to-work initiatives from Australia, Canada, France, Italy and the United States and an extensive debate that enabled delegates to compare and contrast approaches and to assess what works.

This publication provides a synthesis of the discussions that took place and presents the main papers prepared. It aims to draw out some main points of policy advice to central government policy-makers and local practitioners involved in designing and delivering welfare-to-work programmes. The lessons fall in three areas. Firstly, there is a need to be more innovative than has been the case in the past. This can be achieved by giving local agencies more flexibility within a clear and supportive central framework. Secondly, partnership working should be enhanced at the local level and the private sector fully engaged. Thirdly, there are a number of promising policy instruments that can be employed at the local level, including social enterprises, personal advisers, placements for training-in-work and methods to encourage labour mobility.

The publication was prepared by Jon Potter of the OECD LEED Programme Secretariat based on the contributions of all the participants in the conference. Sergio Arzeni, Head of the OECD LEED Programme, and Robert Butcher, Divisional Manager for TECs and Lifelong Learning at the Department for Education and Employment (DfEE) in Sheffield directed the preparation of the conference and publication. In addition, John Doherty, Danny McFall and Luisa Papa of DfEE, and Sylvain Giguère of the OECD LEED Programme all played a central role in preparing the conference. Chapters 6-11 were prepared by independent authors and the views expressed do not necessarily reflect those of the DfEE or of the OECD and its Member countries.

TABLE OF CONTENTS

PART I

LOCAL APPROACHES TO WELFARE-TO-WORK.
AN ASSESSMENT OF RECENT INNOVATIONS

PART II

CASE STUDY PAPERS

Boxes

CHAPTER 1
INTRODUCTION

The concept of welfare-to-work: an overview of international trends and issues

Combating long term unemployment and welfare dependency is a key policy challenge

This book deals with one of the most important current policy challenges for OECD countries; countering long term unemployment, youth unemployment and the danger of social exclusion. Governments must respond to these challenges if they are to maintain the social fabric and social cohesion of our societies. It was to explore these issues that the OECD launched a major *Jobs Study* in the early 1990s, whose conclusions were endorsed by OECD Ministers in 1994. The central finding of this work was that there is a pressing need to deal with the inability of OECD economies and workforces to adjust sufficiently rapidly to changing circumstances and thus to prevent the emergence of unemployment, and particularly long term unemployment. A wide-ranging programme of actions was proposed, including the expansion and refocusing of active labour market policies, improving labour force skills and competencies and reforming welfare benefit systems. Although there is no precise definition, the term welfare-to-work has been used by many politicians and commentators to refer to such policies, where their aim is to assist welfare recipients into the labour market. During the 1990s there has indeed been a significant movement to introduce this type of measure. However, governments still have much to learn from each other on the practicalities of implementing effective welfare-to-work policies.

There is a need to adjust welfare systems to new labour market conditions

What is clear, and has been one of the key driving forces behind the introduction of welfare-to-work strategies, is that traditional welfare systems are no longer adequate to the social, economic and labour market circumstances we find today. The welfare systems and employment policies developed in the 1960s and 1970s were based on the provision of passive income support, or a basic safety net to help people experiencing temporary labour market difficulties. Since that period, OECD countries have witnessed the emergence of high and persistent unemployment, especially in continental Europe, rising inactivity rates and an ageing of societies. This dependency leads to a heavy financial cost that constrains other public investments. At the same time, new technologies, intense competition and globalisation have changed labour market needs and in particular have been associated with an increased demand for skills and more labour flexibility. However, traditional welfare and employment policy models have not provided the intensive support required to help those who are detached from the labour market to improve their skills and employability and overcome other barriers to employment. Moreover many of the work incentives and signals provided by our welfare systems can also be criticised for discouraging people from taking work and encouraging long term welfare dependence.

Active labour market policies (ALMPs) and incentive changes will help

The introduction of well managed active labour market policies (ALMPs), such as job matching, training and employment subsidies, together with changes in tax and benefits incentives can help in reducing long term unemployment and combating exclusion. Governments are therefore piloting a number of new approaches in these areas. ALMP measures can help raise the skills and employability of welfare recipients and provide channels for them to access job vacancies. However, several studies suggest that often they do not achieve their objectives for reasons such as inappropriate delivery mechanisms, lack of tailoring to the needs of specific groups, inappropriate financing or a lack of local employment opportunities (OECD, 1996a). It is therefore important that lessons are learned for effective management and policy design. It is also important that incentives within the tax and benefit systems are appropriately designed so that they do not act as unintentional barriers to people taking work. For example, rules that prevent people from returning to benefits if they leave their jobs within a short period of starting or the imposition of high taxes on low paid jobs can discourage people on welfare from taking work.

There are differences between OECD countries in the measures introduced . . .

Of course, there are many differences between OECD Member governments in concrete terms in the way that they are going about introducing measures to help bridge the gap between welfare and work. There are significant differences, for example, in the extent to which Member countries are involved in adjusting their tax and benefits regimes to increase work incentives. Indeed this is the source of much of the controversy to be found in current welfare-to-work debates. On the one hand the United States, the United Kingdom and Australia have each introduced compulsion to certain parts of their welfare-to-work programmes. This involves imposing a requirement on unemployed people to undertake activities to improve their employability or to carry out work of community benefit in return for welfare payments. The term 'workfare' is sometimes used to describe this approach. On the other hand, many of the continental European countries in particular are quite strongly opposed to the idea of suppressing existing welfare benefits in order to induce a person to take work. They nonetheless share a focus on the 'activation' of support to the long term unemployed and welfare recipients, in terms of targeting ALMPs on these groups. There are also differences in the policy tools that are in place in different countries and even between different localities within countries. For example, in France and Italy there is strong emphasis on job creation measures through social enterprises and the creation of new activities of community benefit. In the United Kingdom and the United States policy focuses more on improving employability and job search.

. . . but also common challenges in policy development

Whilst there are differences in context, there are also many common challenges for the implementation of welfare-to-work policies for tackling youth and long term unemployment in OECD countries. Their approaches are being driven by the need to reduce welfare costs and to adapt provision to new labour market needs. In doing so, an important common challenge is to determine how much freedom to give to local actors whilst at the same time providing an appropriate national framework and limiting the emergence of inequities, funding problems or skill deficiencies for example. Another common challenge is to create structures that harness the potential benefits of partnership between the public, private and voluntary sectors without creating problems of co-ordination or legitimacy. All areas are also seeking to identify work experience, training, guidance and job match tools that are effective in helping excluded people to find work.

The United Kingdom: an interesting example of welfare-to-work reform

The UK welfare-to-work strategy aims to address the problem of the persistence of high unemployment and exclusion amongst certain groups of people and in certain localities even in a relatively healthy national labour market in which quite large numbers of jobs are being created. The total number of people employed in the United Kingdom recently reached its highest ever level and overall around 6 million people move into a new job every year. However, against this background, there are mismatches between the jobs available and

11

the people and skills to fill them. Long term unemployment is still too high and is heavily concentrated in large cities. Moreover, nearly 3 million children are growing up in work-less households. Some groups of individuals, young people without basic skills and motivation, men over 50, disabled people, lone parents, continue to have poor labour market prospects and the longer the period of their unemployment, the more difficult it is for them to find work.

A comprehensive programme has been put in place

In seeking to address the problems of those who have become detached from the labour market, a strategy has been put in place with the following four main elements:

- Investment in education and skills.

- Reform of the tax and benefit system including a Working Families Tax Credit.

- A national minimum wage.

- Active labour market policy initiatives targeted on those who are detached from the labour market and measures to regenerate the poorest and most disadvantaged communities.

The New Deal programme is one of the keys to this welfare-to-work strategy, representing a new and concerted effort to apply much more extensively the principles of active labour market policy to the long term unemployed, the young unemployed and other excluded groups (Box 1). Its aim is to provide guidance, work experience and training that will not simply move people off benefit and into work, but will also improve their skills and long term employability. Recent figures show that in the first year of the New Deal for 18-24 year olds nearly 70,000 young people who were previously unemployed for at least six months moved into sustained jobs, of which approximately 56,000 were unsubsidised jobs and approximately 13,000 subsidised. Some 64,000 received training or work experience to improve their employability, with 12,400 on the Environment Task Force, 13,100 on the Voluntary Sector Option and 39,100 in Full Time Education and Training. Some 740 young people had been given help by the New Deal in acquiring the skills for self-employment, with 108 moving to independent employment. In the New Deal for the Long Term Unemployed, 10,500 people had moved into sustained jobs by the end of March 1999. Nearly 50,000 employers had signed Employers Agreements by the end of April 1999.

There are a number of policy challenges for implementation of this programme

The UK welfare-to-work programme aims to tackle social exclusion and benefit dependency and bring economic benefits by helping to raise the sustainable level of employment. It is critical to this effort to improve the functioning of the labour market so that high levels of unemployment do not persist alongside large numbers of job vacancies. Three areas that have been identified by United Kingdom authorities as needing further policy development in this respect are:

1. *Improving labour mobility.* Widening the area that people travel to seek work would increase their chances of finding a job and would help to meet skill shortages, especially in London and other large cities. The indications are that many people are willing to travel further given the opportunities and incentives. Travel concessions have already made an important contribution to the New Deal for 18-24 Year Olds and touch screen technology also seems to encourage wider job search. These innovations need to be consolidated and extended.

2. *Matching vacancies and job seekers.* This appears to be the key to getting people off the carousel from benefit into work and back again as well as to helping employers to fill their vacancies more efficiently. The United Kingdom is experimenting with centralised telephone links, or call-centres, to deal with vacancy information more effectively. IT systems and the training of personal advisers are also being improved. Again it is important to develop these tools.

3. *Using the Internet for the benefit of target groups.* The Internet opens up the possibility of job-seekers getting access to many more vacancies and employers selecting from many more candidates for the vacancies they have. The risk is that those who are detached from the labour market, the New Deal priority groups, might lose out. It is important to act to make sure that does not happen.

Box 1. The UK New Deal

The New Deal is at the heart of the United Kingdom Government's strategy to tackle long term unemployment and social exclusion, with substantial funding commitments of some UK£3.5 billion over four years. It aims to increase peoples' employability and help them find work. It is made up of a number of different strands.

The New Deal for 18-24 year olds. This was put into place nationally in April 1998, and accounts for some 70% of all New Deal funding. The target group, the young long term unemployed, includes some young people experiencing multiple disadvantage. The government has set a target of finding work for 250,000 young long term unemployed people between its launch and the end of the lifetime of this parliament.

An important feature of the programme is its initial 'Gateway' period under which young people are given individual counselling for up to four months, including support and encouragement to apply for jobs (a majority of those who move into work go to unsubsidised jobs). In identifying and responding to individual circumstances and needs, the Gateway aims:

- To help those who are already well equipped to find jobs to do so.

- To provide appropriate help for those who, with the necessary support, could quickly improve their immediate job prospects - and then help them to find jobs.

- For those who take up the subsequent New Deal options, to provide the support and help required to enable them to make appropriate choices and to prepare them to gain the maximum benefit from the option in terms of developing skills, employability and job prospects.

During the Gateway, young people can also be referred to a very wide range of provision designed to help them to find work and to help them to overcome any specific difficulties that are making it harder for them to obtain and retain employment. For example, some young people will take advantage of short basic skills courses during the Gateway; some will be matched with an independent mentor to help them to maximise the benefit they gain from New Deal; and some will be referred to specialist agencies to help them tackle such problems as drug or alcohol dependency, or homelessness, at the same time as they seek work and aim to improve their employability.

Box 1. (continued)

Following the Gateway, if the participants are not job-ready or fail to find a 'normal' job they are required to take up one of the following options:

- A job, subsidised for up to 6 months, with one day a week of good quality training leading to a recognised qualification, receiving a wage at least equivalent to the subsidy. The subsidy is UK£60 a week for 6 months plus UK£750 training subsidy. This option can include support to become self-employed.

- Work for up to 6 months with the voluntary sector, including one day a week of training, a work placement to benefit the local community, and receiving a wage or an allowance.

- Work and training for up to 6 months with an organisation or project that is part of a new Environmental Task Force, including a work placement to contribute to the improvement of the environment, receiving a wage or an allowance.

- Full time education and training for up to 12 months, including accreditation of key skills, support for basic skills, job search skills and training in a realistic work environment or work experience with an employer, receiving an allowance equivalent to usual benefit.

Each young person is allocated a personal adviser to resolve problems and help with childcare is available. Advice and financial assistance is also available for those who want to take up self-employment.

The New Deal for the Long term Unemployed. This was launched nationally in June 1998 and is aimed at people aged 25 and over who have been unemployed for 2 years or more. It offers personal advisers, a subsidised job, full-time education and training and continuing job search guidance. It does not involve the withdrawal of benefit for people who refuse an option. At the end of November 1998 a range of pilots were introduced to test the effects of extending support to a wider group of those unemployed for over 18 months or 12 months in some areas. Whilst it would be desirable to extend support to all these groups, it has to be recognised that the numbers of people participating in policy are much greater if the intervention is an early one. The flow past the 18-month point is only one-half of that of the flow past the 12-month point. These pilots are therefore testing the effectiveness of intervention relative to expenditure at those different points in time.

Box 1. (continued)

The New Deal for Lone Parents. This was launched nation-wide in October 1998. All lone parents on income support with children of school age are offered a personalised service on a voluntary basis. There is a series of interviews with a New Deal Personal Adviser to discuss job vacancies, training and childcare and to advise on benefits to make sure that work pays. There is also job search and training support and an aftercare service once they have found work.

The New Deal for Disabled People. This is currently being piloted. It offers an individually tailored personal advisor service for disabled people who want to find work. Six personal adviser pilots are being run by the public Employment Service and six by the voluntary sector. They are trained to provide specialist advice to disabled people and their employers to help disabled people retain or return to work. They can provide access to a range of extra support, for example by arranging access to appropriate retraining.

The New Deal for Partners of the Unemployed. In the past the benefits system has assumed that partners of unemployed people cannot or do not want to work, denying them help and opportunities. This was launched early in 1999 in order to provide support to this group. Partners of people who have been unemployed for six months or more will have the opportunity, on a voluntary basis, to receive guidance and advice on job search from specialist Employment Service Personal Advisers. At an initial interview Advisers will look at how to break down barriers to employment through discussing Employment Service programmes, training opportunities, in-work benefits and where appropriate information on local childcare provision.

A parallel initiative, the New Deal for Communities is being piloted in 17 small and severely deprived communities, to tackle unemployment within a broader programme of neighbourhood renewal. There are also other wider programmes targeted on particular geographical areas with severe and multiple economic and social problems, such as the Single Regeneration Budget.

In the United States some deep-seated welfare-to-work reforms have been introduced at federal and state levels, including time limits on the receipt of federal welfare payments and a shift towards a philosophy of 'work-first'.

In the United States, the 1996 Personal Responsibility and Work Opportunity Reconciliation Act (PRWORA) significantly changed federal welfare policy for low-income families with children, building on and expanding earlier state-level reforms. Under the main welfare support programme, Temporary Assistance for Needy Families (TANF), federal welfare funding is now provided as a block grant to states, and is no longer tied to the delivery of specific federal programmes. Under this system states have much greater flexibility in determining how to use the TANF funding, although they must meet certain federal requirements in terms of the reduction of welfare registers and levels of participation in work or work-related activities. One important result of these changes is that whereas previous programmes often focused on training and skills development activities, with the aim of improving the subsequent chances of welfare recipients finding work, there is now a strong emphasis on getting welfare recipients quickly into work, known as 'work-first'. To make 'work-first' successful, states are increasing their effort in the area of client guidance and support services. The federal government has also made available a welfare-to-work block grant to provide additional resources for innovative programmes from organisations and partnerships operating below state level. Box 2 describes TANF and the new 'work-first' approach.

There have been substantial falls in United States welfare rolls since the enactment of the reforms

Many of the changes are still relatively recent and there is a lack of comprehensive evaluation evidence on their impacts. Moreover, there are no federal requirements for states to report on the status of former welfare recipients, making it difficult to effectively track outcomes at national level. What is known is that there has been a dramatic fall in the welfare claimant numbers in the United States since the introduction of the new welfare-to-work programmes. From its peak in March 1994, the national caseload for AFDC and its replacement TANF decreased by 43% to September 1998, or from some 5 million 2.7 million families. A large part of the fall occurred after the enactment of the federal reform in August 1996, with the national caseload declining by 32% between January 1997 and December 1998. It is difficult to assess what part of this decline is the result of the programmes themselves and what part is due to an improvement in economic conditions.

A majority of leavers appear to be in employment, but there are concerns about the quality and durability of some of the jobs found . . .

Several studies suggest that most people leaving the welfare registers are in employment at the time of follow-up. Studies in seven states, reviewed by GAO (1999a) indicate that between 61% and 71% of adults in families remaining off the welfare register were employed at the time of follow-up. However, the percentages of families who initially left welfare and then returned to the rolls were significant, ranging from 19% after 3 months in Maryland to 30% after 15 months in Wisconsin. Another review of twelve United States studies, by Brauner and Loprest (1999), gave similar employment rates of between 51% and 75% at the time of follow-up, but according to both reviews the average incomes of these workers are relatively low and may not raise family incomes much above poverty levels. There is also the danger that many leavers may return to welfare.

. . . and a number of policy challenges are still to be met

The recent OECD review of the public employment service in the United States (OECD, 1999a) identifies six main issues and challenges for its current welfare reforms:

1. *Supporting welfare recipients to find permanent, well-paid jobs.* Although it should be possible for many welfare recipients to move into work, a greater challenge will be to help people stay in work for a sustained period of time and lift them out of poverty.

2. M*eeting the challenge of a downturn.* Evidence suggests that much of the recent reduction in welfare caseloads are the result of favourable general economic conditions as opposed to changes in welfare systems themselves. In less favourable conditions welfare caseloads may rise steeply. In such conditions states could find it difficult to the needs of welfare clients under the new work based systems.

3. *Encouraging skills development.* A key principle behind welfare reform is a 'work-first' approach with a 'learn later' goal. However, when there is a down-turn it may become very difficult for low skilled welfare recipients to find jobs.

4. *Evaluating the new programmes.* Evaluation will be difficult because there are many new programmes and they aim to bring about long term behavioural changes. States will need to collect good administrative data to support evaluation.

5. *Cost shifting.* To meet work-participation requirements, states could try to shift some of the caseload to programmes funded at local or federal levels of government. They could also shift some of the case load to their own separately administered programmes. It remains unclear what will happen if large numbers of welfare recipients reach their time limit.

6. *Access to support services.* A key issue whether there is adequate childcare capacity to meet the needs of all those people moving into work or work based activities. Welfare recipients are also likely to face transportation problem which can be exacerbated by non-standard working hours.

Box 2. Temporary Assistance for Needy Families (TANF) and 'work-first' in the United States

During the late 1980s and early 1990s the traditional welfare system in the United States came under much criticism for its rising cost, its perceived adverse effects on attitudes to work and its inability to tackle poverty. In response, from the late 1980s a number of states began to introduce work-related activities to their welfare programmes under federal waivers that allowed experimentation with job placement, work requirement and work incentive approaches. An increasing number of such measures were introduced in the 1990s. However, the decisive change was the introduction of the 1996 federal welfare law, the Personal Responsibility and Work Opportunity Reconciliation Act (PRWORA). This ended automatic entitlement to welfare benefits for families with children, which previously had been guaranteed by the Aid to Families with Dependent Children (AFDC) programme. The replacement programme, called Temporary Assistance for Needy Families (TANF), was designed to help families reduce their dependence on welfare and move to self-sufficiency. TANF allocations to states are now paid as block grants, which states can use to support the programmes that they design within the remit of the federal legislation.

Under the new arrangements states must impose certain federal requirements on participation in work or work based activities by welfare recipients. For most adults a maximum lifetime limit of five years must be imposed on the receipt of federal welfare assistance under TANF, and states are free to impose a lower limit. Furthermore, a system of penalties has been introduced whereby states lose part of their welfare block grant from federal authorities if they do not meet given requirements for the proportion of TANF welfare recipients leaving the welfare register or undertaking work-related activities. By 2002, 50% of the heads of single parent families claiming welfare support must be engaged in work or work-related activities and 90% of adults in two parent families. Eligible work-related activities include subsidised employment, on-the-job training, work experience, community service and vocational training.

Box 2. (continued)

 The legislation allows states and local areas to use TANF funds for a wide range of support activities including employer subsidies and public sector employment programmes as well as employability activities such as job search/job placement, job readiness, education and training and work experience. States are also free to impose financial sanctions on families refusing to co-operate. The practices themselves vary widely between states, and individual states and local areas may choose not to implement all of the activities allowable. Some cities and states have introduced controversial 'Workfare' employment programmes where welfare recipients are required to work in community service jobs as a condition of eligibility for benefits and services. Almost all states have moved towards a 'work-first' philosophy in their welfare programmes where work activities are favoured over training and skills development programmes for the unemployed and 'social contracts' or other personal responsibility agreements are enforced in which recipients agree to take specific steps towards self-sufficiency.

There have also been some radical changes affecting the delivery of employment services in Australia, involving the contracting-out of previously publicly delivered programmes

Welfare-to-work measures in Australia have been implemented against the background of radical institutional reforms put in place in 1997. In the past, most employment services were delivered through the local offices of the public employment service, the Commonwealth Employment Service (CES). Since 1997, a new market has been created in which referral and placement previously carried out by the CES are contracted out to a network of competing agencies, known as Employment Service Providers (ESPs), which includes a new semi-public body set up to take over the services of the CES. These agencies can provide a range of employment services, from matching job seekers to vacancies on the national register, to training provision or organisation of work experience placements. Part of their fee is made as an up-front payment, with the rest dependent on achieving certain outcomes, and in particular the completion of a period of six months without claiming unemployment benefit. The residual unemployment registration functions of CES have also been integrated with the local welfare administration services of the Department for Social Security (DSS) to form a single first point of contact or one-stop-shop for the unemployed, named Centrelink. As well as administering welfare payments they will now register job-seekers, provide self-help job search facilities and refer people requiring further assistance to providers in the new employment services market.

Against this new institutional background, Australian employment policy has introduced the concept of 'mutual obligation' and more rigorous work and job search requirements.

Under the concept of mutual obligation, Australian job seekers who have been receiving benefit payments for at least six months are now asked to meet some additional Activity Test by participating in an activity while they look for work, for example training or community work (Box 3). Unemployment payments are conditional on meeting the requirements of these Activity Tests. The aim is to make welfare recipients more active in their job search and in improving their employability. Key issues in the Australian case are how far the new activity requirements will help stimulate more people to find jobs, and how well the new contracting-out system will work in providing the services required to help people, and particularly disadvantaged people, bridge the gap to the labour market.

Box 3. The Australian Mutual Obligation and Work for the Dole initiatives

A key recent innovation in Australia has been the introduction of the principle of 'mutual obligation' for young people aged 18-24 years who have been unemployed for six months. This has imposed additional obligations for the receipt of unemployment allowances to require young people to look for work more actively and to participate in activities that will improve their skills and work habits. From July 1998 young people have been expected to fulfil their obligation by participating in an activity drawn from the following menu of options:

Part-time work - A minimum of six hours a week for at least 14 out of 26 weeks.

Voluntary work - A minimum of six hours a week for at least 14 out of 26 weeks.

Education or training - A minimum of six hours contact a week in an accredited course. Completion of a course of at least 14 weeks, or a full semester for longer courses, is required or supplementation with another activity for shorter courses.

Box 3. (continued)

Relocation - Movement to another area which has a higher demand for the young person's skills or significantly better employment prospects, followed by 14 weeks of more intensive job search.

Literacy and numeracy training - Up to two semesters involving 6 to 10 hours of activity a week. Expected number of places in 1998-99: 12,000.

Work for the Dole - Participation for the length of the project (generally six months) involving on average 12 to 15 hours of activity a week. Expected number of places in 1998-99: 20,000.

FLEX 2 - job search training - Participation for the length of the course (usually three weeks) followed by 14 weeks of more intensive job search. Expected number of places in 1998-99: 20,400.

FLEX 3 - intensive support - Up to two years of individualised job preparation and support. Expected number of places in 1998-99: 36,000.

Job Placement, Employment and Training (JPET) programme - Participation for the length of the programme with contact hours per week varying depending on individual need. Young people who cease to participate in JPET before the end of 26 weeks will need to undertake another mutual obligation activity. Expected number of places in 1998-99: 20,200.

Green Corps - Green Corps participants do not have to satisfy mutual obligation requirements while receiving a training allowance. Expected number of places in 1998-99: 300.

In addition, 1000 mutual obligation clients were to be assisted under the Mentoring pilot programme in 1998-99 with a further 6,500 young people to be provided with career counselling. Career counselling and mentoring should supplement mutual obligation activities and cannot satisfy a young person's obligation by themselves.

In 1998-99 the total government budget for these initiatives was A$112.4 million for 56,500 participant places. In the next four years to 2002 the budget is A$465.5 million for 206,500 places. The first four activities are self-funded by the participants.

Box 3. (continued)

The Work for the Dole programme is a particularly interesting and new initiative with substantial local involvement. It funds community projects in activities such as heritage, the environment, community care, tourism, sport, provision of community services and restoration of community facilities. Funding is provided for quality projects specifically targeting young

unemployed people and at the same time providing the opportunity for older workers to participate. Projects are located primarily in areas of high youth unemployment. The objectives of the Work for the Dole Programme are to foster work habits and attitudes, improve participants' self esteem and contribute to local communities by the establishment of projects of value to the community. The projects are sponsored by local government and community groups (charities, religious groups and local associations). Work for the Dole had a budget of A\$61.8 million in 1998-99 and A\$259.5 for the period 1998-2002.

In France, there is less emphasis on the compulsion aspects of welfare-to-work, but rather a much stronger focus on the creation of new employment opportunities directly for excluded people

One aspect of in the United Kingdom, the United States and Australia is the notion of a 'contract' requiring people to undertake work activities or improve their employability in return for the receipt of benefits. There is much less emphasis on this in the French case. Thus income support assistance, the *Revenu Minimum d'Insertion (RMI)*, is generally not made conditional on undertaking any corresponding activities. Instead RMI claimants are offered the possibility of participating in a range of ALMPs (*Insertion par l'économique*), in particular vocational training, to get them back in the labour market. The distinctive feature of the French approach is the strong emphasis that has recently been placed on the creation of jobs directly for groups of 60

people who experience exclusion. The jobs are created through exploitation of new activities that meet new social needs. A major strand of this job creation approach is the innovative new programme to create jobs for young people in new service areas described in Box 4, *Nouveaux Services - Emplois Jeunes*. There is a similar programme for more disadvantaged long term unemployed youths and adults, *Contrats Emploi Solidarité*. A third strand is support for social enterprises, operating at the boundary between the public and the private sectors, which provide work opportunities for disadvantaged people at the same time as a product or service of community value.

The success of the job creation approach will largely depend on how sustainable the jobs are in the longer term

The key test of this approach will be the durability of the jobs created. Whilst the jobs are initially subsidised, the objective of policy is to help new markets and enterprises emerge that in the long run can provide sustainable employment. In addition, concerns can be raised about the possibility that people working in these subsidised posts will be perceived badly by employers and will find it difficult to get jobs in the mainstream labour market.

Box 4. The *'Nouveaux Services - Emplois Jeunes'* programme in France

In October 1997 a new employment programme was introduced in France, *Nouveaux Services - Emplois Jeunes* (New Services - Youth Jobs). It represents a significant break from previous programmes in that its emphasis is neither on providing income support nor on improving the employability of severely disadvantaged people (who are the target of the *contrats emploi-solidarité*). Instead it aims to create entirely new jobs that will employ large numbers of young people on a long term basis whilst also providing socially useful services.

The target is to create some 350,000 jobs for young people, aged 18-26 years, during the period 1997-2000. At the beginning of 1997, nearly 600,000 young people under 26 years old were looking for jobs in France, with a corresponding rate of unemployment of more than 26%. Of these, some 47% had virtually no secondary education qualifications. The programme aims to allow these people to get jobs quite quickly and to acquire recognised professional training whilst undertaking them.

The opportunity to create this employment without displacing existing jobs stems from recent social changes, for example in terms of lifestyles and age structures, which are leading to the emergence of new social needs and expectations that are not currently satisfied. These new needs are mainly in the areas of housing, health, welfare, security, education, environment, leisure, sport and culture. Without public support a fully developed market has not been able to emerge for these services because they are in areas that are not immediately profitable, where demand is latent or poorly-defined or where supply is poorly structured. The programme is therefore based on a concern to encourage the emergence and development of new services through public support for youth employment in these activities.

Voluntary organisations, local government authorities and public bodies are called on to develop projects for job creation in these services and national education and police services are strong contributors. They receive a substantial public wage subsidy over a period of five years in order to make the activities viable. The annual amount of assistance given per job is relatively high, at approximately 92,000 Francs per year.

Box 4. (continued)

By the end of March 1999, some 175,000 jobs had been created in the programme, towards a target of 350,000 by the end of the year 2000. The main activities developed are in para-education, sports, mediation, safety, the preservation and enhancement of natural spaces, recycling and the protection of cultural and historical heritage.

Because of the very high subsidies offered, the projects are expected to be able to offer some sort of longer-term sustainability that will last beyond the five years of programme support. Success will be judged by the extent to which the projects do indeed continue in the longer term, for example by finding new funding partners, by bringing the activity into the normal local government budgets, or by creating a private enterprise within the market sector.

According to an early evaluation, there seems to have been little substitution of programme participants for other workers and a majority of employers state a desire to hire the young person at the end of the supported contract (*Ministère de l'Emploi et de la Solidarité*, 1999a).

In addition to the above examples, many new policy directions are being pursued for welfare-to-work in other OECD countries.

These welfare-to-work policy innovations are not isolated examples. The trend towards activating labour market policies, redesigning welfare benefits and adjusting the institutional structure of support is widespread in OECD countries and many other country examples could be cited. For example in Denmark major labour market reforms were put into place in 1994, with the Active Labour Market Policy act, the Leave Schemes Act and the Act for Activation at the Local Level. In New Zealand a Community Wage has been introduced to replace existing unemployment benefits, paid in return for participation in community work or training, and a one-stop-shop has been created integrating the public employment and income support services. In the Netherlands, the receipt of unemployment benefits is conditional on more rigorous assessments of job search activity and capacity to work, linked with a range of measures aimed at improving the employability and job prospects of those out of work for long periods. The strategy includes direct job creation in the public sector for the long term unemployed, changes in the tax and benefits system and incentives for employers to take on unemployed people.

The local dimension

The local dimension is essential to the effective delivery of welfare-to-work policies

Welfare-to-work policies are ultimately delivered at the local level. They must therefore be adapted to local needs and able to draw on the energies and initiatives of local unemployed people, local enterprises and organisations and local employment service providers. There are three main qualities of the local level that can be harnessed for employment policies. Firstly, at the local level it is often possible to better judge specific needs and opportunities in the labour market and hence to adapt policies to take advantage of them. It can be easier to identify skill shortages or oversupplies, the recruitment needs of major employers and the small business sector or the gaps in community provision that could provide new employment opportunities. If local policy-makers are given flexibility, they can design approaches that respond to these needs and opportunities or bend mainstream programmes to local circumstances. Secondly, there is a capacity to bring together and co-ordinate the range of different national, regional and local policies affecting employment in an area so that duplications are avoided and synergies are maximised. In the localities experiencing the most severe employment difficulties there are many actors and instruments aimed at tackling the linked problems of exclusion, and local partnerships can be used to co-ordinate them more effectively. Thirdly, there are common issues and forums at local level that can play a role in mobilising local people, employers and community groups in support of policy goals. Box 5 shows how the United Kingdom has sought to build these local strengths into its New Deal programme.

Box 5. The local dimension in the UK New Deal

One of the major new elements of the New Deal in comparison with earlier public employment service initiatives is its emphasis on local flexibility in policy design and delivery within nationally set standards and guidelines. In order to achieve local flexibility, it was chosen not to deliver the New Deal exclusively through the national public employment service, but rather to develop a collection of some 140 local programmes, with design and delivery entrusted to partnerships of agencies, companies and organisations operating in each locality. In each local unit of delivery, the managers of the local offices of the public employment service had responsibility for forming a partnership, following a wide consultation with interested and appropriate agencies. The partnerships are responsible for assessing local needs and designing the details of New Deal provision in their locality within a national design framework.

Box 5. (continued)

The size and make-up of the partnerships varies between areas. However, the principle actors are employers, trades unions, voluntary organisations, education and training providers, government careers services, Training and Enterprise Councils (TECs), Chambers of Commerce, local authorities and local offices of the government's Employment Service. Various partners are also involved in delivering specific measures. In some of the more deprived areas many of the partners have already had some history of working together to deliver other regeneration programmes.

Local managers of the public employment service could choose to set up partnerships according to one of three models:

- *A series of individual contracts*: where the public employment service delivers services through contracts with single organisations or with consortia that form to deliver a specific New Deal option.

- *A Consortium led by a single organisation*: where the public employment service has a single contract with either a legally constituted consortium or designated lead organisation.

- *A Joint Venture approach*: where the public employment service works with a consortium to jointly develop the delivery plan and to implement the plan through a joint venture agreement.

In addition, the government decided that in 10 of the 140 local areas, private sector organisations, particularly private employment agencies, should be given the lead in managing provision. This allows the merits of private sector involvement to be tested.

There is also considerable local flexibility in selecting appropriate organisations to deliver activities with New Deal funding. Some elements of provision are delivered directly by the public employment service, as has been normal with past programmes. However, other elements are now contracted out to other organisations when the partnership feels that they are in a better position to deliver the objectives of the government.

Overall, local partnerships were given considerable flexibility to plan provision according to their assessment of local needs and possibilities. They were able to involve a wide range of appropriate local bodies and link with existing initiatives in their area. Their proposals were outlined in District Delivery Plans. These allowed local people to see what was being planned for their area and quality to be controlled by Regional Assessment Panels and ministers.

There has been a strong trend towards decentralising the design and management of employment policy to local areas

It is these qualities that governments have sought to exploit through recent efforts to decentralise aspects of employment policy design and management to regions and localities. OECD (1998) and OECD (1999b) have reviewed recent trends in decentralisation of employment policy and show that it has been occurring to a different extent and in a different form in different OECD countries and in different circumstances. The main trends can be characterised as follows:

- *Bottom-up approach.* In some cases the trend has been towards lower levels of government, or local partnerships, becoming more actively involved in the development and management of national programmes and policies. This can range from advanced notification, to extensive consultation or to a full-fledged bottom-up approach to policy making.

- *Freedom to implement.* In other cases lower levels of government are given more room to manoeuvre in implementing national policies. Here again, a wide range of options is available: local decision making power regarding the appropriate institutional set-up for implementing national policies; freedom to switch resources between a number of programmes within a given budget envelope; freedom to decide on staffing policy etc.

- *Freedom to design.* Policy making authority in certain areas is completely devolved to lower levels of government with the result that a uniform national policy in these particular areas no longer exists.

Box 6 illustrates in the case of the United States the new flexibility that is being given to state and local governments in delivering welfare-to-work programmes. Aspects of each of the three main decentralisation trends are involved.

Box 6. The local dimension in United States TANF and other welfare-to-work programmes

The 1996 Personal Responsibility and Work Opportunity Reconciliation Act (PRWORA) introduced a substantial decentralisation of TANF programme design from the federal to state and local levels. The key change has been the provision of the federal TANF budget to states as a block grant rather than for provision of specific welfare payments and services. States have the additional flexibility to carry forward any savings that they realise from their block grant from one year to the next and can choose to supplement federal funds with their own resources.

The change to a block grant system and accompanying regulatory changes have given states a number of new freedoms:

- States are now free to decide what welfare payments to make out of the block grant, including the levels and duration of payments and the basic eligibility criteria. As a consequence there is no longer any automatic federal entitlement to welfare assistance.

- States are free to determine what active labour market policy initiatives to provide from the block grant.

- It is largely up to states to determine what the public-private mix is in relation to their welfare-to-work activities, the extent to which the state wishes to make use of private firms, non-profit organisations, religious groups and so on.

- It is now largely up to each state to determine what the boundaries will be between state and local. If a state wishes to delegate decisions on welfare payments, the types of services provided and the agencies used to deliver them then it is free to do so. Equally, if the state wishes to retain most of them at the state level it is free to do this. States have often passed down responsibilities for the detailed design and delivery of their TANF welfare-to-work programmes to local governments.

As a result, welfare-to-work programmes vary considerably between states and local areas in the amount of financial assistance they provide to welfare recipients and the rules they set. For example, federal funding cannot be used to provide welfare assistance to families for more than five years. Eight states have introduced limits shorter than 36 months (Connecticut, Massachusetts, Virginia, Louisiana, Arkansas, Nebraska, Idaho, Oregon), whilst two states (Michigan and Vermont) will extend benefits indefinitely using their own resources (OECD, 1999a). States also vary in the sanctions imposed on welfare

29

Box 6. (continued)

recipients who do not comply with the conditions for obtaining benefits. For example, seven states apply a lifetime ban on further payments for continued non-compliance, whilst fifteen only apply partial benefits sanctions over a limited period. The labour market services offered through TANF grants also vary considerably. Apart from TANF there is a wide range of other welfare-to-work programmes funded by states and local governments. To promote this type of innovative local initiative, federal assistance has been made available direct to organisations operating at sub-state level through a $3 billion federal Welfare-to-Work block grant. Some 75% of the funding is allocated to states, which are required to spend at least 85% of it through local Workforce Development Boards, or an acceptable alternative. The other 25% is allocated through 'Competitive Grants to Local Communities', and is awarded directly to local governments, private entities or community based organisations. The funds have to be spent on employment and job search programmes that assist people to move from welfare to work. Workforce Development Boards have also been encouraged to develop local one-stop centres that combine delivery of a wide range of different federal employment services in one office. The aim is to increase the accessibility of the services to users and improve customer choice and service integration. Services offered through these new one-stop centres include basic self-service information on vacancies and opportunities, staff guidance and intensive services. Other welfare and employment agencies are commonly networked with these one-stop centres.

Partnerships of local agencies are often asked to participate in strategy development and delivery and innovation is encouraged

A strong feature of many of these decentralisation approaches is the creation of partnerships of local agencies from the public, private and community and non-profit sectors that are becoming involved in various aspects of economic and employment development. The local partnerships often work together to identify needs and design strategies for intervention. In some cases they may put together resources to create new joint delivery projects. Partners are also being encouraged to use the flexibility and powers given to them to be innovative in developing new activities for their local area. Thus during the conference, United Kingdom Employment Minister Andrew Smith stated that, for United Kingdom employment policy:

'Delivery is best managed locally, through partnership between the Public Employment Service, the private and voluntary sectors and other agencies. These local partnerships are responsive to local needs in ways that central government cannot be . . . Partnership working helps to stimulate innovation and creativity, improve customer service and add value to basic provision.'

Partnership is also an important aspect of the Australian Work for the Dole initiative (Box 7).

Box 7. The local dimension in the Australian Job Network and Work for the Dole

Provision of labour market services in Australia has recently undergone a major shift with the introduction in May 1998 of the 'Job Network', under which services have been contracted out to a network of Employment Service Providers in the private and voluntary sectors. This new market replaces the fifty-year old public employment services provider, the Commonwealth Employment Service (CES), its case management arm (Employment Assistance Australia) and most labour market programmes. It has effectively decentralised responsibility for design and delivery of services from the public employment service to individual providers. The aim is to facilitate a more client-focussed rather than programme driven approach that will improve employment outcomes.

Job Network is a national network of around 300 private, community and government organisations contracted by the Australian government through a competitive tendering exercise. The services provided by contractors cover Job Matching, Job Search Training, Intensive Assistance (which is a new enterprise incentive scheme to support unemployed people to set up their own business), Project Contracting (which supplies out-of-area labour to harvest crops) and New Apprenticeship Centres (which provide traineeship support services for employers and job seekers). A complementary one-stop-shop, called Centrelink, has been established as the first point of contact for the vast bulk of clients. Through Centrelink, job seekers may choose which Job Network provider in their area they want to see. Employers can choose which providers they wish to work with.

Under Job Network the public sector continues to play a role in the delivery of employment services through the corporatised entity Employment National, which could be described as a public utility. In the interests of maintaining a fully contestable market for the delivery of employment services, Employment National is required to operate on exactly the same terms and conditions as its private and community sector competitors. The public employment service staff that has been retained is only very small and is concerned with monitoring, setting frameworks and organising the contracting.

Box 7. (continued)

Contracting out has the advantage of making employment services far more contestable. It also gives the possibility of using new agencies and players to help deliver government employment programmes. Another benefit of Job Network is better coverage of services for job seekers. For example there are now around 1,4000 Job Network sites compared to 300 sites with the CES. However, it is more difficult for the government to impose operational changes or practices on service providers, which must rely on central guidelines and contracting frameworks.

Work for the Dole, one of the principal welfare-to-work measures in Australia, was introduced in this new decentralised institutional context. It operates through a major national tendering exercise, through which community organisations, local governments, state governments, church organisations and so on are asked to come forward with project proposals for suitable work experience initiatives. Proposals are selected by the Department of Education, Employment and Youth Affairs (DEETYA) using the local labour market knowledge of civil servants working in its local offices and taking account of recommendations sought from outside bodies. An overriding requirement is to try and locate Work for the Dole projects in localities where there are concentrations of young unemployed people and few other opportunities such as part-time work. The other main selection criteria are that projects should benefit the community, offer valuable work experience for young people, offer some post-placement support for participants and should be cost-effective.

By contracting out Work for the Dole, the public employment service is able to gain the support and ideas of the community. At the same time it draws heavily on the local labour market knowledge of civil servants working in local offices of the government employment service in order to select the most promising project ideas. The outcome is that there are some 500 different projects, offering a much wider variety of project types and activities for young people than has been available previously under centrally designed programmes.

Local involvement is a common characteristic of emerging welfare-to-work approaches

Recent welfare-to-work approaches can be seen as an attempt to break with the passive employment and welfare policies of the past and to make them more responsive to current labour market needs. Doing this involves a certain amount of experimentation with institutional frameworks and policy instruments. Decentralisation represents one of the key methods that governments are using in attempting to manage this experimentation. The local dimension is very clear in the welfare-to-work initiatives that have already been cited, although the precise form of local involvement of course varies between each case. Box 8 describes another example of the local dimension in employment welfare-to-work policy, the *Nouveaux Services - Emplois Jeunes* programme in France.

Box 8. The local dimension in the *'Nouveaux Services - Emplois Jeunes'* programme in France

The *'Nouveaux Services - Emplois Jeunes'* ('New Services - Youth Jobs') programme aims to combat youth unemployment by supporting innovative social projects that offer both immediate jobs and longer-term professional prospects for young people. It follows very much a local logic:

- The appeal for projects is launched at local level, where there is the most detailed knowledge of needs and gaps in provision and where actors can best be mobilised. Local actors include mayors and elected local government members, managers of voluntary organisations, social partners and officials from public agencies operating locally.

- The geographic zones for programme implementation are defined in collaboration with local partners in order to take account of the existing traditions of partnership for employment and local development. They commonly cover a travel to work area, an urban district or conurbation or an area already used for other programmes.

- A local co-ordinator (or 'pilot'), who is generally either a civil servant or an elected Member of Parliament, is appointed for each zone and is responsible for networking with local actors in the fields where activities could be established. The local co-ordinator normally develops a team of animators to provide technical assistance to actors responding to the call for projects.

Active local partnerships are built up, based on 'framework agreements' between the state and networks of voluntary organisations and public employers and on 'statements of priorities' between state Prefects and local government authorities. Many of the proposed services are at the interface between the activities of different agencies (local authorities, voluntary organisations, private firms, the public sector) and these many operators must therefore be included in the development of local programmes in order to give their opinions and ensure co-ordination.

Box 8. (continued)

The first stage of operation, which largely took place during the first 12-18 months of the programme, largely focused on mobilising projects. This was done through information and awareness campaigns, setting up local animation teams, providing technical support to project promoters and building local partnerships. A critical part of this first stage was the study of needs. This had to integrate an assessment of local characteristics (unsatisfied needs, financing opportunities, barriers to the creation of activities) with an assessment of developments and opportunities in different sectors of activity (needs of the population in a given sector of activity and barriers to the creation of activities in this sector). The local needs analyses included a survey of users and potential users, an assessment of links with wider local development projects underway in the area and an analysis of existing activities in the same fields.

The second phase has been that of project development and selection. Project promoters are given advice by the local co-ordinator and animation team on how to structure their project so that it links with a professional platform being put in place for the services and so that the services can continue to operate at the end of the wage subsidy period. The local and regional authorities help to support the local co-ordinator and animation team. Decisions on funding are based on an assessment of the quality of the opportunity for the project, its potential for development and the probability of the project leading to permanent services. The selection of projects is framed within a collective assessment of how well the interventions fit with a broader strategy for local development. The local partners participate in this collective assessment. In this way complementarities can be encouraged and competition or duplication can be minimised (*Ministère de l'Emploi et de la Solidarité*, 1999b).

But careful management is required in order to bring out the potential of local approaches without inducing harmful trade-offs

The advantages sought from local involvement - in terms of better co-ordination, tailoring to local needs and increased mobilisation of local groups - will not necessarily emerge unprompted from a simple decentralisation of policy design and delivery to the local level. It is important that the right structures and tools are in place to support the achievement of these goals. Otherwise potential counter effects could emerge, such as concerns over unequal or inconsistent treatment for client groups, funding problems, lack of appropriate skills, duplication of activities or poor co-ordination or lack of accountability of legitimacy for local interventions. It is therefore important to examine carefully what works and what does not work in terms of local involvement and how it can best be managed.

The three central questions

To improve our understanding of the potential of local approaches to welfare-to-work and of how best to implement them the following key questions need to be addressed. They are at the core of this book:

1.   What are the strengths and weaknesses of policy design and management at a local level and what is the appropriate balance between local and central agencies?

Local management can make welfare-to-work policies more effective, but a balance has to be struck between local flexibility and a national framework. It can be argued that local bodies must be allowed flexibility if they are really to innovate and find new local solutions. On the other hand, a national framework helps to ensure a certain equity and consistency across the country and the provision of adequate funding and technical support for local initiatives. It can also help to ensure that national government policy objectives are met when increased responsibility is given to the local level.

2.   How effective are local partnership mechanisms in stimulating policy innovation, adapting policies to local conditions and mobilising social partners?

Local partnerships can play an important role in co-ordinating policy and developing strategy, in increasing the scale of intervention and in filling resource or policy gaps. However, making partnerships work is not always straightforward. In circumstances where there is poor co-operation between partners, co-ordination and local adaptation of policy can actually become more difficult than when carried out by agencies of central bodies. It is also common to see partnerships becoming dominated by one major local player, leading to distortion of objectives and limited participation by other social partners. It is therefore important to understand the circumstances under which partnerships work best.

3.   What locally based policy tools work well in promoting the recruitment of excluded youths and adults?

Perhaps above all, OECD governments are looking to local initiatives to create the new opportunities that will increase the numbers of people leaving welfare for work. There are many innovations at local level that, if they can be shown to be successful, could be adopted elsewhere. In moving from passive policy approaches to active labour market policies much depends on the systems put in place at local level, for example for one-stop-shops, personal advisers, job matching techniques, training and work experience projects or methods of improving job mobility. These local ALMPs can be complemented by measures to support job creation for unemployed people, for example jobs in social enterprises or in organisations supplying new social needs. There is still a need to identify and assess appropriate local tools.

Structure of the book

Given the substantial recent international innovation and experimentation in welfare-to-work and local design and delivery, there is clearly scope for policy makers to learn from experiences in other countries. This book aims to support this exchange by examining key issues for local approaches to welfare-to-work now being adopted in OECD countries, with a particular emphasis on the United Kingdom, the United States, Italy, France, the Netherlands and Australia.

The remainder of the book is organised in two parts. The first part provides a synthesis of the arguments, experiences and debates presented in the November 1998 OECD-DfEE Sheffield conference on the Local Dimension to Welfare-to-Work. Chapters 2-4 each tackle a critical issue. Chapter 2 investigates the strengths and weaknesses of the local approach and what should be the appropriate balance between local and central agencies. Chapter 3 examines the issue of local partnerships of agencies co-operating to design and deliver programmes that are innovative, adapted to local needs and that mobilise local social partners. Whilst the concept of partnership is often praised there is much that still needs to be understood in terms of how local partnerships can be made to work in practical terms. Chapter 4 then seeks to identify some locally-based policy tools that work well in promoting the employment of excluded youths and adults. These include social enterprises and Intermediate Labour Markets, the personal adviser, local training-in-work projects, methods for encouraging local labour mobility, use of the Internet for job matching and local experiments with in-work financial incentives. Then Chapter 5 draws some key conclusions and outlines some perspectives for the future.

The second part of the book is devoted to case study papers that tackle in more detail some specific aspects of local approaches to welfare-to-work. Chapters 6 and 7 examine the role of local agencies in delivering recent welfare-to-work reforms. Dan Finn compares local approaches to welfare-to-work in the United States, the United Kingdom and the Netherlands. Robert Straits offers an overview of the evolution of welfare-to-work in the United States and identifies key issues for local programme administrators and advisory boards. Then Chapters 8 and 9 explore the question of creating and sustaining effective local welfare-to-work partnerships. Mike Campbell draws some lessons for local welfare-to-work partnerships from recent experience in the United Kingdom. Lyn Hogan then examines United States experience in engaging the business sector in welfare-to-work policies. Finally, Chapters 10 and 11 turn to the issue of finding effective local tools for welfare-to-work. Carlo Borzaga examines social enterprises in Europe as a local tool for welfare-to-work policies. Nakamura, Wong and Diewert examine the local dimension of recent welfare-to-work initiatives in Canada, including incentive approaches and Internet recruiting services for job matching.

A short annex sets out the programme of the Sheffield conference and identifies the speakers whose contributions have been synthesised in Part 1.

PART I

LOCAL APPROACHES TO WELFARE-TO-WORK.
AN ASSESSMENT OF RECENT INNOVATIONS

CREATING THE BALANCE BETWEEN LOCAL FLEXIBILITY AND A CENTRAL FRAMEWORK

Introduction

Chapter 1 has outlined the importance of the local dimension to the effective delivery of welfare-to-work policies and given examples of how local flexibility has been built in to programmes. It also raised the question as to what are the strengths and weaknesses of policy design and management at a local level and what is the appropriate balance between local and central agencies. Whilst it can be argued that local discretion and autonomy can make welfare-to-work policies more responsive to local needs and opportunities there can also be certain trade-offs, for example an unevenness in provision across a country or a reduction in accountability for public money. A balance therefore has to be struck between local flexibility and a national framework. This chapter focuses on how to find this balance.

Strengths of local flexibility

Until recently, employment policies have tended to differentiate certain labour market segments, such as youth, but have not adapted to differing local needs and opportunities. By contrast, a key strength often attributed to local involvement in the design and management of welfare-to-work policies is the ability to design services that are more adapted to different local circumstances. This is partly based on the idea that local actors have greater information than central ones on these issues, by virtue of their proximity to local employers, community groups, employment service providers and so on, and because of their wide range of overlapping competencies. The local partnership approach, in particular, is seen as a way of capitalising on this local knowledge. It also reflects the idea that programme regulations designed rigidly at the central level risk prohibiting activities that could be appropriate in particular local circumstances that are difficult to predict and legislate for centrally. By giving local groups the flexibility to design provision within a broad range of permitted activities, programmes can tap into local facilities or activities that might otherwise be missed.

A second key strength of local involvement in the design and management of welfare-to-work policies is the capacity to co-ordinate locally the range of different national, regional and local policies affecting employment in an area. In the past, policies affecting employment have often suffered because delivery has been fragmented between different institutions without enough local co-ordination and integration. Local partnerships of agencies can act as forums for planning and delivery through which synergy and inter-linkage between projects can be planned from the outset and duplication minimised.

A third key strength of local involvement in the design and management of welfare-to-work policies is the ability to mobilise people, employers and community groups in support of national policy objectives, based on the exploitation of common local issues and objectives and the existence of local forums and networks. This can help access additional local expertise, resources and support from the social partners to increase the scale of delivery and to address local problems that are preventing policy from working effectively.

Fourthly, the process of experimentation with new policy approaches at the local level may help to fill gaps in the existing policy framework and generate innovative project ideas that potentially can be transferred or adapted elsewhere.

Finally, adopting an approach that differentiates between different local areas offers the possibility of channelling additional resources to areas with a particular need. Often the problems experienced by unemployed and excluded people are not just related to their own personal characteristics but to a breakdown in the functioning of a local economy and a major local jobs deficit. In these cases additional resources may be required to create employment opportunities. This type of local area targeting is not possible when policy is directed to particular target groups, wherever they are located, rather than to disadvantaged areas.

These types of innovations resulting from local involvement in design and management are illustrated in Box 9 in the case of the UK New Deal programme.

One of the principal conclusions of the OECD Jobs Study was that OECD economies must improve their capacity to adapt rapidly to structural change if unemployment is to be reduced. Local involvement in policy can help achieve this by securing a series of local adjustments that respond more closely to distinct local labour market conditions and by releasing real creativity and innovation in programmes. By better dealing with labour market mismatching problems local programmes can reduce frictional and structural unemployment in different localities and can thus increase national employment without crowding out other activities through increasing inflationary pressures. These benefits seem to be confirmed by recent evidence on the effects of labour market policies in Denmark over the last five years that suggests that ALMPs focused on local delivery have helped significantly to reduce national inflation and structural unemployment (*Socialforskningsinstituttet*, 1998).

Box 9. Innovations stemming from local flexibility and involvement in the UK New Deal

The UK New Deal for 18-24 year olds illustrates some of the innovations that can stem from local flexibility and involvement in policy design and management.

Tailored provision: The increased local flexibility and involvement built into the New Deal through local consultations and local design of District Delivery Plans have helped to tailor provision towards the needs of each labour market. As a consequence, what is delivered by New Deal differs quite significantly between localities, or units of delivery. The emphasis between the Gateway and the four different options differs markedly from place to place and what goes into each of those four different options also varies significantly. Local flexibility and involvement also allow policy to build on existing initiatives in many localities, where they have been shown to be successful and could be expanded or supported more fully. In the most distressed localities, where unemployment and exclusion are concentrated, there is a wide range of such initiatives supported through local regeneration programmes. For example, the city of Sheffield has an 'urban farm' that has operated for some years and is very sympathetic to the needs of the poor and unemployed in the city. It is a distinctive local resource that does not exist in many other areas. Decentralising policy design to the local level has enabled the Sheffield 'urban farm' to be used for work experience and training projects for New Deal clients, and at the same time its activities have been supported. Use of this type of special facility can be allowed for with local involvement in programme design, but it would be difficult to legislate centrally for this such 'one-off' projects.

Box 9. (continued)

Co-ordination with existing policies and institutional structures: Local flexibility and involvement in New Deal design and management have also helped to improve the co-ordination of New Deal with other local area policies. For example, the Phoenix Regeneration Company in Rotherham operates as a New Deal consortium, set up by the partners as an independent company to combine funding for New Deal with other social and economic regeneration funding from central British government and European sources. That has allowed the partners to create an Intermediate Labour Market centred on the urban regeneration of Rotherham, something that would not have been possible without a flexible delivery approach. In addition, the fact that there are now three different contracting models for the delivery of the New Deal for young unemployed adults in the United Kingdom allows policy to take into account the fact that existing institutional structures vary between localities and to find an arrangement that best fits with local potential. In the majority of localities, New Deal provision is organised by the local office of the public employment service, which contracts with individual providers according to the delivery plan drawn up following local consultations. However, in some cases private sector companies have been given the lead in designing delivery plans and managing contracts. In other cases there is a joint venture partnership arrangement where the major players from the social partners have formally contracted, as a consortium, to jointly develop and implement the delivery plan. The presence of different contracting models allows experimentation to test the strengths and weaknesses of the different approaches in different circumstances.

Mobilisation of local social partners: Another type of innovation in the New Deal is the opening up of new links between the public sector Employment Service and the local communities in which it operates. A specific example is the participation of organisations for unemployed people in the consultations for the New Deal, which provides a channel for taking on board some of the proposals of these organisations to improve delivery. In many localities the links between the Employment Service and unemployed groups had previously been quite limited. Another example is consultation with community groups about the community projects to be carried out as part of New Deal. This helps both to ensure that work is carried out that the community wants and to gain the support of relevant community groups. The sense of local ownership that results can be important for the motivation of participants as well as promising to bring in additional resources.

The limitations of policy design and management at a local level

Whilst decentralisation of policy design and management to the local level offers many potential benefits, these benefits may be counterbalanced by certain negative impacts if the right frameworks are not in place. There are seven main issues that come into play, concerning the global nature of aspects of the welfare-to-work problem, the possibility of uneven provision, establishing accountability, undertaking robust evaluation, deviation from national objectives, duplication and limits to awareness of needs and opportunities.

The global nature of aspects of the welfare-to-work problem: One of the main contentions of this book is that national macroeconomic and structural policies alone are not adequate to overcome barriers to employment, particularly in those localities with the highest concentrations of unemployment and exclusion. Policies have to be adjusted to local conditions and local initiatives need to be encouraged. However, it is also the case that local initiatives on their own are not sufficient to tackle the problem. Tight labour markets need to be achieved if job opportunities are to be found for previous welfare recipients and this task is as much national as local.   The OECD Jobs Study identified a range of conditions that contribute to reducing unemployment at national and international level, including a stable and conducive macroeconomic environment, flexible product and labour markets and investment in skills and innovation (OECD, 1995).   Equally, nationally-set tax and benefits regimes have important impacts on the demand for work. In sum, local initiatives need to be complemented with appropriate national and international policies.

The possibility of uneven provision: The problem of uneven provision is one that may arise when operating decentralised policies. When local areas are responsible for designing their own services what is on offer will clearly vary between localities. Consequently people wishing to access a particular service may be able to do so in one area but not in another. Equally, it may be perceived that the overall quality of provision in one area is poorer than that available in another. Further to the differences arising from local choices about the range and mix of services to be provided, uneven provision may result from different institutional competencies in different local areas. Partnerships are likely to work better in some areas than in others and the professional capacities of people working in local agencies may also differ. There can also be funding issues if local resources are required to substitute for or supplement national resources. Clearly some areas may be in a better position to find funding than others, perhaps because of a larger tax base or because of greater availability of resources from complementary regeneration programmes.

Some argue that any marked unevenness in provision should be rejected. Many countries have a tradition that people from the same eligible groups should benefit from the same services wherever they live. Others argue that unevenness must be accepted as the counterpart to local flexibility, since this is likely to bring improvements to most areas. What is really needed is a way of securing the benefits of local design and management whilst at the same time preventing provision in any particular area from declining below a given standard.

Establishing accountability: A third problem that can arise with local design and management is that it can become more difficult to assess what are the outputs for public money and to hold the various local agencies and partners to account. If local partnerships or agencies are given autonomy to use central budgets for the activities they choose then a situation could arise where the activities are supported are not those intended by central government. Similarly the activities could be pursued with low efficiency or could become dominated by particular interest groups or organisations leading to unbalanced provision. The issue of accountability is one that still needs to be explored in the context of substantial local discretion, the involvement of a large number of organisations and a range of integrated funding packages.

Undertaking robust evaluation: A related problem concerns the existence of a wide range of local variations that make it difficult to have a robust evaluation of impacts at national level. For example, there are variations in economic conditions, in the baseline situation of the client group, in local tools and facilities, in complementary funds and programmes and in the way that policy is implemented, including a variety of different partnership arrangements. This suggests that a series of local evaluations is therefore needed, with methodologies designed to reflect the different circumstances in each local area. The problem for national policy-makers is that it can then prove difficult to summarise the overall national impact of the programme.

Deviation from national objectives: A fifth danger is that once given flexibility, local groups will choose to carry out activities different to those that the central government originally intended for them. In Ireland, local partnerships to combat unemployment have in certain cases been criticised by unemployed groups for deviating from stated objectives for tackling unemployment towards wider community development objectives.

Duplication: Another issue that can arise is that of duplication of activities. Designing delivery plans, undertaking consultations with social partners, setting up administrative models, evaluating performance, assessing labour market needs and so on may be carried out separately in each local area. However, if combined there may be efficiency savings. This duplication may be criticised on efficiency grounds in certain cases. The counter-argument is that although there may be duplication, effectiveness should be enhanced, and there may be scope for co-operation between different areas where this makes sense, for example in the joint design and reporting of evaluation studies.

Limits to awareness of needs and opportunities: A final issue is that local proximity may not always equate to better awareness of local needs and opportunities or a greater capability to design appropriate solutions. In many cases local agencies have only a partial view of the situation in their area or of the tools that could be applied to tackle their problems. They may in fact be less well placed than national bodies to understand some of the key drivers that affect a local labour market, which can be as much driven by national and global forces as by local ones. Furthermore, they may not have the resources or capabilities to undertake a more detailed examination of the area or assessment of the merits of different services. There are clearly limitations to what local agencies can be expected to achieve without appropriate national information and guidance.

The role of a central framework

The role of central authorities should be to support local actors to design provision in line with local needs and opportunities and to implement it effectively and efficiently. It should thus help to limit the occurrence of the potential counter effects cited above. There are three main functions of a central framework. It should ensure that local initiatives are supported by other policies operating at a national level so that they are working with, rather than against, national policies. It should use appropriate national controls, consultations and guidelines to ensure that the local initiatives undertaken are consistent with broad national objectives, to ensure that there is accountability and to secure minimum standards of provision. It should also ensure that central authorities provide certain services to support local actors, where they are best placed to do so, to minimise unnecessary duplication of tasks and provide information that could help local planning and implementation.

Supporting policies at national level

The global nature of many aspects of the welfare-to-work problem has been highlighted above. It is therefore important that links are created between local approaches to welfare-to-work and other aspects of the welfare-to-work policy environment that operate at a larger scale. The right framework conditions are required to reduce unemployment nationally otherwise local welfare-to-work initiatives will be working within a very difficult environment. There is a range of relevant policies in this respect, for flexible product and labour markets, to support skills and competencies and for investment in innovation. National tax and benefits regulations also have to be appropriate so as not to act as a barrier to people taking work. Similarly, it is important that funding rules for key national programmes are not drawn up in such a way as to prevent local agencies from creating the innovative or joint projects that the overall thrust of policy aims to encourage.

National controls, consultations and guidelines

Appropriate national controls, national-local consultations and guidelines can help overcome the potential weaknesses of local approaches in terms of possible uneven provision between different local areas, lack of accountability for spending or deviation from national objectives whilst at the same time recognising the decision-making flexibility of local bodies.

One of the main control methods used for national steering of local approaches to welfare-to-work is the use of funding regimes. Where local programmes depend on significant national funding, regulations and incentives can be attached and they can be fine-tuned to provide quite refined signals to local policy-makers. One common funding method is output related funding. Under this system local agencies are paid block grants, rather than a series of separate budgets linked to particular services, and are free to provide the services they choose. However, they are rewarded according to the achievement of certain target outputs (e.g. number of qualifications obtained, number of people finding work). This allows central government to steer provision towards national objectives and to instil accountability for the efficiency and effectiveness with which these results are achieved. The local area nonetheless retains the flexibility to choose how to deliver these results. Various regulations, bonuses and penalties can be built into funding regimes to encourage local programmes to meet certain national priorities or to make certain provision. These funding systems can also be used to control quality when provision of services is contracted out to non-public sector organisations.

Administrative based rules can also be imposed on local bodies and compliance verified by government or courts. These can set out methods of working and responsibilities of different organisations. They can be imposed independently of funding levers. In the UK New Deal for 18-14 year olds, for example, central administrative rules have imposed eligibility criteria and the basic structure that local New Deal programmes must implement.

Box 10 illustrates how funding and administrative controls have been used in the United States TANF programme to steer state and local government towards programme designs that meet key federal objectives.

**Box 10. The balance between central and local in the
United States TANF programme**

There are some very important elements of local flexibility in the United States Temporary Assistance for Needy Families (TANF) programme. Federal funding is now provided to states as block grants. States are free to determine how to use these grants in terms of what welfare payments to make and what active labour market services to provide. States are also free to choose the government agencies that deliver services or to contract out many parts of service provision to appropriate private firms or non-profit organisations. States have often passed down responsibilities for the design and delivery of TANF programmes to local governments.

However, although there is greater flexibility within TANF, states also have to operate within a framework of national regulations, bonuses and penalties:

Time limits: National policy imposes restrictions on states and local governments that limit the amount of time that assistance can be provided and the groups that are potentially eligible. Federal cash assistance cannot be paid to welfare recipients for more than 2 years on any claim and beyond a maximum limit of 5 years over a lifetime.

Work participation targets: States risk federal budget penalties if they do not meet federally-set and rising targets for proportions of public assistance recipients in work or work-related activities. According to these targets, 25% of all single-parent families must be engaged in work activities or have left welfare rolls in fiscal year 1997, rising by 5 percentage points a year to 50% in 2002. For two-parent families, 75% must be working in 1997, rising to 90% in 1999. There are detailed federal guidelines on what constitutes work and work-related activities. Since education and training activities do not count towards the work participation targets, the federal government is sending cues to states to emphasise 'work first'.

Minimum spending: States' own-resources spending cannot drop below a minimum of 80% of their spending in fiscal year 1994, or 75% if they meet the work participation targets.

Box 10. (continued)

Performance bonuses: There are a number of performance bonuses to states that also influence provision. In particular, one bonus is largely focused on work by rewarding employment entries and job retention.

It should also be recognised that state and local programmes for TANF assistance for needy families are conceived of as part of a much broader federal welfare-to-work initiative. That broader initiative includes federal efforts to reform the tax system around the earned income tax credit, federal policy for childcare and healthcare and other federal measures to reform aspects of the employment and training system.

Design and management of welfare-to-work programmes in the United States has always involved some degree of co-operation between federal, state and local governments and there has been a large local role for a long time. However, the 1996 PRWORA legislation that set up the TANF has shifted the balance towards an increased role for state and local choice.

National authorities can also influence local programmes more informally through consultations and non-binding guidelines.   Consultations can be important to help clarify broad national goals to local agencies and as a way of allowing local agencies to raise any concerns about the design of national policy.   For example, a range of informal and formal consultations were undertaken across the United Kingdom involving both local organisations and national representatives concerned with the establishment of the UK New Deal. The dissemination of national guidelines can also influence what is undertaken by local agencies, even where no formal controls are attached. In Australia, local organisations putting together bids for Work for the Dole projects were given clear guidelines on what sort of initiatives the central government was seeking to support.   This allowed them to use their local knowledge and resources to draw up appropriate bids.

Specific national services to support local actors

There are certain services that in many circumstances may best be provided at central rather than local level. Together with appropriate controls, consultations and guidelines they can help prevent the emergence of areas where provision is weak. By providing these functions centrally it is also possible to minimise unnecessary duplication of tasks and provide information that could help local planning and implementation. Some of the main such functions are outlined below.

Funding provision: A key central role is the provision of funding to local areas to allow them to implement programmes at a scale commensurate with the requirements. Tackling unemployment and exclusion is a major policy challenge and it is likely that in most cases local actors alone will not have the capability to undertake the necessary level of activity without some national financial support. The funding role of central authorities can encompass several components. National budgets can be used to ensure that there is at least a minimum level of activity in each local area. Appropriate financial incentives can be used to draw out as much additional locally funded activity as possible. Additional funding can be given to local areas with the greatest local funding constraints compared with needs or opportunities. Incentives can be offered for activities that are national priorities, in order to encourage local areas to start to develop the provision considered necessary by national policy-makers, e.g. childcare and intensive support services, or alternatively penalties and regulations can be imposed on access to national funding. In the latter case there is of course a potential conflict with encouraging local flexibility and this must be managed carefully.

National awareness campaigns: welfare-to-work programmes require a high degree of awareness amongst employers, welfare recipients and other organisations such as community bodies. It makes sense for such publicity to be co-ordinated nationally rather than separate efforts being made in each locality.

Quality control: Central authorities should play a role in the monitoring of local programmes to ensure that basic standards are met and to require adjustments to poor performing programmes if necessary. If quality control is undertaken entirely at the local level then in some cases poor results may not fully be heeded by local actors and in other cases local actors may lack the capabilities to overcome problems even when they are recognised.

Programme evaluation: Whilst it can be argued that evaluations should be undertaken at the local level in order to take into account variations in local circumstances and implementation arrangements, there is nevertheless still an important evaluation role for central authorities. Central advocacy and financing may be required in order to ensure that evaluations are commissioned, undertaken and acted on by local partnerships. Central involvement is also important for the co-ordination of evaluations, so that a minimum set of common issues are covered and there are certain basic common measures, where this does not constrain the ability of evaluators to take into account local variations. National co-ordination will increase the value of the evaluation findings in terms of the scope for comparisons between areas and the ability to build up a national picture of impacts and issues to resolve. There should also be considerable local involvement in evaluation efforts so that issues of local importance can be investigated and so that local ownership is established. Local ownership is important if results are to be acted on.

Technical assistance: National authorities are in a better position than individual local areas to identify and understand what policy approaches appear to work best and where there are problems to avoid. This stems from their ability to oversee how policy is progressing across the whole country and to commit resources to assessing drivers of change. It follows that national authorities should also help to disseminate information on tools and processes to local areas, either through forums such as publications and seminars or through programme guidelines and incentives. National authorities may also provide information to help planning by local groups, for example on national or regional labour market trends, to complement what is available locally.

Achieving the right balance between local flexibility and central framework

It is clear from the above discussion that there are certain tensions between local flexibility and a central framework. Fundamentally there is a tension between giving local areas the flexibility to tailor and co-ordinate policies, to mobilise new actors and to experiment, whilst at the same time ensuring that local approaches are consistent with national objectives, securing minimum standards of provision and establishing accountability and efficiency. Where the balance is struck between local flexibility and central direction depends on policy priorities and the level of risk that national agencies are prepared to take in order to secure benefits. However, it can be argued that in general terms local flexibility should be most marked firstly where there is the greatest scope to increase innovation, local tailoring and co-ordination and mobilise new local players and secondly where local actors have the greatest design and management capabilities.

Governments can nonetheless take steps to support local approaches by building local institutional capacity. A first aspect of this involves supporting the professional capacities of the staff working in local agencies. Designing local policy and managing flexible funding regimes requires different skills than managing top-down, nationally prescribed programmes. Staff and managers in local public, private and voluntary sector organisations involved in designing and delivering local programmes are asked to make important changes in the way they operate. Appropriate training and resources are required to support them. A second aspect involves developing local partnerships by encouraging local bodies to work together, plan together and build joint projects. Resources and guidance are required. The next chapter looks at this issue in some detail.

However, it must be recognised that building local flexibility takes time. Partnerships have to be created, local needs and opportunities must be assessed and provision planned, new projects have to be developed and new actors involved. Managers and staff have to learn new skills. It also takes time to generate innovative ideas and test their strengths and weaknesses. Governments may therefore need to allow local flexibility to evolve gradually, gradually shifting the balance towards more local autonomy. Pilot programmes and small scale programmes can be useful to build understanding of the changed working methods required.

Practical examples of the balance between local and central

Where the balance between local flexibility and a strong national framework is set in practice depends on the country and the programme. Two different examples are given below, both from the United Kingdom. This balance has been struck differently in each case. The first is the UK New Deal for 18-24 year olds. This programme allows significant local flexibility within quite a strong central framework. The second is the UK Employment Zones pilot programme where central guidelines have been reduced and there is much greater scope for local flexibility. In the case of the New Deal for 18-24 year olds local discretion is mainly in terms of aspects of policy delivery. In the case of Employment Zones there is substantial discretion both in policy design and delivery. The Employment Zones initiative is smaller, more experimental and has a wider remit than the New Deal and is intended to help the government to test the impact of increased flexibility in difficult areas and with a difficult target group.

Local flexibility within a strong central framework: the UK New Deal for 18-24 year olds

Box 11 shows the mechanisms used to promote local flexibility within a strong central framework in the UK New Deal for 18-24 year olds.

Box 11. The balance between central and local in the UK New Deal for 18-24 year olds

The overall strategy for the UK New Deal for 18-24 year olds has been determined centrally, but draws heavily on ideas developed locally. The central framework is very clear:

- All welfare-to-work participants in Scotland, Wales and the English regions have the same eligibility entitlements, the same rights and the same responsibilities. That is one of the main advantages of a coherent national strategy. The eligibility for New Deal is the same across the whole country. It is for people aged between 18 and 24 years old who have been unemployed and claiming the Job-Seekers Allowance for 6 months. There are some exceptions to that. For example, young adults who are at serious risk of unemployment because they have recently been in prison are eligible as soon as they come out of prison. However, where exceptions are made they are the same across the whole country.

- The basic structure of the programme is the same across the whole country. In every locality there is an initial period of intensive advice and counselling, known as the Gateway, where personal advisers try to identify and break down barriers to employment for the young unemployed people. If it is not possible to help the young man or woman straight into work then they are prepared for one of the four so-called 'Options' or 'Pathways to Work'. Again those four options are the same in all localities (a subsidised job with an employer; full-time education or training; work with an Environmental Task Force; work with the voluntary sector). These different elements of the programme are all available for the same length of time – the Gateway for four months, the subsidised employment for six months.

- There is also very strong national branding for New Deal. All the publicity materials have the same sets of colours and typescripts, for example, and there has been a lot of powerful national advertising. Indeed, it is likely that the successful take up of the New Deal is in part due to the national rather than local nature of its overall design and advertising, which allows a simple clear understanding by employers and unemployed people of what the programme involves.

However, at the same time as having a strong central framework, there are many important aspects of local flexibility, which have been described in Box 9. In summary, the local dimension involves:

Box 11. (continued)

- Delivery through a collection of 130 separate local programmes rather than one national programme.

- Design and delivery of provision entrusted to partnerships of agencies, companies and organisations operating in each locality.

- Different partnership models in different localities, including a private sector lead in 10 of the 130 localities.

- Contracting out of service provision to non-public sector organisations where the local partnership feels this is appropriate.

Local proposals for provision are outlined in District Delivery Plans, which are reviewed by Regional Assessment Panels and approved at national level. These reviews and approvals can be seen as a further part of the process of achieving a balance between a central framework and local flexibility. They allow central authorities to ensure that each local partnership has followed the overall national design structure and to the quality standards that had been established. There is a potential conflict here between achieving full local ownership and having final control by a national government. The balance though, appears to have been very much in favour of local design.

As is the case in the United States, it is also important to recognise that the New Deal for 18-24 year olds is just one part of a much broader national programme of welfare-to-work measures. The overall response has four main elements:

- Investment in education and skills.

- Reform of the tax and benefits system and a national minimum wage, to make work pay.

- Welfare-to-work initiatives targeted on a range of groups of people who are detached from the labour market (e.g. adult unemployed, lone parents) and on local areas suffering from high unemployment.

- Maintenance of the link between benefit payment and job placement, reinforced by active management.

Enhanced local flexibility: UK Employment Zones

Compared with the New Deal for 18-24 year olds, the Employment Zone programme is a much smaller and more experimental strand of the United Kingdom government's welfare-to-work strategy. Five prototype Employment Zones have been established in areas with high concentrations of long term unemployment. Their function is to combine in innovative ways the training and regeneration programmes that already exist in these areas and to test a range of new approaches to delivering them. It is hoped that by allowing much greater local flexibility in policy design and delivery, lessons can be learned for the design of future strategies to tackle long term unemployment. The basic structure and objectives of the Employment Zone programme are outlined in Box 12.

Box 12. Description of the UK Employment Zones programme

Five prototype Employment Zones began operation in February 1998 and to run for at least two years. They are located in the urban areas of Glasgow, Liverpool and Sefton and Plymouth, in a mixed urban-rural area in South Teeside and in the remote rural area of North West Wales. These areas have slightly different problems, but all are characterised by high levels of long term unemployment and social exclusion. The aim is to help people in these areas to find and keep work. The programme has since been extended to cover 15 local areas in total.

Employment Zones work by combining in innovative ways the training and regeneration programmes that already exist in these areas and testing a range of new approaches to delivering them. The programme is open to long term unemployed people over 25 years old. This covers people claiming the Job Seekers' Allowance, the main benefit for unemployed people in the United Kingdom, as well as people on other benefits who are not required to look for work but who may wish to try and get back into the labour market. The latter includes lone parents on Income Support and disabled people on Incapacity Benefit.

The programme is entirely voluntary. If people choose to participate they complete an action plan that charts their route back into work. They then receive an allowance worth UK£15 pounds per week more than their benefit would have been. Once in the Zone, people are offered considerable personal advisor time, not just as they enter the programme but throughout the length of their stay. The personal adviser helps to identify appropriate support tailored to their needs.

A partnership board is responsible for designing and co-ordinating service provision on Employment Zones. The partnerships include Training and Enterprise Councils, local authorities, the voluntary sector, the education sector and the private sector. They come together using a joint venture agreement so, unlike the majority of New Deal units of delivery, there is no lead partner.

Box 12. (continued)

Partnership is critical to achieving greater co-ordination of the different employment, training and regeneration programmes that operate in the Employment Zone areas. There are many programmes involved. For example, the inter-departmental Single Regeneration Budget, public employment service programmes such as Work Based Training for Adults and the New Deal for 18-24 year olds, initiatives funded by the European Social Fund and new programmes such as Education Action Zones, Health Action Zones and the New Deal for Communities. By working in partnership, all the agencies and groups dealing with programmes to combat long term unemployment in an area can map out their various activities and co-ordinate their implementation, pooling and co-ordinating resources where appropriate.

Local partnerships have been encouraged to design activities in three main areas:

-   'Neighbourhood Match' - Supported work experience and training that benefits the wider community. In particular, this area promotes the Intermediate Labour Market or social enterprises approach. The projects are usually, but not exclusively, in the voluntary sector and use subsidies to create jobs that provide a community product or service but would not exist without support. They teach people practical skills and help them smooth the transition between benefit and employment.

-   'Learning for Work'- Education and training to improve employability. The government is not putting in place prescribed programmes but letting local communities and local groups decide what is best for their areas.

-   'Business Enterprise' - Help for people to start businesses or become self-employed. Research suggests that there are substantial numbers of the long term unemployed, who given the right kind of skills and opportunity would welcome the chance to start-up in business for themselves.

Zones have been encouraged to develop further innovations where particularly relevant to their local needs. For instance they can help people through driving tests or pay for work tools or meet the cost of attending interviews.

Among the new approaches to programme delivery are public transport initiatives to improve access to employer locations, outreach and community based facilities, personal mentors, childcare vouchers, Intermediate Labour Markets and 'enterprise tasters' where unemployed people spend time with small businesses to find out if they want to consider self-employment. The emphasis is on bottom-up strategic planning and partnership, a strong focus on clients and local flexibility to combine Employment Zone funding with budgets from certain existing regeneration programmes.

Box 12. (continued)

One of the features of Employment Zones policy is a new flexibility to combine funds from different programmes. In the past, programmes and associated funding streams have often been quite rigidly and narrowly defined. They have often followed a sector logic (for example, health initiatives, business development initiatives, training initiatives or employment initiatives), rather than trying to develop projects that link together measures to tackle different aspects of a problem. The Employment Zones experiment seeks to overcome this problem by facilitating the movement of funding from one programme to another. This gives decision-makers the opportunity to think more strategically about issues and problems. At present, this funding flexibility covers budgets from current regeneration programmes and the new money associated with the Employment Zone pilot.

In the near future, the government intends to take this funding flexibility further by creating 'Personal Job Accounts'. These will combine money currently paid out in welfare benefits with other money already spent on long term unemployment, such as training programmes and Job Centre advice, into an individual block resource that can be used to offer participants solutions more tailored to their own particular unemployment problems. Through discussions with their personal advisers, individuals will be given the opportunity to help decide the way that the money is spent. It is hoped that this will lead to more sensible and imaginative decisions about provision and will help to motivate participants, because people will be more involved in the decisions that affect them. The 'Personal Job Accounts' could for example be used as support for self-employment or as a job subsidy for an employer and may also be used to lever in resources from other programmes by acting as a source of matched funds. This additional funding flexibility will require new parliamentary legislation and some revisions to regulations applying to certain central government funds.

The Employment Zone programme is on a much smaller scale than the New Deal. There are currently only five Zones with a direct budget of UK£58 million until April 2000. However, the programme is of great interest because of its experimental nature in giving communities more flexibility to devise innovative and tailored solutions for their areas and to combine existing budgets and programmes. There is strong potential for the lessons learned to be integrated into mainstream provision.

There are a number of innovations that are being tested in the overall design of the Employment Zone experiment in order to encourage local partners to use their increased flexibility to develop locally tailored actions:

Partnership: What is innovative about the approach to partnership in Employment Zones is that each partner signs a joint venture contract that makes them jointly responsible for delivery of specified outputs. Partnership is therefore formal. The use of a joint venture structure is also intended to act as a brake on the emergence of a lead or dominant partner.

Pooling of funds: Many independent agencies already survive by drawing on a wide range of different funding streams from government. However, what Zones are testing are ways in which these funds can be brought together at the local level before they reach the individual provider in order that they work together in a more coherent way.

Personal advisers: Whilst personal advisers have been introduced in the New Deal for 18-24 year olds, the Employment Zones apply the concept to a more difficult target group. These are long term unemployed people over 25 years old and in areas of the highest long term unemployment. The work of Employment Zone personal advisers is more extensive than for personal advisers within the New Deal, covering the entire time that participants are on the programme and advising on a wider range of possible activities and support than is available through New Deal.

Increased choice of opportunities: Employment Zones are based on offering a greater choice to unemployed people. The key to increasing employability is taking the appropriate steps for each individual. But this means that there needs to be flexibility of provision and an appropriate supply of opportunities locally. This poses some critical challenges for the local provider infrastructure. Purchasing for the individual, rather than block purchasing from the provider takes us one step further towards establishing a market in the purchasing of opportunities for unemployed people. Individual providers will have to be more responsive, with the right package and at the right time and with the right support mechanisms.

Benefits: Moving from welfare into work can represent a significant financial risk for an individual or a household. That risk is greater and feels greater the longer somebody has been unemployed, so the risks need to be minimised and risk-taking needs to be rewarded. Zones are exploring different ways in which social security regulations can be changed to make that transition easier.

Filling gaps in provision: A whole range of local initiatives is being developed which concentrate on the sorts of local issues that are important for local economies. The emphasis is on filling the gaps that exist in local provision. To identify these gaps, Zones have had to analyse what is needed and what is supplied. This is an ongoing process that will take time to develop.

Focus on the individual: Zones seek to provide what the individual and the personal adviser have agreed in terms of what is necessary to get someone into a sustainable job. The degree of flexibility provided to the Zone goes a long way beyond what national programmes have given in the past.

The role of the private sector: The government has made it clear that they want to see an increased role for the private sector both in terms of membership of partnerships and also in providing opportunities to unemployed people. All Zones are exploring this and have a high degree of private sector involvement.

CHAPTER 3
MAKING LOCAL PARTNERSHIPS WORK

The importance of local partnerships to welfare-to-work policy

Local partnership is a relatively new concept that has been widely taken up during the 1990s in the field of employment and social policies, based on evidence that they can improve the effectiveness of policy (OECD, 1996b, OECD, 1998). Within Europe, most OECD Member countries now have local partnerships to combat social exclusion and to stimulate economic regeneration in disadvantaged areas. In many cases their establishment has been supported by the European Structural Funds, which introduced a focus on partnership in their 1992 reforms, but there are also many nationally and locally funded initiatives. Partnerships for local development, urban regeneration and workforce development are also common in North America. Helping people on welfare to find employment is an important objective for many of these initiatives. In some areas the public employment service is also working through local partnerships to deliver mainstream employment policies, including the Mutual Obligation and Work for the Dole policies in Australia, the state welfare programmes in the United States and the New Deal and Employment Zone approaches in the United Kingdom. How well these local partnerships work will help determine the success of welfare-to-work programmes.

The following main potential advantages of local partnership approaches can be listed:

- Firstly, there are enormous variations in labour market conditions and needs across localities within OECD countries and this requires locally differentiated design of labour market policies. Local agencies are close to the various different aspects of the unemployment problem. Partnerships that encourage exchange of information, experience and knowledge between them can therefore help to design policy that is well aligned with local conditions.

61

- Secondly, the local partnership approach enables local people to be involved in the decisions that affect them. This includes not only the unemployed but also the employers who will be the recipients of the participants in welfare-to-work programmes and the local agencies that are preparing and developing initiatives. Local participation creates a greater sense of ownership and a greater sense of commitment to what is being done.

- Thirdly, the problems that people face in the transition from welfare to work are often multifaceted, including for example issues of childcare, transport, skills, matching with vacancies and availability of job opportunities. Local partnership is a mechanism for agencies to work together to provide 'joined up' and coherent solutions, at a minimum to co-ordinate their actions and at best to adopt an integrated and comprehensive approach.

It is therefore important that these potential advantages are drawn out in the way that local partnerships are established and supported.

There are many different partnership models for bringing together local actors to design and deliver policies in the field of economic and social development. For example, there are different ways that partners relate to each other and differences in the number of partners involved. There are also differences in management structures, in terms of the composition of boards, working groups management procedures. Hutchinson and Campbell (1998), for example, distinguish between the 'Federation' structure and the 'Hub Network' structure. The 'Federation' is a structure with a relatively large number of inter-dependent organisations, where the management organisation is created and sustained by a network. There is pressure to achieve consensus and compromise. The 'Hub Network' involves a number of different organisations but one of them acts as the core partner, co-ordinating and integrating the activities of all the others. What is most important in all these different models is that the partnership model is manageable and fit for purpose.

Box 13 gives an example of the process of setting up a welfare-to-work partnership under the UK New Deal programme.

Box 13. Setting up a New Deal partnership in Wearside, United Kingdom

Wearside is in the north east of England, centred on the city of Sunderland. It contains a diverse range of settlements, including inner city areas, ex coal-mining villages, Washington New Town and rural areas. The area has experienced severe recent industrial decline with the loss of some 30,000 jobs over the last 20 years, culminating in the final closure of its main industries, shipbuilding and coal-mining, in the late 1980s and early 1990s. Its economic development strategy, led by the local government authority, has been to create jobs through the establishment of an advanced manufacturing sector, including the Nissan car factory and local suppliers, and a major call centre sector. The Wearside labour market is characterised by high levels of long term structural unemployment, which co-exist with skill shortages in certain expanding sectors and occupations. One of the key roles of the local New Deal partnership is to assist labour market adjustment in this context.

The recognition of a public problem was an important catalyst for the initial establishment of partnership working in Wearside in 1994, three years prior to the New Deal programme. At this time, the city council led the establishment of a Sunderland City Partnership, bringing together public, private and community sectors with the common goal of improving and sustaining quality of life for the people of Sunderland. It was chaired by one of the city's major employers. A process of partnership working was established which has been successful in attracting 50 million pounds into the city, from the national government's Single Regeneration Budget and national lottery funding as well as from the European Structural Funds. However, it is noteworthy that there was no public employment service representation on this partnership.

With the introduction of New Deal in 1997, the public employment service was identified as the lead agency. This new initiative could potentially have presented some local tensions with the existing partnership arrangements. At the heart of New Deal was the requirement to set up an inclusive and extensive basis to develop an integrated strategic approach. The challenge was to achieve this more inclusive and extensive approach whilst keeping the support and co-operation of the existing and very effective partnership.

Box 13. (continued)

One way of setting up the New Deal partnership would have been to take-over an existing partnership that could then be labelled as New Deal. The difficulty was that all interests across the city were not on any one group and therefore the objective of being inclusive and extensive would not have been achieved. A different approach was therefore chosen. The manager of the local office of the public employment service arranged bilateral meetings with the most senior representatives of the key organisations and agencies across the city, beginning with the chairman of the existing Sunderland City Partnership. Their views, hopes and concerns were sought, and local public employment service ideas were put forward on how to form a new broader-based New Deal partnership steering group on which they would have representation. In this way, the manager of the local office of the public employment service was able to work up a consensus for a new partnership structure. Following these meetings, the City of Sunderland New Deal Partnership steering group was established with a much broader representational base than the original partnership.

A vision, mission and values were agreed to provide an enduring reference point with strategic goals that were above personal or organisational interests. The agreed mission was to operate through an inclusive partnership that would deliver New Deal through quality opportunities, supporting client progression out of unemployment and into sustainable employment, and to use New Deal as a catalyst for improved social cohesion and a more efficient economy. Everybody in the group signed up to the work by these principles which complemented the original and ongoing work of the City of Sunderland Partnership.

The Sunderland New Deal Partnership steering group is organised as a federation, with a documented and agreed constitution. The steering group is supported by a number of additional design and advisory groups. There are also regular discussions and meetings on a wide range of other local initiatives that have an impact on employment and the New Deal and the local office of the public employment service is now a key player in many of these initiatives. Strong personal relationships have been built up between partners, based on mutual trust and a common understanding of shared goals, so that problems can be identified and dealt with through open and honest communication.

Box 13. (continued)

Among the initiatives developed by the Sunderland New Deal partnership are:

-   Work with the private sector to design appropriate training provision. For example, design of a customised New Deal training programme with an association of local automotive industry manufacturers in response to a major expansion.

-   Combination of funding from the Single Regeneration Budget, local authorities, the European Union Structural Funds and the New Deal Environmental Task Force in order to develop an Intermediate Labour Market initiative covering environmental projects, childcare provision and call centre work.

-   Creation of a New Deal voluntary sector development agency, working with over 100 separate voluntary sector organisations to provide them with support to develop quality job opportunities for young people. As well as capacity building within the voluntary sector it has provided New Deal clients with opportunities to demonstrate, learn and rehearse work skills to prove their suitability and reliability to enter the commercial labour market.

The advantages of partnership working are perceived locally to be a widened understanding and approach towards the issues, the application of holistic solutions to problems and the opportunity to pool knowledge and resources and share risks.

After one year of activity a 'partnership day' was organised in order to revisit the strategic objectives and the mission, vision and values in order to check their relevance for the next 12 months and beyond. The event was organised in order to examine and review the effectiveness of the partnership against the original plans, to set out future goals, measures and quality standards, to re-establish inclusivity and to look again at developing innovative approaches to common problems.

Key lessons for the operation of welfare-to-work partnerships

Campbell in Chapter 8 of this book sets out some key good practice lessons for welfare-to-work partnerships based on recent experience in the United Kingdom. Partnerships should be encouraged to operate in this way. In summary:

- Localities should treat partnership as a process of building relationships of trust and building for the future, rather than as a static structure.

- Partnerships should be given enough local discretion and autonomy to create synergies in the design of policy.

- Partnerships should seek to meet local objectives at the same time as national objectives in order to secure both bottom-up and top-down support.

- It is important that the people who are involved in partnerships have the power to change the situation for the long term unemployed. Partnerships that seek to include everybody with an interest may become unwieldy.

- It is very important to have a strategic approach and clear objectives.

- Partnerships need to be results oriented with clear targets, good management information and strong review systems.

- Strong management is very important, including leadership that is oriented to the local culture and a skilled management team.

- The means need to be found to sustain partnership activity in the long run by deepening ownership and commitment to those partnership, engaging in team building and embedding the culture of partnership in localities.

However, local areas vary in their capacity to put into place partnerships operating according to the good practices identified above. In particular, an existing history of effective partnership working is an important determinant of future success, whether this is just in terms of sharing information or whether it extends to sharing resources and decision-making. For example, early experience with the Employment Zones experiment in the United Kingdom suggests that initially whilst all partnerships were positive about the programme and the opportunities it offers them, in some areas there were greater difficulties starting up the initiative than in others. The Employment Zone experiment seeks to establish a model of partnership where all partners take joint and equal responsibility for the design and management of provision and all partners take a clear role. Moving towards this model appears to have been more difficult in areas where there is not a strong tradition of working in partnership or in areas where there is one very strong partner that tends to dominate the others. Overall, local areas with a history of successful networking between agencies, and the individuals within them, are more likely to be successful than either those with little history of partnership or those where problems have emerged.

There are nonetheless certain capacity building measures that can be undertaken to improve performance where there are weaknesses in the operation of partnerships. It is important therefore that the partnerships are monitored and evaluated in terms of their structures (e.g. depth of membership, communication channels), staff skills and management procedures (e.g. understanding of local conditions, project management, financial control) and financial resources. Identified problems may then be addressed, for example by the measures outlined below in order to bring poorly performing localities up to the standards of the others (European Commission, 1998; LEDA Partenariat, 1998a, 1998b). These measures can be initiated and pursued either by central agencies or by local partners themselves.

- *Building structures.* A structure for co-ordinating the resources and actions of the multiple partners involved must be established. There are various possible structures, and where partnership is not working well in a locality it may be possible to change to a different structure. For example, where there is a very wide and inclusive partnership it may be better to reduce decision-making to a smaller group, but to include others through appropriate forums and subcommittees. It may also be appropriate to establish a strong lead partner to move partnership forward where otherwise little progress would be made. Partnerships often break down where there is poor communication between agencies. It is therefore also very important that partnerships have a communication system that allows information to be transmitted with clarity and consistency between partners and externally. Guidelines and advice may be required on how to share information and with whom to ensure that no partner has privileged access to important decision-making information and that no partner is excluded.

- *Building staff skills and management procedures.* Collective in-service staff training can be used to enhance the partnership skills required amongst the people involved, for example in servicing the diverse needs of individual members, managing relationships between partners, developing consensus and strategic planning. Staff exchanges between different agencies involved in partnerships can also help promote understanding of different needs, ways of working and cultures. Local seminars on key issues for the development of effective partnership can be held bringing together staff from different agencies. Advice and guidelines can also be given on management procedures, for example mechanisms for monitoring and evaluating policy performance and partnership functioning, establishing decision-making structures, managing internal relationships including how to mediate conflicts/tensions between individuals, ensuring quality and dealing with dominant partners. Seminars, publications and exchanges can be used to help areas learn from experiences elsewhere.

– *Provision of financial resources.* Resources are required to support a central partnership structure, to support the activities undertaken and the time devoted to partnership working by individual partners and to support the implementation of actions. Difficulties operating and sustaining partnership may sometimes reflect under-resourcing. One way of tackling this is to encourage accessing of additional resources by extending the partnership. It may also be possible to provide some additional central funding support if particular barriers need to be overcome in certain localities.

– *Temporary delegation of a representative from central authorities.* Where local partnership is performing very poorly, central authorities could take a direct role in the decision-making bodies of the partnerships set up by the local actors, by delegating a representative of the central authority.

Measures such as those listed above can have an important role. However, it is important that both central and local agencies invest in the development of partnership. It is also important to be aware that effective partnership working can take time and that the time required may vary between different localities according to their different local histories and contexts. As experience grows structures and processes are likely to evolve and strengthen and the capacity to assess local needs and introduce innovative actions is likely to increase.

Engaging the private sector

If local partnerships are to be successful in tackling long term unemployment, it is critical that they engage the interest and involvement of employers.

Employer representation on local partnerships helps to ensure that the support activities designed for individual long term unemployed clients is directly focused on work that is likely to be available with employers. The involvement of employers designing the nature and quality of provision also makes it more likely that they will eventually take on welfare recipients moving through the programmes.

This employer role is widely accepted within the design of employment policy provision by local partnerships. For example, in the United States legislation requires that the private sector makes up the majority of members on local Workforce Development Boards in order to bring to a recognition of the local labour market demand in the design of training programmes. Employers have also been brought in to the local partnerships for the New Deal for 18-24 year olds in the United Kingdom (see the example in Box 14). They benefit from the opportunity to influence the nature of training provision and employability measures and thus to influence the supply of labour in their locality as well as from the opportunity to demonstrate a commitment to the development of the community in which they are based. It is often larger employers that are most concerned with these two goals but it is important not to limit partnership participation to just a few large employers, since they may not be representative of the labour market needs across the local economy as a whole.

**Box 14. An example of employer involvement
in a UK New Deal partnership**

The Sheffield New Deal Partnership established a Consultative Task Team (CTT) bringing together a range of partners to help design provision. The CTT was broken down into different working groups. Six employers worked on the Employment Option working group to look at the details of provision under this option and how they could benefit from New Deal at the same time as providing employment to people between 18 and 24 who had been jobless for more than 6 months. The main issues covered in their discussions were:

- The form, quality and content of training provision and how employers may contribute, source and pay for it.

- General employer perceptions concerning the initiative and how to overcome the barrier of poor perceptions of previous initiatives.

- How New Deal should be sold to employers so that they take advantage of the possibility to hire welfare recipients through a supported programme.

- The work activities that should be undertaken under the Employment Option so that the new employee will achieve sustained employment beyond the subsidy period.

The employers made a number of recommendations for provision, including the introduction of a mentoring system for clients. In addition, the employers advised on how the programme should interface with employers in order to secure the best response. They suggested that there should be a single contact point for employers, that there should be a clear information pack or help-line and that there should be a simple system for employers with minimal bureaucracy and paperwork. The benefits of New Deal for employers were identified and a list of potential obstacles to employers was drawn up so that they could be tackled prior to the launch.

Critically, welfare-to-work programmes need to convince employers to recruit welfare recipients. One of the keys to this is to demonstrate quality in the support provided to participants in programmes. This includes appropriate guidance, so that people are motivated and capable of pursuing the opportunities recommended, activities to develop skills and employability and adequate support services so that welfare recipients are not prevented from taking and keeping work by other problems, such as family or transport. It is also critical to provide good quality support to employers taking on welfare recipients through welfare-to-work programmes, including good information on the programme, referral of people who are appropriate for vacancies offered and help overcoming problems if they emerge. Box 15 looks at the strategies employed by a not-for-profit intermediary in the United States to help and encourage businesses to engage successfully in welfare-to-work programmes. In Chapter 9 of this book Lyn Hogan describes in more detail the issues and methodologies employed.

Box 15. The approach of the Welfare-to-Work Partnership to engaging the private sector in the United States

The Welfare-to-Work Partnership in Washington is a non-profit entity established at the request of President Clinton to help implement the 1996 PRWORA legislation. The organisation was deliberately created outside of the government and does not receive government funding. Instead it is funded by its business membership. This is because it was felt that the business community sometimes has a negative or uncomfortable reaction working directly with government and that using an organisation funded and organised by the business community was probably the best approach to really engaging businesses on a wide scale. To date, the Welfare-to-Work Partnership has brought together over 7,000 businesses throughout the country, businesses of all sizes and in all industries, in order to encourage them to hire welfare recipients and to retain these recipients. These businesses receive technical assistance, information and written materials and conferences and discussions are organised to help them understand the welfare population and to structure appropriate programmes within their companies.

In the United States, evidence suggests that most businesses are reluctant to become involved in welfare-to-work, even if they have a need for workers. They generally buy into existing stereotypes of welfare recipients, believing that hiring welfare recipients may disrupt their work environments and believing that welfare recipients may not be the best workers available. They also tend to consider involvement in welfare-to-work programmes as charity rather than as good for their business. The Welfare-to-Work Partnership seeks to overcome these barriers. Its main methods of work are:

- Breaking down existing stereotypes about welfare recipients by providing information to the business community about welfare recipients and their backgrounds. This shows that welfare recipients do want to work, that often they have some work experience and that what they need is a step up or a connection to the labour market.

Box 15. (continued)

- Sharing positive examples with businesses. Encouraging businesses with a positive experience to engage additional businesses in this movement has been very successful.

- Emphasising the results of research that show the benefits of hiring welfare recipients for company profitability. Research conducted by three different organisations in the United States shows that involvement in welfare-to-work programmes can result in long term savings for companies by increasing job retention and by providing a ready source of workers.

- Providing public relations and press access to businesses and organisations working in welfare-to-work programmes.

- Research by the Welfare-to-Work Partnership suggests that there are several success factors for business involvement in welfare-to-work programmes. Firstly, a representative from the high levels of the company, or a corporate champion, should make the decision to hire welfare recipients. Without a corporate champion at the top levels of the company, businesses tend to be slow to become involved or tend not to take a comprehensive approach. Secondly, companies should develop strategic plans for integrating welfare recipients into the business. Thirdly, businesses should maintain high employee management standards. They should not lower their standards to accommodate welfare recipients. Finally, companies should enter into partnerships with the government and/or a community organisation to help them set up and deliver on their strategic plan.

- Developing partnerships with government or community organisations is crucial if businesses are to structure their programmes appropriately and provide the sort of benefits necessary to retain the employees. Businesses generally work with partners to understand the needs of people recruited from welfare and how to retain them. They also typically rely on them to provide them with information on affordable childcare for the new hires and the transport services that are available. They may even enter into partnerships with local organisations to provide transportation or create new transportation solutions. Generally businesses will also rely on local organisations to provide counselling and mentoring to the new employees.

- The Welfare-to-Work Partnership encourages businesses to structure their involvement in welfare-to-work programmes in this way. The organisation seeks a commitment from senior people in the business for participation in welfare-to-work, it stresses the need for a strategic plan, it encourages them to maintain their employee standards and it acts as a broker between the business and community organisations and the government.

Further issues for partnership approaches

This chapter has identified the importance of local partnership for effective design and management of welfare-to-work programmes and outlined some key lessons for partnership development and for involving the private sector. Overall, governments must be prepared to invest in partnerships, to support the actors involved, and to allow time for effective partnership working to emerge. This is particularly important in cases where there has been relatively little history of partnership working in the past. This section deals with two further issues that are emerging as the use of local partnerships becomes more widespread and as a number of partnerships mature. More work needs to be done in the future in order to find appropriate approaches to deal with these issues.

Competition together with collaboration

Whilst the purpose of introducing the partnership approach is to encourage collaboration between key players in the provision of services to combat long term unemployment, it is important not to overlook the role of competition and markets in securing dynamic and efficient provision. Key players within partnerships often collaborate but they may sometimes compete and it is important to get this balance right. Competition helps ensure that provision does not stagnate and that prices do not rise. In the long-run collaboration through partnership may impede this competition. Collaboration between employers and providers may also become dominated by certain groups of firms and organisations and provision may end up being distorted towards the needs of these players rather than reflecting demand as a whole. Overall, the local partnership concept is still relatively new. More work is required to identify the situations in which partners should compete and those in which they should collaborate and to establish which types of framework best support this type of flexibility.

Accountability and evaluation

The question of accountability and evaluation of partnerships is also one that requires more investigation and development. Evaluation is important for providing accountability, for justifying public expenditures by demonstrating benefits and for helping adjust programmes to overcome problems and take advantage of areas of success. However, on a technical level, evaluation becomes difficult in partnership situations because outputs result from combinations of actors and inputs and the relative impact of each actor or input can be difficult to disentangle from the others. Similarly, a number of questions are raised with respect to who is accountable for problems. Appropriate channels of accountability need to be explored and evaluation methods developed for these situations. On an empirical level, more evaluation evidence is still needed to assess the overall value-added that is brought from using partnerships. A great deal of organisational, managerial and resource effort goes into creating and running partnerships. It therefore needs to be demonstrated that partnership is both effective and efficient in terms of getting welfare recipients into work, compared with other organisational structures that may be developed.

CHAPTER 4
PROMISING LOCAL POLICY TOOLS

Clearly it is critical to the effective operation of welfare-to-work programmes that appropriate tools are used. The evolution in the tools of local employment policy has been rapid in recent years and a range of new and modified tools are now being used to help people move from welfare to work. They can be grouped under the following main headings:

- *Work placements and employment subsidies*; for example placements with employers, wage subsidies to employers, wage incentives to employees, loans or grants for entering self-employment, Intermediate Labour Markets and social enterprises.

- *Guidance, job search and placement*; for example careers guidance, personal advisers, job match databases, mentoring.

- *Training and employability skills*; for example vocational training, confidence building, personal development courses.

- *Access assistance*; for example public transport and mobility assistance, childcare support.

There is nonetheless still considerable variation in the nature of tools used by local actors in different countries, implying significant scope for international transfer of ideas and lessons. This chapter looks at some innovative tools being used by local welfare-to-work programmes in each of these areas.

Social enterprises and the creation of new work opportunities

One of the functions of welfare-to-work programmes is to link long term unemployed and excluded people with existing vacancies and labour market opportunities. However, in many localities with very high concentrations of unemployment there are simply not sufficient opportunities either for long term unemployed people to find work experience placements or for them to obtain a permanent job. In response to this situation, initiatives have emerged during the last ten years that attempt to create new opportunities directly for the long term unemployed by involving them in providing new socially useful products and services to the local community. For example, these services may include developing new social services for individuals and families, improving the environment or enhancing cultural assets. The advantages of these activities for local employment creation are that the services involved are labour-intensive, they must be supplied locally rather than imported and they often do not require much start-up capital and therefore have low barriers to entry.

The activities themselves are sometimes undertaken in the public sector, as is the case with the *'Nouveaux Services-Emplois Jeunes'* initiative in France outlined in Chapter 1 (Box 4). However, there is an increasing movement to develop this type of service in independent companies or not-for-profit organisations, known as social enterprises. They generate their own revenues by selling their services in the market and to the public sector and by making use of public sector subsidies where available. They have an entrepreneurial character in that they are voluntarily created, autonomously governed and the founders risk their capital or labour to exploit market gaps or emerging markets. At the same time they are not profit-maximising, but have a social goal. Their recent emergence reflects two key trends; growing demand for social and community services and privatisation of social services provision.

Not all social enterprises aim to create employment or help integrate the long term unemployed in the labour market. For many, the aim is simply to provide new services for community benefit. However, there is an important sub-set of social enterprises that combine this with offering the unemployed and excluded a bridge into the mainstream labour market. It is this group of social enterprises that is of interest for welfare-to-work programmes. They either provide temporary work experience and training for people detached from the labour market, to make it easier for them to find a job, or they provide permanent job opportunities for this group at the same time as meeting a community need. In all cases, a critical principle is that the activities carried out in social enterprises should not displace existing jobs.

Certain European countries have already built up a significant base of social enterprises, albeit within a wide variety of legal and organisational frameworks, and some useful lessons can be learned from them. In particular, in Italy there were some 750 'work integration co-operatives' in 1996, according to estimates from the *Istituto di Previdenza Sociale* (INPS), and in France the *Comité nationale des entreprises d'insertion* (CNEI) identified approximately 800 'insertion enterprises' in the same year. Both provide temporary jobs for disadvantaged or unemployed workers as well as social and community products and services. Other European countries also operate initiatives corresponding to the social enterprise concept, in particular Belgium, Spain, Germany, Portugal, Ireland, Sweden and Austria. There are further social enterprise initiatives in Canada and the United States, mainly focused on disadvantaged communities, and in Mexico. In the United Kingdom, until very recently, there have been only a very small number of schemes in operation. One of them, Glasgow Works, is described in Box 16. Nonetheless, a large number of new initiatives are now planned within New Deal and Employment Zone strategies, known as 'Intermediate Labour Markets'.

**Box 16. United Kingdom Intermediate Labour Markets:
the case of Glasgow Works**

Glasgow Works is an Intermediate Labour Market initiative operating in Glasgow, which is the largest city in Scotland and has a particularly high concentration of long term unemployment. The initiative aims to develop new services of benefit to the city at the same time as providing long term unemployed people with skills that are in demand in the local labour market. The projects are designed to have the potential to raise their own income and create permanent job placement places.

Glasgow Works has developed projects across a range of activities, but one key feature of its approach is to access, wherever possible, funding from benefits and social programmes that are already available in the city. For example, it has developed a programme where long term unemployed people undertake housing improvement work on behalf of people living in damp properties, accessing finance from social grants already available to people in those properties but that they would not otherwise be able to take up. Other examples of Glasgow Works projects include:

- Disability support: 15 people supporting disabled people at work.

- Childcare: 43 people in 6 new after-school care schemes and 2 crèches.

- Youth education: 24 people assisting professionals in youth work and combating school drop-out.

- Recycling manufacture: 26 people refurbishing refrigerators, washing machines and cookers.

- Health action: 10 link-workers for the city's black and Asian community.

Box 16. (continued)

There is a wide range of projects, normally with around 15-20 operating at any time. In 1997 there were some 500 work places in the Glasgow Works programme.

A critical determinant in establishing these projects has been the development of partnership. At the city level the partnership created by Glasgow Works brings together the major actors, including Glasgow Development Agency, the local government authority, the public employment service and the Scottish Trades Union Congress. Glasgow Works has also developed partnerships with community groups, non-profit companies, private companies and development agencies in the local areas where it is active.

Under the normal Glasgow Works process, the long term unemployed (12 months plus) go through 3-4 weeks of pre-assessment, counselling and guidance before being recruited onto a project following a competitive interview. They are then employed for up to one year, undertaking work on a project for a wage, with some training and some personal development activity. At the end of that period they receive ongoing support for up to 6 months within a job, further education or self-employment or for continuing job search.

Glasgow Works functions on a diverse package of funding. Currently about one-third comes from Europe Union sources, mainly from the European Social Fund. Local public agencies put in about 15%. Approximately 20% is drawn from unemployment benefits. Approximately 15% is from national programmes. The rest comes from a range of public and private revenues. However, this mix of funding is likely to change over time.

Another key characteristic of the Glasgow Works programme is that it is managed by a very small central team. There are therefore relatively low administrative overheads (only 8% of the budget goes on central staff and management costs). The role of the central team is to bring funding together for projects and to transfer good practice. Most of the actual delivery is undertaken by local organisations on the ground that recruit the workers, manage the work and pay, achieve training and job outputs, provide personal counselling and support and administer the project budget. The initiative is therefore characterised by central guidance but local delivery.

Box 16. (continued)

The personal development activity in Glasgow Works is very important and makes a big difference to peoples' employability in the long term. Glasgow Works, and the Intermediate Labour Market approach in general, operates with the philosophy that employability increases through work experience, not just training, based on evidence that it is the core skills associated with work that employers look for rather than specific qualifications.

Evaluation results suggest that Glasgow Works has been very successful in helping long term unemployed people to find work. Some 69% of leavers had a job in the mainstream labour market at the survey date and 62% entered employment at the point of leaving. Amongst the group of people unemployed for at least three years the proportion gaining a job at the point of leaving was approximately 53%. This conversion rate is three times better than for normal government programmes for this group. Some 80% of the jobs obtained were full-time and permanent. It should be noted, however, that there is competitive recruitment onto the programme through interview, so there will be some element of 'creaming' of participants who are more likely to succeed.

Factors in the success of the Glasgow Works programme appear to be:

- A strong focus on activities that are recognised by participants and external employers as being real jobs, with a focus on transferable skills rather than specialised training.

- A competent management team, clear structures and local partnerships.

- The presence of personal support throughout the programme and continued support after the programme to help successful transition to the mainstream labour market.

The category of social enterprises providing work opportunities for people who are detached from the labour market includes sheltered employment workshops employing handicapped people. This concept has existed for many years. Much newer are two other categories of social enterprise that Borzaga, in Chapter 10 of this book, names 'closed work integration social enterprises' and 'open work integration social enterprises'. 'Closed work integration social enterprises' provide permanent and regularly paid employment for disadvantaged people on their own premises and for life. 'Open work integration social enterprises' employ hard to place people on a temporary basis with the aim of increasing their employability by training on the job and helping them in this way to re-enter the open labour market. Whereas closed work integration social enterprises effectively create new jobs, open work integration social enterprises create mainly work places. The person is trained for a limited period and then the work place is made free for another person. This is the case with the Glasgow Works programme described in the box.

One of the key advantages of social enterprises from the point of view of welfare-to-work programmes is that they are often able to overcome information deficiencies in the labour market that discriminate against people who are unemployed or who are involved in traditional government programmes. Often employers will seek to reduce the costs and risks of selection and training of recruits by excluding people who cannot provide evidence of recent work experience and work skills. Evidence of recent work and training in social enterprises allows previously long term unemployed people to give positive signals to employers and can therefore open new opportunities to them. Many training schemes and traditional government programmes are less well respected by employers and do not provide the same signals.

Given the advantages of social enterprises and Intermediate Labour Markets for social and employment policy, governments have recently begun to take initiatives to foster their development. In Italy, a new government agency has been set up in order to expand employment by promoting the creation of new activities for long term unemployed people by providing for unmet community needs. Box 17 identifies the role of this new organisation, Italia Lavoro, as a practical example of how governments can encourage the emergence of social enterprises at a local level.

Box 17. New activities for employment creation: the role of Italia Lavoro

Italia Lavoro was set up in November 1997 as a wholly state-owned enterprise working in close co-operation with the Italian Ministry of Labour. Its principal mission is to enable long term unemployed people working in 'socially useful jobs' (*lavori socialmente utili*) programmes to find permanent employment in the market economy. Socially useful jobs offer long term unemployed people part-time work with local authorities and other public bodies on a temporary basis. There were some 100,000 such workers in 1997. However, because of the high public cost of providing jobs in the public sector and because of the difficulty of making available sufficient socially-useful jobs placements relative to the demand, the government is seeking to provide alternative market sector employment opportunities to as many of these workers as possible. To do this, Italia Lavoro supports projects to create employment in innovative and entrepreneurial activities that are in the community interest and are still relatively undeveloped, for example new activities stemming from the ageing population, concern for the environment and the need to protect the country's artistic heritage.

Italia Lavoro works with territorial bodies (regions, provinces, communes), central government agencies involved in employment development for long term unemployed people, private firms, including employment agencies, and non-profit organisations, advising them on how to establish and manage projects to create new kinds of employment for the unemployed. This support consists of the following:

- Certification of business plans
- Legal, administrative, planning and economic assistance to public bodies and particularly to communes
- Venture capital contributions to new public-private ventures for the management of local public services
- Support to workers to set up co-operatives and to start-up self-employed craft or business activities
- Information to public bodies and private firms on the instruments aimed at promoting the hiring of the long term unemployed, including incentives, tax relief, use of European, national and regional funds
- Participation in territorial agreements, area contracts and negotiated planning agreements
- Guidance to workers in socially useful jobs, including training and reskilling tailored to the possible employment opportunity.

Box 17. (continued)

To make its action more effective, Italia Lavoro has established a Consortium that assists and advises co-operatives. It is also a shareholder in a firm that prepares feasibility studies and business plans and in the newly established *Banca Etica* ('Ethical Bank'). It is involved in the territorial agreements of the north-eastern area of the province of Naples and the Agro Nocerino Sarnese area and in the neighbourhood contracts of the Scampia and Ponticelli districts of Naples.

A key aspect of the work of Italia Lavoro is research to identify local market niches where there are opportunities for new activities based on meeting social needs. Its principal sectors of intervention are town renewal and heritage, environmental protection, development of rural and mountain zones and personal services.

Italia Lavoro is currently compiling a register of the individuals involved in socially useful jobs, all of whom will be contacted in order to review with them their potential and opportunities. At the same time it is contacting all government administrations that have launched socially useful jobs projects to assess their potential and the potential for initiating new services (either as new socially useful jobs projects or as market sector employment for people currently in socially useful jobs). On the basis of this two-fold survey, a large programme of individual guidance and training for the unemployed will be implemented, carefully targeting the possible job opportunities identified. The main types of possible job opportunities that have been identified are:

- The establishment of public/private sector joint ventures that hire socially useful job workers.

- The hiring of carefully selected and suitably trained socially useful job workers by private businesses.

- The establishment of service or production co-operatives run by socially useful job workers.

- The start-up of individual craft or business initiatives, possibly using a 'loan of honour'.

- The hiring of socially useful jobs workers by social co-operatives.

Box 17. (continued)

This work of Italia Lavoro involves organising a network and will therefore take some time to be completed. In the meantime it is actively seeking out and developing all the opportunities that arise in the course of the contacts it makes in establishing this network. In the initial stages of the programme, and within the first year, the following results have been achieved:

- 12 joint ventures established, which will ultimately employ 2 170 workers, of whom 1 905 have already been hired.

- 14 joint ventures planned or being set up, which will ultimately employ 1 207 workers

- Slightly over 100 individuals hired directly by industrial firms

- The preparation of over 1 000 business plans for socially useful job projects that should provide jobs for over 20 000 people, mostly in the form of co-operatives.

Social enterprises for labour market integration are a relatively new phenomenon and a significant body of evaluation evidence is yet to be established on their effectiveness and efficiency and on whether certain approaches are more successful than others. A number of evaluations of individual local programmes have demonstrated positive results in terms of the employment secured for participants and the community benefits provided in relation to the costs incurred. However, there are also some potential weaknesses of the social enterprise approach that need to be explored and assessed further.

Are social enterprises associated with poor quality job attainments? Social enterprises, particularly those of the 'open work integration' type, play the very important function of helping disadvantaged people to access jobs in the mainstream labour market. The emphasis is usually placed on support in the form of work experience and whilst some training is often involved it is much less intensive than is the case with standard government training programmes. Without significant training it could be argued that programme leavers are likely to attain only jobs requiring relatively low skill levels, commanding relatively low wages and possibly of short duration. If leavers subsequently receive training in the job attained or move up the job and wage ladder this problem is not necessarily serious. However, in order to assess these issues, more evidence is required on the long term job history of people leaving social enterprise projects. In the case of 'closed work integration social enterprises' permanent jobs are offered to disadvantaged people, but they may be at a lower rate of pay than prevails in the private sector. Again it is important to assess the relative quality of the opportunities involved and the possibilities of participants moving on to other jobs.

How important are the potential displacement and substitution effects? The establishment and operation of social enterprises may lead to the displacement of employment and output in existing private enterprises or public sector operations if work previously undertaken by them is transferred to the social enterprise. In assessing the potential contribution of social enterprises to reducing long term unemployment and to increasing the availability of community services it is therefore important to investigate the effects on competitor suppliers. It may be the case that displacement is actually quite low. This is because social enterprises attempt to be innovative in bringing together new packages of funding to meet needs that are not currently met by the market or the public sector. Moreover, it could be argued that even if some of the activities undertaken by social enterprises were otherwise carried out by the private or public sector, it is unlikely that the long term unemployed would participate. Social enterprises therefore have an important role in attaching the most disadvantaged to the labour market even where there is some displacement. A similar potential counter-effect of social enterprises relates to substitution. This can occur where people who are helped to obtain employment in the mainstream labour market substitute for other potential recruits. Again it could be argued that even where this occurs social enterprises are likely to improve the overall access of long term unemployed people to new vacancies. More evaluation is nevertheless needed to assess the scale of these displacement and substitution effects.

To what extent does the success of such initiatives rely on 'creaming' the most employable candidates and avoiding those who are most disadvantaged? Further evidence is also required on the extent to which the reported success of social enterprises in helping people to obtain employment reflects prior screening and selection of those people who would be most likely to succeed anyway. If this were the case, then it would imply that attempts to increase the scale of social enterprise initiatives could run into decreasing returns and that they may therefore be inappropriate as a large scale tool for combating long term unemployment. More information is therefore needed on the contexts in which social enterprises best operate and with which groups of people.

Notwithstanding the need for more evaluation evidence on the above issues, there would appear to be some potential to make the social enterprise tool available to a larger group of beneficiaries. Social enterprises provide many social benefits, including work integration, and as 'positive externalities' they are not always rewarded for them. The existence of such 'positive externalities' is a justification for public sector intervention to support social enterprises. The greatest potential for expansion would appear to be in geographical areas where social enterprises are not currently being used and in new market niches where there is the opportunity to meet community needs that are not currently being met by the market or the public sector. It is also important that social enterprise initiatives should not be seen as a solution on their own but as part of a portfolio of activities to combat unemployment. They may not be suitable in all contexts or for all groups of long term unemployed people.

In Chapter 10, Borzaga points to a number of steps that public agencies can take to increase the number and effectiveness of social enterprises in welfare-to-work programmes. In summary:

–   Distinguish work integration social enterprises from the rest of the social enterprise or non-profit sector and link them to the network of institutional relations centred on welfare-to-work programmes.

–   Contractually define the contribution of work integration social enterprises to the employability of disadvantaged people and make a public subsidy corresponding to the expenditure on training and increase the employability of these workers.

–   Regulate the activities of work integration social enterprises to ensure that they use certain instruments to increase the employability of disadvantaged workers, for example personalised skill development programmes.

–   Develop programmes to link work integration social enterprises with traditional firms. Work integration social enterprises appear to have a greater chance of success if they are strongly connected with normal private businesses, for example through subcontracting links.

In-work financial incentives

Getting the structure of tax and benefits right is an important aspect of welfare-to-work policy. It is widely recognised that unless programmes make work pay better than passive income support then they are likely to fail to induce people to move into the labour market. High out of work incomes relative to wage earnings can lead to an 'unemployment trap', where there is little immediate financial incentive to take paid employment. Tackling this problem requires a change in the balance between incomes in and out of work. There are two possible approaches to this. Firstly, unemployment and related welfare benefits could be reduced where they are considered to be over-generous, or restrictions could be placed on the length of time benefits are available to people who are not working. Secondly, net incomes in work could be increased through changes in tax and benefits.

The provision of in-work financial incentives to welfare recipients taking jobs is part of the second of these two approaches. The underlying concept is to make people certain that moving from welfare to work will make them financially better off compared with staying in the passive system. The incentive approach aims to help people to earn enough by working to support themselves and their families. This is important in the context of OECD labour markets where there is an increasing incidence of low wage employment for some groups, particularly poorly educated young males, and people may therefore need to combine continued welfare payments with their wages from work to realise a liveable income. An incentive approach requires governments to be willing to invest in getting people back to work. However, the public costs of changes in tax and benefits can be limited when they are closely targeted on those groups exposed to financial work disincentives. Moreover, there should be new entrants to the labour market and for those people persuaded to move into work because of the changes, the public cost will be reduced to the 'top-up' rather than the full welfare benefit. Where incomes subsequently increase the 'top up' can be phased out.

Employment-conditional tax credits or benefits have been introduced in Ireland, the United Kingdom, Canada, Mexico and the United States. For example, in Ireland families with low incomes are entitled to Family Income Supplement. In the United Kingdom a Working Families Tax Credit (WFTC) is being introduced in 1999 as part of recent welfare-to-work reform to replace the previous family credit with the effect of increasing incomes for poor working families. Jobs publicised in public employment service Job Centres will be advertised with the extra WFTC earnings added, so that people with children can immediately see how much better off they would be working. The recent introduction of a national minimum wage is an important complement to this. In the United States there has recently been an expansion of the federal Earned Income Tax Credit (EITC) for low-income workers.

In some OECD Member countries, particularly the United States and Canada, the provision of in-work incentives is not just a national responsibility but is shared with regional and local governments as part of their own welfare approaches. Thus in the United States, Wisconsin, for example, is one of four states to offer its own income tax credit, which applies on top of the federal

EITC. The Wisconsin tax credit is worth 4% of the federal EITC for working families with one child and increases to 14% for 2 children and 43% for 3 or more children, up to a maximum of US$ 1529 in 1999. In Connecticut, welfare recipients taking work are allowed to keep all earnings up to the federal poverty level in addition to their state welfare payments (for up to 21 months), childcare support (for low income households) and Medicaid (for up to 2 years after leaving welfare) (OECD, 1999a).

In Canada, devolution and decentralisation of responsibilities for labour market and social programmes during the 1990s has effectively created a situation of 'asymmetrical federalism', where different power relationships are evolving between each province and the federal government. Certain elements of the social safety net remain a federal responsibility, for example the new employment insurance system introduced in 1996. But other responsibilities are mainly with the provinces, including design of labour market services and welfare programmes, or are shared with the federal government, for example initiatives directed towards child poverty or to social excluded groups such as people with disabilities. Within this context reforms to the social safety net are proceeding at very different paces in different provinces. Overall, however, there is a common orientation towards improving work incentives and, apart from the 'workfare' programme in Ontario, there is very little popularity in imposing obligatory work or employment programme activities.

Nakamura, Wong and Diewert, in Chapter 11 of this book, describe one such local experiment with work incentives, known as the Self Sufficiency Project. This initiative operates in the Vancouver area of British Columbia and southern New Brunswick. It aims to test the impact of generous in-work incentives on overcoming the 'welfare trap' that discourages welfare recipients from taking low paid jobs. The design and preliminary results of this experiment are outlined in Box 18. There are also several United States random assignment experiments that have examined the effects of making more extensive use of work incentives that ensure that people are better off when they enter employment. Recent results from these programmes, including the New York State Child Assistance Programme, Minnesota's Family Investment Programme and the Michigan To Strengthen Michigan Families Programme, suggest that there may be significant impacts (Bloom, 1997).

Box 18. The Self Sufficiency Experiment in British Columbia and New Brunswick, Canada

The Self Sufficiency Experiment is a response to the existence of a 'welfare trap' in the current Canadian system that, beyond very modest earnings, imposes an implicit 100% tax-back on earnings for people on low wages. This is likely to discourage people from taking low wage jobs, although they might lead to eventual wage progression. The experiment aims to test the impacts on work and incomes of a three-year income supplement to lone parents on welfare who take full-time work. The experiment follows a random assignment methodology. One group of lone parents is given the possibility of receiving the incentives whilst another group acts as a control. Those assigned to the treatment group are given up to a year from the date of notification of eligibility to obtain full-time work, of at least 30 hours a week, and to discontinue their welfare claims. They can then make a claim for the earnings supplement. The earnings supplement is very generous, effectively doubling the income for individuals that work full-time and leave welfare. The supplement is limited to three years and is only paid during periods of full-time work. The experiment started in November 1992 and will follow 9,400 families over 5 years.

Some initial results are available from 18 months of tracking of the first 2,000 families, enrolled in the period between November 1992 and December 1993. This shows that the treatment group were working more and earning more than the control group. Fully one-third of people that were eligible for an earnings supplement indeed left welfare by working full-time, with the result that the average monthly welfare receipt was reduced by 14%. The treatment members were twice as likely to work full-time as members of the control group. They were mainly working in low paying jobs, just above the minimum wage on average, but there was a net earnings gain of approximately 58%, or C$137 per month. Total monthly income was 23% higher on average than that of the control group. The treatment group also worked more hours than the control group. There is also a separate experiment that tries to measure whether there are some unintended consequences in terms of people trying to gain eligibility in order to take advantage of the bonus. The initial finding is that there is very little effect (about 3%) on increase in entry to this project. Follow-up results will be based on 36 months and the 54 months of tracking. At this stage there will be much more information on whether there have been wage progressions.

The personal adviser or counsellor

Welfare-to-work programmes involve the activation of support to welfare recipients by making available a range of job search, training and employability measures to help recipients into work. However, the best solutions are likely to vary according to the individuals and local areas concerned, since different people face different obstacles and different local areas have different opportunities. 'Personal advisers' or 'counsellors' can play a key role in developing more tailored solutions by working together with the client to identify their needs and possible responses, drawing on the most appropriate assistance available in each local area. The use of personal advisers or counsellors in welfare-to-work programmes therefore facilitates the shift from general programmes that treat each member of the target group in the same way towards more client-focused provision. They need to operate at local level so that there can be direct face-to-face access between the client and the adviser, and so that the adviser can build good links with the employers and service providers relevant to their client. Local proximity is also important to the understanding of local needs, barriers and opportunities.

There are two further key benefits of personal advisers and counsellors for the effectiveness of welfare-to-work programmes. Firstly, they can hold service providers to account for the quality of the services that are provided to the client and for delivering what the client needs. Secondly, they can offer personal advice and mentoring. This can help motivate unemployed people and identify possible solutions to a wide range of problems that act as barriers to employment, many of which may not be directly related to accessing the standard service provision of labour market programmes and may not otherwise be picked up.

The experience of many people entering the labour market from the welfare system is of short duration jobs, often with low pay and few skill requirements. They may therefore need to negotiate their way through a series of jobs in order to stay off welfare and move up the wage ladder. It can therefore be argued that the adviser role should continue beyond the achievement of an initial job placement or a placement in an appropriate labour market programme, so that further advice and mentoring is available to help people retain jobs, build their skills and move on to new jobs.

'Personal advisers' play a pivotal role in UK New Deal approaches, providing client contact and guidance during the Gateway process in the New Deal for 18-24 year olds and in the New Deals for the long term unemployed, lone parents, the disabled, and partners of the unemployed. They are also a key element in the Employment Zones pilots. Their role is to help focus their clients on job search, provide guidance on how to overcome a range of barriers to work and identify and access appropriate provision from labour market programmes. In some programmes they provide continuing support after the initial work placement. In the United States, 'counsellors' play a similar role in many local welfare-to-work programmes as a pivotal person in the lives of the unemployed, acting as a role model, a mentor and an adviser.

The extensive use of personal advisers and counsellors in welfare-to-work programmes is still relatively new and could be extended to welfare-to-work programmes in other countries. In seeking to establish effective adviser measures, however, it is important to consider three key design issues - the need to provide appropriate tools for advisers, the need to provide training to advisers and the need to identify the appropriate client group.

Appropriate tools for advisers: The adviser has to access a substantial amount of information and appropriate tools are needed to help them to manage this. They need to have information on local employer vacancies and local labour market services that might help their client (e.g. training opportunities and work placements) and information on various local support services that might help the client (e.g. childcare and transport). Computer databases are therefore required and need to be integrated with a wide range of other local organisations. The adviser also needs to carry out assessment of the needs of individual clients and the barriers that they may be facing. There are various assessment tools that can be developed to help them in this task. For example, at a general level, statistical profiling may be a useful tool to identify job-seekers at risk of becoming long term unemployed and therefore with the greatest need of early intervention and intensive services (Box 19). There are also various questionnaire-type approaches that can be used to assess attitudes, preferences and constraints.

**Box 19. Profiling as a tool for establishing priorities
for intensive assistance**

There is a targeting paradox that poses a key challenge for the design of welfare-to-work programmes. On the one hand, intensive support is expensive and therefore cannot be provided to all clients, a large proportion of whom will leave welfare within a relatively short period of time without needing intensive assistance. On the other hand, intensive support is more effective if applied early in the period of unemployment rather than being made available only after a given duration of unemployment has been exceeded. Early identification of the individuals most likely to reach long term unemployment is an answer to this challenge because it enables early intervention with intensive services whilst keeping eligibility to a limited target group.

Profiling is a statistical technique that can be used by local programme administrators or advisers to carry out this early identification where to concentrate intervention. The technique essentially attaches to each individual at their point of entry to the welfare system a probability of remaining unemployed. This probability is based on the combination of particular characteristics in each individual (e.g. previous job tenure, educational attainments, skills, age, number of children requiring care, presence of a disability etc.). The assessments made in this way may be better and less contestable than the qualitative judgements of personal advisers or counsellors. One of the key characteristics often associated with a high probability of long term unemployment is the length of recent work experience or the existence of other recent periods of unemployment.

Profiling has been used extensively by states and local programmes in the United States. It is also used in the Australian Job Network system. Job Network clients are classified at registration using the Job Seeker Classification Instrument (JSCI), to identify those whose personal circumstances and labour market skills suggest that they could have barriers to attaining employment. Based on their JSCI score, some job seekers are referred for 'Intensive Assistance'.

Training for advisers: Advisers must have skills in assessing client needs, in identifying possible solutions, in motivating clients, in maintaining relationships with clients, in negotiating provision with service providers and in providing services and liaison with employers. Advisers need to be multi-skilled in all these areas. Appropriate training is therefore critical. Training programmes or modules are needed in a range of areas, including for example client service, employer relations, personal assessment, information technology and negotiation. Where advisers were previously already working within the public employment service fulfilling more tightly defined tasks, such as job-seeker registration or benefit administration, then a culture shift will also be involved.

Identifying the appropriate client group: The use of personal advisers and counsellors also raises the issue of cost. Adviser services are relatively intensive and therefore relatively expensive whilst a certain part of the unemployed target group, where they are reasonably well motivated and confident, may be quite well served by self-service facilities. Although personal advisers can probably contribute something useful in all cases, if finance has to be generated locally it may be necessary to limit the size of the group benefiting from this service to those who have most need of it. In the United States and Australia, for example, less disadvantaged job-seekers are commonly offered self service facilities such as access to computer databases listing job vacancies and training opportunities. The profiling techniques outlined above are one way to identify the client group most at need of intensive assistance, including personal adviser and other services. Another method is to make people eligible after a given duration of unemployment.

New electronic technologies and job matching

New electronic technologies for computing and telecommunications provide the opportunity to improve the effectiveness and efficiency of job matching. Compared with traditional paper-display labour exchange systems in public employment service offices, newspaper advertisements or the use of informal networks, new electronic technologies make it possible for people to search much more widely for jobs and for employers to search from a much greater number of potential candidates. For employers, electronic technologies can lower recruitment costs, reduce the length of time required for the recruitment process and give access to a larger number of better targeted candidates. For job seekers, electronic technologies can help identify new opportunities both within and external to their local area. Private placement agencies are already developing job-matching services based on the Internet and without an involvement from the public sector there is the risk that those who are detached from the labour market will lose out because they have less access to the Internet and computer technologies.

Public employment services in a number of OECD countries are currently experimenting with the potential of computer and telecommunications or Internet based systems for job matching. In many cases the databases are national with local offices providing accompanying support to unemployed job seekers. In the United Kingdom, for example, centralised telephone links, or call centres, are being developed to deal with vacancy information more effectively and information technology systems are being improved. In Denmark, unmanned 'job-boxes' have been installed in public places, such as large shopping centres, with computer touch-screen technologies inviting job seekers to contact their local employment office to follow up vacancies of interest. Recent developments in Canada and Sweden are outlined in Box 20.

Box 20. Publicly accessible computer based job-matching services in Canada and Sweden

The Canadian public employment service, Human Resources Development Canada (HRDC), has created a new state-of-the-art system called the Electronic Labour Exchange (ELE) for unemployed job seekers. The system runs on the World Wide Web and enables job seekers and employers to post their employment needs on an open, computer searchable electronic bulletin board. Those who are unemployed and receiving unemployment insurance benefits as well as other job seekers can use the system to search online for suitable work opportunities. If need be, job seekers can access the system or receive assistance using it at the regional offices for the unemployment insurance programme. Kiosks have also been set up in places such as shopping malls that can be used for accessing the ELE. A separate system has also been set up for students and graduates in the post secondary education sector, subsidised by the government industry department, Industry Canada, called Campus WorkLink. It is widely available to students and recent graduates of a large portion of the post secondary institutions in all of the Canadian provinces. It allows employers to post job openings to the students and alumni of the institutions that are WorkLink members. In Chapter 11 of this book Nakamura, Wong and Diewert describe the importance of these developments and remaining barriers.

The Swedish government has decided to put special resources into the development of Internet services offered by the public employment service (AMS) (*Observatoire européen de l'emploi*, 1998, 1999). It is putting in place a full Internet site for placement, professional orientation and information on training and the labour market. This will allow agents of the public employment services to concentrate more on providing individual support to job seekers and employers. The Internet site includes a database of job seekers that employers can consult, as well as separate databases for people seeking temporary work and an illustrated database for artists.

In Spring 1999, the Internet site had some 250,000 visitors per month, but the potential is thought to be even greater. A key objective is to convince more employers to use the database of job seekers, increasing their number from 3,500 in Autumn 1998 to 50,000 at the end of the year 2000. A national call centre has also been established to improve information services for job seekers and employers. It will progressively be integrated into the Internet services by means of a technique called 'click and call' that will enable direct dialogue on the Internet with a member of the public employment service.

Developments in computer-based and Internet job matching have been particularly rapid in the United States (OECD, 1999a). The federal Department of Labor (DOL) has sponsored the development of a national Internet job match system centred on two key databases, America's Job Bank (AJB), which posts vacancy information, and America's Talent Bank (ATB), which posts job seeker details. These are open-access national databases, accessible free-of-charge via the Internet or self-service tools in one-stop centres and other service points such as kiosks in public libraries. Development of the system has been carried out in conjunction with State Employment Security Agencies (SESAs) and many functions have been contracted out to states, local governments and private companies. As of June 1998, the system had nearly 712,500 vacancies and 71,000 job seeker curricula vitae. Local agencies and states are also developing systems for local and intra-state search, with the latter linking in to the national AJB and ATB databases. A notable difference between many public agencies and one-stop centres in the United States and those in other OECD countries is the absence of posted paper copies of vacancy listings, which have largely shifted to computer databases.

When accessing the AJB database, and associated state and local job banks, job seekers are able to search for jobs by location, job title, occupational codes and key words. The searches can be narrowed to screen for recently listed jobs, educational requirements, experience requirements, salary range and nature of the job (i.e. full-time/part-time and temporary/permanent). Employers can search the ATB database for candidates by skill categories, job seeker preferences for location, job duration and salary or job seeker characteristics (e.g. education or occupation) and so on. Employers usually need to register to have access to the services.

Job seekers and employers may be left to make their own matches each time they consult the system. However, search systems can also be set up to automatically notify a job seeker or employer when a suitable match is found, according to pre-specified search criteria. The one-stop centre in Hartford,

Connecticut provides an illustration of this job-matching process (OECD, 1999a). At the centre, job orders and job-seeker information are entered in the automated system daily. Each night a batch job is run, usually screening by occupational code or skills but with other screens possible including education, desired shift, geographic location, salary or veterans' preference among others. Job seekers in actively managed welfare-to-work programmes are notified by counselling staff when promising matches occur. Unemployment Insurance staff are notified if they refuse to apply.

In countries operating local as well as national databases, it is clearly important to find a mechanism to link them together. Otherwise, job seekers may be constrained in their search, unable to access vacancy information for employers listed on parallel databases, whilst employers may miss out on candidates with more appropriate skills and background than those listed on the databases to which they have access. A great number of separate systems may also create confusion amongst users, and reduce take-up. Most importantly, without national co-ordination and integration, geographical mobility of labour is likely to be reduced. In particular, for localities with high concentrations of long term unemployed but low volumes of job vacancies it is important not to restrict long term unemployed people from being able to identify job opportunities outside of their immediate local area of residence. Governments should therefore encourage local database operators to link up with national systems, using compatible technologies and formats and where possible presenting a seamless interface for the user. At the same time, local services providing support and guidance to users should also be encouraged.

One of the main challenges for public employment services in setting up effective systems for job matching using new electronic technologies is how to ensure that long term unemployed and other disadvantaged people do not lose out in accessing the vacancies put through the system. The following aspects of design and implementation would appear to be important.

Support universal access: It needs to be recognised that electronically accessed job-matching services are increasingly being developed by private placement agencies, funded largely through employer subscriptions, as well as by the career services of higher and further education institutions. These systems offer many advantages to employers in terms of the effectiveness and efficiency of the recruitment process and are likely to become increasingly popular. However, job seekers using these services tend already to have a job or to have completed or to be about to obtain a further education qualification. Long term unemployed people are unlikely to access these systems. If disadvantaged people are not to lose out on vacancy notifications as private job matching systems shift towards the use of electronically accessed databases, it is important that employers have the possibility of using equivalent databases that include significant access by the long term unemployed.

Provide facilities in local offices for people without computers or Internet access: The use of electronically accessed or Internet job match systems offers some users the potential for greater accessibility from home or work. However, a relatively small proportion of welfare recipients has access to computer equipment and the Internet. There is a consequent need to provide access to these technologies through local offices.

Make access simple, for example with touch screen technologies: Some welfare recipients may lack the experience and confidence to use computer-based job match systems. Touch screen computers can help to overcome this problem. In some areas, particularly where there are significant ethnic minority populations, vacancies may also need to be posted in minority languages.

Provide accompanying advice and support: While some people will be sufficiently able and confident to use self-service facilities, others will require a range of advice and support, for example on how to identify appropriate jobs and how to apply for them, as well as building of confidence and motivation. This cannot be achieved simply by providing technical facilities for database access. More intensive staff support will be required for this group. People who are unable to read will need access to counsellor services. Follow-up is required for all job seekers to ensure that people who require support are able to access it.

Get the right balance between self-service and active matching: Some electronic job match databases are entirely self-service, in the sense that full details of vacancies and how to contact employers are provided to job seekers, who are expected to make a direct approach to the employer. The public employment service will not necessarily even monitor who makes applications. Other systems are set up so that the public employment service takes a more active role. In these cases job seekers do not see certain vacancies, or see only limited information requiring them to register their interest with the public employment service, and public employment service officers make the final match between candidates and employers. Open listings are cheaper for the public employment service and save staff time. They also serve to emphasise the individual's own responsibility to search for work. On the other hand, disadvantaged people may lose out if they fail to identify or apply for appropriate vacancies or if they are forced to compete with people who have more recent work experience. For some people a self-service approach will be suitable, but for others more active matching is likely to be required using semi-open or closed vacancies. A balance needs to be struck between the two approaches.

Local one-stop-shops

The introduction of local one-stop-shops is a key component of the new institutional arrangements associated with the activation and client-focus of welfare-to-work approaches. They provide a single locus for accessing job matching databases and the labour market services operated locally by a range of different national, regional and local agencies. One-stop-shops usually take the form of a network of local offices where clients and their advisers can view information and carry out registration for services. The contribution of one-stop-shops to the effective functioning of welfare-to-work programmes is the co-ordination of the various different labour market services available in a local area so that clients and their advisers can easily see and access what is available without needing to make several separate enquiries. The result is that clients are more likely to participate in programmes and are more likely to access the services that are the most appropriate to them. One-stop-shops can also act as a tool for strengthening partnership and collaboration between agencies. The increased visibility of services and the fact that clients are being drawn from a central pool can act as an incentive for agencies to develop joint services or to design their services to link together. It also promotes innovation and competition between providers.

Local one-stop-shops are part of welfare-to-work programmes in many OECD countries. For example, Finn, in Chapter 6 of this book, notes that one of the key elements of welfare-to-work reform in the Netherlands is the co-ordination of the complex range of agencies and institutions that work with the unemployed. This includes the creation of a 'one counter system' by the year 2000 comprising a national network of offices combining benefits administration with all local and regional labour market initiatives. The reform is intended to integrate intake and diagnosis, information exchange and client monitoring, enhance the enforcement of job search and availability rules and create greater competition in the provision of placement services. In Australia, Centrelink has been established as a one-stop shop and first point of client contact for the Job Network (a network of around 300 private, community and government suppliers of labour market services). It is through Centrelink that job seekers and employers choose which Job Network provider in their area they want to work with.

In the United States a one-stop career centre system was gradually put into place between 1994 and 1998 through Workforce Development Boards, with the incentive of federal grants to cover set up costs during the first three years of operation. The aim was to provide universal access to core services and to make the system more transparent to clients. To receive federal grants, the one-stop career centres had to include mainstream Department of Labour programmes (Employment Service, Unemployment Insurance, Job Training Partnership Act programmes for the economically disadvantaged and dislocated workers, Senior Community Service Employment Programme, Veterans Employment and Training Services). States and local administrations have often brought additional local labour market services into these one-stop centres, including local TANF welfare-to-work programmes. The state of Connecticut has been one of the pioneers in setting up a one-stop centre approach (Box 21).

Box 21. The one-stop-shop approach in Connecticut, United States

The one-stop-shop approach in Connecticut is known as Connecticut Works. It is led by the Connecticut Department of Labour (CTDOL) and the nine Regional Workforce Development Boards (RWDBs). A broad coalition of additional partners are also involved, including the state-level Departments of Education, Higher Education, Social Services, Motor Vehicles, Economic and Community Development, the state library system and a range of community organisations. The goal is to offer customer choice and an integrated array of services in support of businesses and individuals.

The system operates through 19 local Connecticut Works centres as well as computerised information kiosks at 102 public libraries. Core CTDOL programmes included in the one-stop career centres are Wagner-Peyser Act employment services, Veterans' Employment and Training Services, Job Training Partnership Act services, Trade Adjustment Assistance, Migrant Seasonal Farmworker Programmes and Unemployment Insurance. Other programmes funded through non-CTDOL channels include the state's training programme for employed workers (Customised Job Training), apprenticeships, adult basic education and welfare employment and training (both federal and state programmes).

Connecticut Works has sought to develop a state of the art technological infrastructure, improve the lay-out of local offices, co-locate the local operations of local partners and build the capacity of the staff through training (including cross-training among partner agency staff.). Automated systems have been developed to expand direct client services, including self-service facilities, and to support internal system operations. The system's wide-area-network is relatively comprehensive and facilitates communications and information sharing among CTDOL and RWDB partners. At the same time, CTDOL's Internet site focuses primarily on the needs of job-seekers and employers rather than the needs of system partners. In terms of the physical infrastructure, the state has made a substantial investment in improving the conditions in the local offices, an initiative that is perceived as having helped to reduce the stigmatisation of the employment service.

Source: OECD (1999a)

Local employer-based training projects

One of the defining features of new welfare-to-work approaches is a focus on getting people quickly off welfare and into work. This has been associated with a change in the nature of training for the long term unemployed. Many welfare-to-work programmes now concentrate on providing just some basic job-readiness training, addressing issues such as punctuality, dress, attitude and so on, before organising in-work training tailored to the needs of specific employers. This contrasts with previous longer duration out-of-job vocational training courses that tended to be standardised rather than adapted to local employer needs. The shift towards training-in-work has been particularly marked in the United States. In Chapter 7 of this book, Straits describes recent shifts towards a 'work-first' philosophy in United States welfare-to-work programmes, reinforced by the enactment of the 1996 Personal Responsibility and Work Opportunities Reconciliation Act and the establishment of Temporary Assistance for Needy Families (TANF). States and local governments responsible for designing welfare-to-work programmes in the United States are now prompted to adopt a 'work-first' approach by time limits on the receipt of federal welfare payments requiring most recipients to be in work or work related activities within two years of first receiving benefits.

The move to 'work-first' in the United States was partly a response to the perceived failings of previous out-of-work training programmes that, although expensive, tended to return many participants to welfare after their training period. At a general level, surveys of what employers look for when they recruit people from welfare have suggested that formal qualifications are valued less than other characteristics of potential recruits, such as honesty, timekeeping and inter-personal relationships. They have also suggested that employers would rather undertake their own training than have it provided externally. These factors, together with a political will to move more in the direction of rapid attachment to the labour force, have led to the development of employer-based training. Essentially the approach is first to link people to the labour market and then to arrange for additional training to be provided, in conjunction with the employer, if this is needed for the recruit to progress in the job. The major benefit is that the welfare recipients are linked with specific employers from the start of their training and receive the training that the employer considers will be appropriate for a specific vacancy. There is some evaluation evidence to suggest that this helps to increase the proportion of programme participants moving into jobs compared with traditional education and training courses for the long term unemployed.

Employer-based training is commonly organised through work placements during which employers give additional training. However, it can also be delivered to the requirements of specific employers by external training providers. Box 22 gives the example of how a customised training project has been developed for a group of employers by a local partnership within the UK New Deal for 18-24 year olds. Because the course has been customised to the needs of local employers, with their full collaboration in course design, the opportunities for local unemployed people to access new job vacancies are maximised.

**Box 22. A customised training project in the UK New Deal
for 18-24 year olds**

This customised training project was established by the Sunderland New Deal Partnership around a major expansion by Nissan, a Japanese automobile manufacturer with a major local production facility. The expansion involved the production of a new vehicle model, creating 800 additional jobs directly and approximately three times that number in the supplier base. Nissan, the company undertaking the expansion, was included in the local partnership responsible for the New Deal policy. The partnership was therefore aware that the existing local skill base was not felt to match the advanced manufacturing requirements of the new facility or of its suppliers. It was also conscious that local long term unemployed people, even those with previous engineering experience, were unlikely to succeed in these companies' stringent recruitment processes without retraining. The aim of this customised training project was therefore two-fold, to help meet the recruitment needs of local employers whilst creating an opportunity for long term unemployed people to access the new job vacancies by providing training in the skills and competencies required to work in this sector.

A public-private partnership was formed to put the training project in place, with the local New Deal partnership on one side and the expanding automobile producer and local suppliers on the other side. This was organised through a newly created umbrella organisation, the Automotive Sector Strategic Alliance (ASSA). The companies came together through this forum to design their own Gateway, i.e. the initial phase of guidance and counselling to long term unemployed young people. During the Gateway, the companies assess the basic skills of clients against the needs of the automotive industry in order to select people for the main training programme. This initial assessment involves literacy, numeracy, manual dexterity and teamwork. Clients who do not pass the initial assessment may be helped with a basic training package and given the chance to be re-assessed for joining the full programme. The clients selected for the full programme then participate in the full-time education and training option of the New Deal, following a training package designed by the companies themselves. A 20-week course has been established consisting of teamwork through outward-bound courses, on-the-job training leading to National Vocational Qualifications and on-line trials with the companies themselves. New Deal participants completing this training programme are given automatic entry to the recruitment process of Nissan and the supplier companies.

Box 22. (continued)

The customised training programme has effectively allowed the companies themselves to design a New Deal training package based on the training they already had in place for their existing employees. They have been involved in arranging the tasks, supplying the tools and technical know-how and commissioning their own approved training suppliers from the private sector and local colleges. Five training centres were established throughout the region, replicating the training provided to existing employees but made available to local long term unemployed people paid for through New Deal with additional elements designed to address the job-readiness and motivational issues that came with the New Deal client.

The employer-based training approach relies on the willingness of local employers to recruit and train the long term unemployed and provide a certain level of in-work training. The incentive for employers to participate is that they will receive public financial support to train people for their own needs and to their own standards. Moreover, as Hogan reports in Chapter 9, there is evidence to suggest that once recruited and trained, long term unemployed people can be highly motivated and committed employees, with relatively low turnover. Welfare-to-work programme managers need to put this message to local employers. Brown et al (1998) discuss some of the main employer categories that United States programme managers can most productively approach to become involved in training and recruiting welfare recipients:

–   Businesses with urgent labour needs, for example those in geographic areas or industry sectors with a need for workers.

–   Businesses with opportunities that match participants' skills.

–   Large businesses, where there is a significant likelihood of a large number of job placements.

–   Small businesses, possibly contacted through intermediaries such as Chambers of Commerce, where there are few large businesses or where small business account for most job growth. Businesses with opportunities that pay above a certain wage. Or that meet other wage, benefit or job advancement criteria.

–   Employers required to hire additional or disadvantaged workers, for example those receiving government assistance through economic development programmes such as Empowerment Zones.

–   Businesses with a commitment to community service or welfare reform.

It is also important that programme managers have regard to the need to minimise dead-weight and substitution effects (principally through funding training for the long term unemployed that would otherwise have taken place anyway or supporting the recruitment of one group of long term unemployed people at the expense of another). The dead-weight and substitution effects will often be small, since many employers would not normally recruit from the long term unemployed labour pool, but they should nonetheless be evaluated so that important cases can be avoided.

Another key issue with employer-based training is how to ensure satisfactory job retention and wage progression once welfare recipients have obtained their initial jobs. Employer-based training tends to be of shorter duration and more focused on achieving employer-specific tasks than traditional education and training courses and this may mean that recruits are less able to change employer following job loss or to move up the wage ladder. In the United States, a key premise used to support the 'work first' model is that after initially obtaining work, welfare recipients will be able to progress to better paid jobs and to find other opportunities if required. However, in fact relatively little is known about the extent to which people leaving welfare for work subsequently move on to better opportunities over time. Indeed some studies suggest that for many of the families that enter low wage jobs, wage mobility over time appears to be extremely limited. A mixed strategy may therefore be most appropriate involving both quick attachment to the workforce and subsequent training to prepare welfare recipients for higher paid jobs (Bloom, 1997). Such activities to encourage employers to undertake employee development programmes for their long term unemployed recruits can fit within broader public sector strategies that encourage lifelong learning and employee development in companies.

Overall, what seems critical is that training programmes have a very strong emphasis on employment and that the education and training components of welfare-to-work programmes are not stand-alone but are closely linked to job vacancies. At the same time there is a need to go beyond immediate job-readiness training and to help provide skills for the longer-term development of recruits.

Promoting the local mobility of labour

Lack of local transportation can be a major barrier to the ability of welfare recipients to access work. Welfare recipients are far less likely than other groups to possess a reliable vehicle of their own and existing public transport systems are often inadequate for their commuting needs. In large cities, the problem is related to the existence of a 'spatial mismatch' between the areas with the greatest concentrations of welfare recipients and the areas with the greatest concentrations of new entry-level jobs. Inner city areas tend to have high concentrations of long term unemployment but have progressively lost their traditional sources of employment in manufacturing, warehousing and back office services to surrounding suburban or rural locations. People living in rural areas can also be forced to travel long distances to work, with public transport availability limited because of the dispersed nature of rural populations. The problems of access to work are compounded by the fact that many entry-level jobs require evening, night or weekend work, when public transport services are either unavailable or limited, and the need for many welfare recipients to accommodate travel to childcare providers as well as employers.

There are two long term measures that can help overcome the problem of spatial mismatch. The first is the creation of jobs in areas of high long term unemployment. A wide range of regeneration policies seek to do this, including those operated by local governments and local agencies and targeted national policies, such as *Zones Franches* in France, *Enterprise Zones* in the United Kingdom and *Empowerment Zones* and *Enterprise Communities* in the United States. Ong and Blumenberg (1998) point out that availability of low skill jobs locally is likely to have a particularly important impact on employment levels for welfare recipients. The second measure involves reducing the barriers to work created by the operation of social housing arrangements which have often tended to concentrate the most disadvantaged people in areas with few local job opportunities. Here, it can be argued that the movement of welfare recipients from 'job poor' to 'job rich' areas through housing opportunities can help increase their employment levels (Newman, 1999). One further practical programme design issue concerns the boundaries of local welfare-to-work programme areas. As Hughes (1996) contends, when spatial mismatch issues are important, programme jurisdictions drawn too tightly can dramatically under-bound the opportunities available to participants from areas with high concentrations of jobs and placements. An appropriate administrative geography is therefore required to solve the employment needs of welfare reform. However, perhaps the most obvious immediate response to the problems of physical access to jobs is to seek to create new transport opportunities for welfare recipients to reach employment sites. A number of such local initiatives are emerging in OECD Member countries.

In the United Kingdom, the New Deal for 18-24 year-olds makes available travel concessions for exceptional travel costs and for the weekly travel costs of participation in the Environmental Task Force and Voluntary Sector options. Some of the UK Employment Zones have also identified travel as a barrier to work in terms of public transport costs and the absence of routes that match patterns of travel to work (both location and timing) and are developing new solutions to help overcome the problems. For example, the Plymouth Employment Zone is developing new bus routes to match times and employer locations in outlying industrial estates, pump-primed by public regeneration funds. It has also developed a special 'Employment Zone Travel Card' that subsidises clients' fares during their participation in the Employment Zone and following into transition to employment.

In the United States local welfare-to-work programmes are particularly advanced in terms of providing support services to meet the needs of welfare recipients in terms of transport to work. Box 23 identifies areas of federal government support to welfare-to-work programmes operating transportation initiatives.

Box 23. Federal support for local transportation initiatives in the United States

According to the United States Census Bureau, in 1992, welfare recipients were disproportionately concentrated in inner cities. Almost one-half of people who received Aid to Families with Dependent Children (AFDC) or state assistance lived in inner cities, compared with 30% of the United States population. At the same time, national trends since 1970 show that most new jobs have been created in the suburbs rather than in the inner cities. Many of these newly created entry-level suburban jobs should attract people moving from welfare to work. However, one 1995 survey suggested that less than 6% of welfare families had a car and recent studies have identified important gaps in existing transport routes. For example, it has been estimated that in 1998, whilst 98% of Boston's welfare recipients lived within one-quarter of a mile of a bus route or transport hub, just 32% of potential employers (in high growth areas for entry-level employment) were within one-quarter of a mile of public transport. These sorts of concerns have led to the following federal initiatives to support transportation strategies for moving welfare recipients into work.

The Department of Health and Human Services (HHS) administers the Temporary Assistance to Needy Families (TANF) programme providing block grants to states for welfare-to-work programmes. Subject to time limits, the states may use TANF funds to provide transportation assistance to people on or moving off of public assistance. For example, states can use TANF funds to provide transit passes for welfare recipients or reimburse TANF recipients for work-related transportation expenses.

In 1997 the Department of Labor (DOL) set up a two-year, US$3 billion welfare-to-work programme. This provides funding for various local programmes providing job placement, on-the-job training and support services, including transport assistance, to those who are the most difficult to move from welfare to work.

The Department of Housing and Urban Development (HUD) has a US$17 million Bridges to Work programme providing funds to support transportation, job placement, and counselling services for a small number of low-income people living in the central cities of Baltimore, Chicago, Denver, Milwaukee ad St. Louis. It is a demonstration programme started in late 1996 and due for completion in 2000. Funding includes transport research and demonstration programmes.

Box 23. (continued)

Between 1995 and 1998 the Federal Transit Authority (FTA) funded a US$3.5 million JOBLINKS demonstration programme funding 16 projects located in urban and rural areas within 12 states. For example, a JOBSLINK project in Louisville, Kentucky, was designed to increase by 25% the number of inner-city residents hired at an industrial park. The project established an express bus from the inner city to the industrial park, thereby reducing a 2-hour commute to 45 minutes. Another JOBLINKS project in Fresno, California, provided transportation services to employment training centres to reduce dropout rates and increase the number of individuals who found jobs. FTA has also helped state and local transportation agencies develop plans for addressing the transport needs of their welfare recipients.

In June 1998 the Transportation Equity Act for the 21st Century (TEA-21) established a welfare-to-work programme known as the Access to Jobs programme with funding of up to US$750 million over 5 years, 1999 to 2003. The programme, administered by the Department of Transportation (DOT), will provide grants to local agencies and authorities, non-profit groups and transit authorities to improve mobility for low-income individuals seeking employment. Both urban and rural areas are covered. Access to Jobs grants fund only 50% of a project's total costs. Other federal funds such as the TANF funds from HHS or welfare-to-work grants from DOL can be used to fund the remaining 50%.

Local co-ordination is considered to be one of the key factors that will help ensure the success of the Access to Jobs initiative. DOT, HHS and DOL have issued joint guidance notes explaining how human service organisations can combine funds. The guidance also encourages local transportation, workforce development and social service providers to co-ordinate their activities. The published grant award criteria for Access to Jobs encourage projects that are the result of a regional planning process including representatives from both transport and social service providers. Projects developed in this way are more likely to receive funding.

Preliminary results from the above programmes suggest that the following factors contribute to success. Firstly, collaboration between transport, employment and other human services organisations. Transport strategies for welfare recipients should be co-ordinated with local job placement and social services provision, including childcare. Secondly, an understanding of local job markets. Initiatives should identify which employers are willing to participate and what are the likely benefits for welfare recipients. Thirdly, the inclusion of wide ranging and flexible transport solutions, without over-reliance on mass transport systems.

Source: GAO (1998, 1999b)

Support with transport is a feature of most local welfare-to-work programmes in the United States, helping participants to attend programme activities and look for a job (Brown, 1997). Support commonly includes public transport passes and mileage reimbursements for participants' vehicles, private van or bus services to programme activities and help for participants to get a driving licence or to have their car repaired. Participants can also be encouraged to form car pools. These strategies facilitate job search and increase participation rates in programme activities, but participants will still need to arrange their own transportation once they get a job.

Brown et al (1998) sets out the following ideas for programme managers to facilitate transportation for welfare recipients:

- **Help welfare recipients buy or repair cars.** Many welfare programmes have increased the limits on the value of a car that recipients can own so that their cars can be more reliable Many also provide one-time assistance for recipients to make car repairs. Other ideas include offering no-interest or low-interest loans so recipients can purchase a car, selling donated cars to recipients at a low cost, or offering affordable leases on cars that recipients then own after a certain amount of time.

- **Consider transportation as a factor in job matching.** When referring welfare recipients for job placement, consider not only their interests and skills, but also their access to transportation. Kansas City LINC includes information on transportation options in its job-matching database. When matching recipients with jobs, programme staff look not only at skills and interests, but also at where jobs are located, whether recipients have access to private transportation, and whether public transportation is available.

- **Co-ordinate work schedules.** Work with employers to co-ordinate the schedules of employees who work in the same company so that they can share transportation. This will allow carpooling, and also make it more cost-effective to operate a van service or other transportation alternatives.

- **Co-ordinate with childcare needs.** Try to match welfare recipients with jobs that will be convenient to childcare or that will minimise the need for childcare. For example, Rachel's Bus Company contracts with Chicago-area schools and hires welfare recipients and other inner city residents. When possible, drivers who have school-age children are assigned routes that involve picking up their own children, thus eliminating the need for baby-sitters before or after school.

- **Co-ordinate among businesses.** Bring together employers and other organisations that are near each other to develop transportation alternatives. For example, neighbouring employers may find it worthwhile to set up a shuttle service serving all their businesses. In Schenectady, New York, UPS and Catholic Charities share a bus. Catholic Charities uses it during the day to deliver Meals on Wheels and UPS uses it at night as a shuttle for workers.

- **Bring businesses and government together to develop solutions.** Business leadership can help persuade government agencies to test new transportation initiatives. For example, when UPS partnered with the Camden, New Jersey, welfare agency and the state employment services to find employees for a new air hub in Philadelphia, they approached the state transportation agency to solve the new workers' transportation problems. With UPS guaranteeing a certain number of seats, the transport agency established a regular bus line.

- **Look for opportunities to expand existing services.** In areas where many welfare recipients live or where many employers are located, it may be cost-effective to develop new transportation routes. For example, JOBLINKS, a collaborative effort in Louisville, Kentucky, resulted in the development of a new bus route between the city and a suburban industrial estate. Passenger numbers have supported ten round trips each day.

- **Be creative.** Make an inventory of transport services and think creatively about how to use those options to meet new needs. In Chicago, the Job Oasis Worker Mobility Project uses old school buses to offer reverse commute services to employers in the suburbs. Welfare recipients ride free while training or looking for work and pay the regular fare when they find work.

- **Build in alternative arrangements.** As much as possible, make sure that workers have backup transportation available if their primary means fall through. Also, remember that workers may need transportation not only to get to work, but also to get to childcare providers. One element of the Bridges to Work demonstration project is support services to deal with issues created by or exacerbated by a daily commute to distant jobs. These include extended childcare arrangements, a guaranteed ride home in an emergency and orientation to suburban communities.

As new welfare-to-work programmes are being introduced in OECD countries, it is becoming apparent that linked support services often need to be strengthened. Better transport is one of the main supports required.

CHAPTER 5
CONCLUSION AND PERSPECTIVES FOR THE FUTURE

The material presented in this book highlights a very important trend in OECD Member countries to move away from traditional passive welfare systems towards new more active approaches involving the local dimension. The innovations are centred on decentralisation of policy design and management to local agencies, involving local partnerships and experimenting with new local active labour market policy tools. There are of course some differences in emphasis in resources and in political commitment, but all OECD Member countries are moving in this direction because of the need to control welfare budgets and to reduce high and persistent unemployment. The policy reforms have been developed at a favourable time in that a number of the countries involved, including the United Kingdom and the United States, have been experiencing a period of growth and reduction in welfare registers. In periods of recession, the need to make welfare programmes more effective will be felt even more strongly and the pressure for the kinds of local experimentation that are being observed is likely to become even more compelling. It is therefore important to take stock of developments internationally and to assess what works best.

The OECD-DfEE Sheffield conference on the Local Dimension of Welfare-to-Work, on which this publication reports, aimed to address three main questions regarding the design and management of local policies for welfare-to-work. The responses that emerged are summarised below.

1.   What are the strengths and weaknesses of policy design and management at a local level and what is the appropriate balance between local and central agencies?

Recent trends towards the local design and management of welfare-to-work policy in many OECD countries point to the wider importance of decentralised governance. In the case of welfare-to-work, the strengths of local involvement are centred on five key characteristics:

- The ability to design services that are more adapted to differing local circumstances.

- The capacity to co-ordinate locally the range of different national, regional and local policies affecting employment in an area.

- The ability to mobilise local people, employers and community groups in support of national policy objectives.

- The ability to experiment and generate innovative project ideas at the local level.

- The possibility to channel additional resources to local areas with a particular need.

The increased policy effectiveness achieved should help better deal with labour market mismatching problems and improve the employability of labour as a factor of production.

However, there are also potential weaknesses and counter effects from policy design and management at a local level, so if local involvement is to be encouraged then proper frameworks must be put in place to minimise any adverse impacts:

- Local initiatives are not on their own sufficient to tackle the problems of exclusion and unemployment and must be accompanied by national measures.

- Uneven provision may emerge and provision may weaken unacceptably in certain localities.

- It can become more difficult to ensure accountability for public money when local agencies and partnerships are responsible for policy management.

- Once given flexibility, local groups may choose to carry out activities different to those that the central government intended.

- Local agencies may duplicate certain functions at the expense of overall efficiency.

- Local proximity may not always equate to better awareness of local needs and opportunities.

Consequently, whilst the role for local agencies is clear, it is equally clear that there must also be a role for central government. In particular, the central framework should provide relevant supporting policies to complement local welfare-to-work initiatives, such as promotion of lifelong learning and adoption of the right national tax and benefits regimes. It should also use appropriate national controls, national-local consultations and guidelines to help overcome the problems of uneven provision, lack of accountability or deviation from national objectives. Regulations and incentives attached to funding of local agencies can provide these controls at the same time as recognising the decision-making flexibility of local bodies. Furthermore, there are certain specific services that in many circumstances may best be provided at central rather than local level. These include funding provision, awareness campaigns, quality control, programme evaluation and technical assistance.

It is clear that there are certain tensions between local flexibility and a central framework. Where the balance is struck depends on policy priorities and the level of risk that national agencies are prepared to take in order to secure the benefits of local flexibility. It can be argued that local flexibility should be most marked firstly where there is the greatest scope to increase innovation, local tailoring and co-ordination and mobilise new local players and secondly where local actors have the greatest design and management capabilities. Governments can of course support local approaches by building local design and management capacity, for example in terms of activities for the professional development of staff working in local agencies. It must also be recognised that the process of building new local approaches to provision takes time.

2. How effective are local partnership mechanisms in stimulating policy innovation, adapting policies to local conditions and mobilising social partners?

One of the key lessons from the approaches examined in the conference and synthesised in this publication is that partnerships of local agencies offer the potential to make a very positive contribution to welfare-to-work policies. They encourage an exchange of information, experience and knowledge that helps to ensure that policy design is well aligned with local conditions. They also involve local people in the decisions that affect them, creating a sense of local ownership or local empowerment that helps mobilise support. Furthermore, multiple problems, such as those faced by people in their transition from welfare-to-work, require multiple agencies to deliver an appropriate response.

It is nevertheless essential that the different agencies called to contribute actually work together towards an integrated approach. In most OECD Member countries this is still a problem area and to solve it requires concentrating on supporting the processes of interaction rather than simply inaugurating a new structure. In some localities partnerships appear to function relatively poorly, for example because of an over-dominant partner or a because of lack of history of agencies working together. There are certain capacity-building measures that can be pursued by central agencies or by the local partners themselves to improve performance in such cases. Partnership structures could be changed, for example by reducing the size of the decision-making group or by appointing a leader. Local staff skills and management procedures could be enhanced, through written guidelines or seminars and exchanges. Additional resources could be provided from central authorities or by extending the partnership. A temporary delegation of a representative from a central authority could be considered.

The involvement of the private sector appears to be fundamental in successful welfare-to-work partnerships. As well as helping to ensure that support and training is designed that is appropriate for the work available with employers, employer involvement is needed for the provision of work placements and so that participants in welfare-to-work programmes are eventually recruited. One of the keys to convincing employers to participate is to demonstrate quality in the support provided to welfare programme participants, including appropriate guidance, activities to support skills and employability and support services, such as for childcare and transport. It is also critical to provide good quality support to employers who take on welfare recipients, including good information on welfare-to-work programmes, referral of people who are appropriate for vacancies offered and help overcoming any problems that emerge.

In order to establish effective partnerships, governments must be prepared to invest, to support the actors involved and to allow time for effective partnership working to emerge. For the future, it is also important to get the right balance between competition and collaboration and to evaluate partnerships and provide accountability.

3.   What locally based policy tools work well in promoting the recruitment of excluded youths and adults?

Certain European countries have developed significant experience of social enterprise or Intermediate Labour Market initiatives and these approaches could be adopted elsewhere. Essentially, these projects seek to create new opportunities directly for the long term unemployed by involving them in providing new socially useful products and services to the local community, such as developing new social services for individuals and families, improving the environment or enhancing cultural assets. They generate their own revenues by selling their services in the market and to the public sector and by making use of public sector subsidies where available. They have a particular role in localities with very high concentrations of unemployment where there are simply not sufficient opportunities either for long term unemployed people to find work experience placements or for them to obtain a permanent job. As the number of these initiatives has increased, there has been a growing public sector awareness of their benefits, both for social policy and for labour market policy, leading to moves in some countries to more formally integrate social enterprises into mainstream government policies.

Local employer-based training projects also help to provide welfare recipients with work experience and job skills and allow them to demonstrate the motivation, honesty, timekeeping and inter-personal relationships that employers say they are seeking in recruits. This fits with a broad shift observable in certain OECD countries, and particularly the United States, towards providing on-the-job training in work rather than prior classroom based training for vocational qualifications. The in-work training approach appears to have the advantage of increased initial attachment of welfare recipients to the labour market, however less is known about the extent to which people retain the jobs found through this route or move on to better paid and higher skilled activities over time. For this, it is likely that some further development of qualifications and skills within work is also important, implying a need for some continued public support for employer-provided training or state training initiatives after long term unemployed people enter employment.

One of the principal objectives of welfare-to-work policies is to help match job seekers to employer vacancies so that situations do not persist where there are concentrations of long term unemployed people alongside growing overall employment and even skill shortages in some occupations. The above initiatives for improving work experience and training contribute indirectly to this objective. Use of new electronic technologies and the Internet aims to intervene in the matching process more directly. Compared with traditional matching techniques, new electronic technologies make it possible for people to search much more widely for jobs and for employers to search from a much greater number of potential candidates. However, there is also the danger that long term unemployed people, who tend to have less access to computers and the Internet, may lose out as these services become more widely developed. To defend against this, welfare-to-work programmes should support electronic job-matching services with universal access, provide facilities in local offices for people without computers or Internet access, make access simple, for example

117

with touch screen technologies, provide accompanying advice and support and get the right balance between self-service and active matching.

Improved matching between unemployed people and available employer vacancies can also be promoted by initiatives to increase the local mobility of labour. Research shows that welfare recipients are far less likely than other groups to possess a reliable vehicle of their own and that existing public transport systems are often inadequate for their commuting needs. Inner cities often have high concentrations of long term unemployed people but have poor public transport access to surrounding concentrations of jobs, whilst people living in rural areas also often have a long and difficult journey to work if they do not posses a vehicle. A number of local initiatives are emerging in OECD countries that could be adapted elsewhere. For example, free public transport passes and mileage reimbursements to welfare recipients, private van or bus services to employment sites and deliberate matching of welfare recipients jobs and placements that will be convenient for childcare.

The role of the personal adviser or counsellor is essential in all these initiatives for work experience, training and job match. They can develop tailored solutions to the barriers faced by each client, working together with the client to identify their needs and possible responses and drawing on the most appropriate assistance available in the local area. Moreover, personal advisers or counsellors can increase programme impacts at relatively low cost by helping to ensure that provision is appropriate for each individual, by improving the motivation of job seekers and by helping them to overcome barriers to employment that may not otherwise be identified. To establish effective adviser or counsellor programmes it is important to provide appropriate tools for advisers, for example for client assessments, to provide them with appropriate training and to identify the appropriate client group to receive this more intensive support. Personal advisers often work within local one-stop-shops. These centres co-ordinate the various different labour market services available in a local area so that clients and their advisors can easily see what is available and access what is most appropriate without needing to make several separate enquiries.

If the above tools are to work it is also necessary that incentive structures are right, to make work pay. Recent evaluation evidence is pointing towards some positive results from local experiments in the United States and Canada in this area, in terms of increasing attachment of welfare recipients to the labour market, although further evidence is still required. These local incentive experiments act to 'top-up' earnings from work so that they are visibly higher than earnings on welfare. In the long run this type of incentive approach may prove more popular and effective than compulsion or sanctions approaches, which risk forcing into poverty those families with individuals who do not work.

Overall, recent welfare-to-work policy reforms in OECD Member countries have released considerable innovation and experimentation at the local level. These are important developments, but there has not been sufficient reliable and consistent evaluation evidence to date on the strengths and weaknesses of the new approaches. It is now important to closely assess which of these new local approaches and tools work best, in what circumstances and for whom, in order to build a basis for future programmes. Decentralisation of policy design and management to a range of local agencies, the creation of new partnership structures and the application of a wide diversity of new local policy tools mean that evaluation will become more complex. Debate is also needed on what should be the measures of success for different programmes, what are their shared objectives and what is different, and how the quality of outputs can be measured. Notwithstanding these complexities, it is very important that rigorous and consistent evaluation is undertaken. The results of local evaluations need to be put together and widely disseminated to policy-makers. The OECD LEED Programme can play a role in helping to promote a culture of evaluation for local programmes across OECD Member countries and in helping to disseminate and exchange findings at an international level on what works and how.

BIBLIOGRAPHY

Bloom, D. (1997)
> *After AFDC: Welfare to Work Choices and Challenges for States*,
> Manpower Demonstration Research Corporation, Washington.

Brown, A. (1997)
> *Work-First: How to Implement an Employment-Focused Approach to Welfare Reform*, Manpower Demonstration Research Corporation, Washington.

Brown, A., Buck, M. and Skinner, E. (1998)
> *Business Partnerships: How to Involve Employers in Welfare Reform*,
> Manpower Demonstration Research Corporation, Washington.

Brauner, S. and Loprest, P. (1999)
> 'Where Are They Now? What States' Studies of People Who Left Welfare Tell Us', *Urban Institute Paper Series A*, No. A-32, May 1999, Urban Institute, Washington.

European Commission (1998)
> 'Forging Strong Local Partnership', Paper No. 1 in the Innovations series of the ADAPT and EMPLOYMENT Community Initiatives, Directorate General V, Brussels.

GAO (1998)
> 'Welfare Reform: Transportation's Role in Moving from Welfare to Work', United States General Accounting Office Report to the Chairman, Committee on the Budget, House of Representatives, GAO/RCED-98-161, United States General Accounting Office, Washington.

GAO (1999a)

'Welfare Reform: States' Implementation Progress and Information on Former Recipients', United States General Accounting Office Testimony before the Subcommittee on Human Resources, Committee on Ways and Means, House of Representatives, GAO/T-HEHS-99-116, United States General Accounting Office, Washington.

GAO (1999b)

'Welfare Reform: Implementing DoT's Access to Jobs Program', United States General Accounting Office Report to Congressional Committees, GAO/RCED-99-36, United States General Accounting Office, Washington.

Hughes, M. A. (1996)

'Learning from the 'Milwaukee Challenge'', *Journal of Policy Analysis and Management*, Vol. 15.4, pp. 562-571.

Hutchinson, J. and Campbell, M. (1998)

Working in Partnership: Lessons from the Literature, Department for Education and Employment Publications, Sudbury, United Kingdom.

LEDA Partenariat (1998a)

Setting Up Local Partnerships for Employment, LEDA Partenariat, Paris.

LEDA Partenariat (1998b)

Managing Local Partnerships for Employment, LEDA Partenariat, Paris.

Ministère de l'Emploi et de la Solidarité (1999a)

'Le programme 'Nouveaux Services-Emplois Jeunes' vu par les employeurs et les jeunes', DARES Paper No. 22.2, June 1999.

Ministère de l'Emploi et de la Solidarité (1999b)

'La mise en oeuvre locale du programme 'Nouveaux Services - Emplois Jeunes'', DARES Paper No. 06.1, February 1999.

Newman, S. J. (Ed.) (1999)

The Home Front: Implications of Welfare Reform for Housing Policy, Urban Institute Press, Washington.

Observatoire européen de l'emploi (1998)

'Internet déleste les services de l'AMS', *InfoMISEP Politiques* n° 63, Automne 1998, Berlin.

Observatoire européen de l'emploi (1999)
'L'AMS renforce sa présence sur Internet', *InfoMISEP Politiques* n° 65, Printemps 1999, Berlin.

OECD (1995)
The OECD Jobs Strategy - Implementing the Strategy, OECD publication, Paris.

OECD (1996a)
The OECD Jobs Strategy - Enhancing the Effectiveness of Active Labour Market Policies, OECD publication, Paris.

OECD (1996b)
Ireland: Local Partnerships and Social Innovation, OECD publication, Paris.

OECD (1998)
Local Management for More Effective Employment Policies, OECD publication, Paris.

OECD (1999a)
The Public Employment Service in the United States, OECD publication, Paris.

OECD (1999b)
Decentralising Employment Policy: New Trends and Challenges - The Venice Conference, OECD publication, Paris.

Ong, P. and Blumenberg, E. (1998)
'Job Access, Commute and Travel Burden among Welfare Recipients', *Urban Studies*, Vol. 35.1, pp. 77-93.

Socialforskningsinstituttet (1998)
Arbejdsmarkedsreformen og arbejdsmarkedet. Evaluering af arbejdsmarkedsreformen III. Socialforskningsinstituttet, København.

PART II

CASE STUDY PAPERS

CHAPTER 6
A COMPARISON OF LOCAL APPROACHES TO WELFARE-TO-WORK IN THE UNITED STATES, THE UNITED KINGDOM AND THE NETHERLANDS

By Dr Dan Finn, Portsmouth University, United Kingdom

Introduction: the local dimension of welfare-to-work

Welfare-to-work, active benefit regimes and institutional reform

Welfare systems in most OECD countries are under pressure. In some countries the key factor has been a long term trend increase in the number of people of working age who are dependent on benefit payments, often for very long periods. In other countries, particularly the USA, the welfare system is deeply unpopular and seen to be ineffective. In response to these changes, and to the growing costs of their social assistance and unemployment compensation systems, governments have embarked on radical reforms aimed at creating work based welfare systems. A key element in the new approaches is the increasing involvement of local partnerships and organisations in designing, developing and implementing programmes.

Governments are also modernising the relationships between their benefit systems and labour markets. Systems are being moved from the payment of passive income support towards more active measures involving new and tougher work tests, especially for the unemployed, linked with voluntary or mandatory attendance at a diverse range of job search, employment and training programmes. The shared aim of what are increasingly described as these welfare-to-work strategies is to create new active benefit regimes which improve employability, reinforce work incentives and reduce costs and welfare dependency. The strategies also include tax and benefit reform aimed at 'making work pay' and fiscal and other policies aimed at maintaining economic growth and stimulating job creation.

Welfare-to-work is not just about the abstract creation of opportunities and incentives. Governments have recognised the need to couple policy with organisational reform and have linked the transition to active benefit regimes with radical changes in the bureaucracies and institutions charged with delivering and administering programmes. The reasons for the perceived inadequacies of existing systems are contested, but at least part of the problem has been attributed to the 'top down' inflexible nature of policy formation and implementation; to the fragmented structure and role of the traditional welfare bureaucracies and national employment services; and to the absence of competition and market forces. Monolithic national service agencies are now being decentralised and public sector monopolies, in the public employment service, have been dismantled, with Australia in particular creating entire new markets in the delivery of employment advice and training services.

Decentralisation, the public employment service (PES) and case management

Throughout the OECD changes are being made to the structure and management of national employment services. This modernisation reflects the need to adjust to fundamental changes in employment, in technologies, and in how people get jobs, but it is also a response to their widely perceived ineffectiveness, their failure to place the long term unemployed, and their inability to respond adequately to the changing needs of the labour market.

OECD countries are introducing more competition in the delivery of PES services, which is often coupled with the creation of a stronger local dimension. In many member States the structure of the PES is being reorganised in ways which combine greater decentralisation with more local discretion to choose among different programmes and options. In Europe, this process is frequently accompanied by 'a closer involvement of the social partners and of local community groups in the search for concrete solutions at the local level' (DGV, 1997, p. 45).

While decentralisation is well established in countries like Sweden, Finland and Denmark, it is now being extended to countries like Ireland, Austria and Belgium. In Germany, for example, a revised 'Labour Promotion Act' now gives local employment offices more autonomy, and within their budgets they are allowed to choose from existing measures those which are most relevant to local needs. They are also allowed to use up to 10% of their active programme resources on innovative measures that they deem necessary. This is linked with new reporting and audit procedures which ensure accountability and it is hoped stimulate competition between local offices (DGV, 1997, p. 46).

In many countries in the OECD there is now also a trend to integrate and co-ordinate the services of a whole range of agencies, from vocational guidance and employment advice through to welfare and social assistance services, into what are described as 'one-stop' or 'one counter' services. The aim is to improve effectiveness and individual and employer access through the creation of a more coherent and integrated gateway to benefits and services.

These organisational reforms are often linked with the introduction of new management techniques and contractual arrangements that are being used both to increase efficiency, reduce costs, and ensure that these public agencies, and their contractors, are more responsive to meeting the needs of the longer-term jobless. Management by objectives coupled with performance targets are putting new pressures on the agencies. In the USA and Holland, for example, the drive towards welfare reform is transforming the work of traditional welfare agencies, and both countries are trying to replace 'bureaucratic compliance systems with innovative, problem solving systems'.

A key element of all these reforms has been to engineer a significant change in the nature of the relationship between individuals and bureaucracies. OECD Labour Ministers advocate the integration of job broking, benefit administration and referral to active measures, to overcome 'the adverse effects' and 'cumbersome management' of disparate administrative systems (Schwanse, 1998, p. 11). This is linked with the opportunity to create a more individualised service for the unemployed where individual action plans or 'routes' can be devised with different measures being linked to the characteristics, motivation and needs of the person. To service this evolving approach many countries have introduced specialised employment advisers or case managers to create new front line services providing the gateway to programmes, jobs and support at the same time as enforcing the new active obligations of those receiving benefits.

These developments are resulting in changes in the actual structure of offices, in new job descriptions, in referral and attendance procedures for clients, and the development of new aids to help secure employment and other placements. At its most dramatic, in the USA, it has involved a huge shift in the culture of welfare offices who now have to call for interview large numbers of lone parents, require them 'to participate in programmes and to work', and then 'supervis(e) their subsequent movements and activities' (Mead, 1997).

Decentralisation, local partnerships and local employment and training initiatives

Historically countries have developed fragmented welfare and employment institutions delivering programmes focused on different groups and often delivered by different agencies drawing on diverse funding streams. Many of the institutions and agencies involved in formulating and implementing employment, training and welfare programmes have done so in an uncoordinated and unsystematic way. The absence of local coherence has often reduced the effectiveness of individual policies and programmes and evaluations have shown that the impact of welfare-to-work programmes has been highly contingent on local labour market conditions and on the capacity of local institutions and networks (MDRC, 1997).

As Governments develop their strategies for tackling social exclusion and welfare dependency one of the central challenges is to reduce this institutional incoherence and to draw together the key local agencies so that they work to a common agenda. However, there are significant differences in the ways that Governments are decentralising and seeking to secure greater local co-ordination.

Drawing on a broad range of comparative evidence, the OECD Local Economic and Employment Development Programme (LEED) identified three ways in which OECD member States were introducing geographical, institutional and programme flexibility into their strategies for combating unemployment and exclusion.

The first approach involved 'geographical targeting of national measures', where the concentration of policy support in the same area and at the same time helps 'overcome market failures and draw in private sector investment' (OECD, 1998a, p. 9). The second approach involves 'devolution of responsibilities to regional and local authorities' which design and implement 'autonomous employment policies'. This devolution allows decisions to be made at a lower level where co-ordination may be achieved more efficiently.

The third approach, which the report saw as offering considerable potential, involves the creation of local partnerships, which are responsible for the implementation of national measures. This type of 'flexible territorialisation' enables 'active labour market policy to profit from the skills, capacities and potential that are specific to local actors in the area, from the public, private or voluntary sector' (1998a, p. 69).

These partnership approaches can most commonly be found in the integrated area based regeneration programmes with which OECD countries have tried to tackle the multiple problems facing disadvantaged areas. However, as Member countries have reorganised their employment, training and welfare systems, some have begun to use the partnership model to provide a framework for creating a more strategic local approach to the development and delivery of welfare-to-work programmes.

In France, for example, both trends are evident. The introduction of large scale and complex employment and insertion programmes has been paralleled by the creation of new forms of organisation and co-ordination. These aim at both facilitating partnerships between central state, regional and local authorities, and at co-ordinating the provision of services by the numerous agencies that participate in 'insertion' (Barbier and Theret, 1998). Area based approaches are best represented by the *'politique de la ville'*, which are city-based and aim to co-ordinate a broad range of regeneration, economic development and employment interventions. There are also local plans of 'insertion' (*Plans locaux d'insertion économique* and *Programmes départementaux d'insertion*) through which local authorities and the state are expected to plan actions and organise individualised 'pathways' especially for those receiving RMI (*revenu minimum d'insertion*).

At the same time that national programmes and services are being made more flexible and co-ordinated locally, it has also become clear that additional actions need to be taken to tackle the entrenched problems faced by particular localities and groups. These local actions or initiatives often draw on a combination of training, job creation and regeneration initiatives and have, according to some evaluations, produced impressive results.

In Europe in particular a range of case study evaluations, capacity building and 'best practice' exchange programmes have explored ways of harnessing the potential of locally based initiatives. In the early 1990s the ERGO programme found that a wide variety of local agencies had been able to create more flexible and effective provision for the long term unemployed than that available through uniform national programmes (1992). They also concluded that 'local actions' were often able to create more 'additionality' because local Cupertino and co-ordination meant that the mix of measures available often better reflected the specific problems faced by the unemployed and employers in the particular area.

Subsequently, the European Commission went on to investigate 'local development and employment initiatives'. While many local schemes have no direct employment creation potential, the report suggested that others did, especially in areas of activity where there were 'new or unmet needs'. It appeared that 'throughout Europe' a new 'bottom-up' approach was emerging 'creating jobs and attempting to meet consumer's needs'. The initiatives were often targeted at the unemployed and were the products of public-private partnerships based 'on a co-operative approach, hinging initially on decentralisation and a change in administrative attitudes' (EC, 1995, p. 21). The report concluded that these local initiatives seemed to have the potential to create new areas of employment, particularly in the caring, environment, leisure and cultural industries. Subsequently, the development of new local area based actions for employment generation moved rapidly up the European policy agenda (Lloyd et al, 1998).

The importance of the local dimension

Although the development of local partnerships, inter-agency collaboration, and of local actions and employment initiatives are not the precisely the same thing they do together constitute an 'increasingly important type of intervention' whose effects can 'complement and amplify those of national measures' (OECD, 1998a). In particular, the success of welfare-to-work strategies, especially in areas of high unemployment, is likely to be enhanced if they are able to harness the innovation associated with local initiatives, and through various partnerships mobilise the commitment, energy, skills and resources of the key local players.

These objectives have been given added urgency at a time when many OECD countries are replacing passive benefit entitlement with new work focused systems, linked either with absolute time limits (as in the USA) or temporary job or training guarantees (as in Europe). Coupled with decentralisation these changes are presenting many localities with a set of far-reaching choices about how to restructure and deliver new active benefit regimes and improve the effectiveness of labour market programmes.

Structure

This chapter assesses the welfare-to-work strategies now being pursued in three case study countries - the USA, the UK, and the Netherlands. Each of these countries was chosen because they have embarked on radical welfare reform even though they have recently experienced economic growth, increased employment and reductions in unemployment.

The chapter describes the changes that are being implemented in the benefit and employment and training systems in each country and explores the ways in which these programmes are being managed and implemented locally. It outlines the approach to partnership formation, the development of 'one-stop' services, and the scope for local innovation.

Finally, the chapter compares and contrasts the approach of each country and outlines some of the key developments and implementation problems that are emerging. It also assesses the potential and problems that local flexibility and innovation will bring to the implementation of welfare-to-work strategies.

Welfare-to-work in the USA

The concept of moving people from welfare-to-work is most closely associated with the USA. This section describes the way in which the US is implementing welfare reform and the ways in which welfare agencies and employment and training services are being restructured. It highlights the role that was played by local experimentation with welfare-to-work programmes, and describes what US welfare-to-work programmes now look like. It also describes the local partnerships that are being created to deliver welfare reform, which are often linked with the parallel creation of 'Workforce Development Boards'. Finally it assesses the initial impact of reform.

Institutional arrangements and labour market programmes

The US has evolved a complex range of benefits and labour market programmes for jobless people. Although responsibility is shared between federal government, the states and local government, the unemployment and welfare systems have traditionally been organised through two separate bureaucracies, both at national and state levels. The public employment service, with about 1700 offices, usually housed both Unemployment Insurance (UI) eligibility and payment services, linked with separate job placement and advice and referral services. Welfare agencies, by contrast, have provided benefits and Food Stamps for the poor, particularly lone parents and their children. Although the agencies have become increasingly work oriented, until recently their principal priorities have been with assessing eligibility and making accurate payment of benefits.

The most significant training and employment programmes for 'disadvantaged groups' have been delivered through a separate network of local Private Industry Councils (PICs) which were established under the 1982 Job Training

Partnership Act. These are now being replaced by Workforce Development Boards. As with the PICs the Boards have majority employer representation, but also include representation from local government, education providers, labour organisations, community based organisations, economic development and other relevant agencies, including advocacy groups. From 1988 each Board now has to develop a five-year strategic plan for delivering over 14 separate federal programmes, including JTPA training programmes, the PES, UI administration, adult education and literacy, vocational education and rehabilitation and some welfare-to-work programmes.

A key element of the new approach is that each Board has to create a one-stop delivery system which must involve at least one physical centre which can be supplemented by networks of affiliated sites and by the use of new communication technologies. The aim is to transform the bureaucratic maze of separate programmes and access points into a single performance-driven and outcome based system characterised by 'universal access' to core services, such as job matching and guidance; 'customer choice' and 'service integration' (SPA, 1997, A-1).

Although workforce development systems vary state by state they are all being directly linked with welfare reform agencies and programmes.

Welfare reform and local experimentation

The focus of US welfare reform has been recipients of Aid for Families with Dependent Children (AFDC) – usually lone parents and their children - and Food Stamps. During the 1980s, a consensus emerged around the need to reform AFDC. Most mothers were in the workforce, including mothers of young children, and 'the Depression-era commitment to helping mothers stay at home was considered obsolete' (DHSS and DoE, 1997, p. 1). The system was also unpopular, was perceived to be rewarding dependency and undermining work incentives, and, in the more extreme versions, was seen to be helping create an urban underclass. By the time President Clinton was first elected the aim was to shift the US social assistance system from one based on entitlement, because of need, towards one based on temporary assistance which enables those in difficulty to become self sufficient.

One crucial feature of this fundamental change in approach was that it was preceded by over 30 years of experimentation at State and local level (Gueron, 1997). By 1996 this local experimentation had created a lengthy series of evaluations of work-focused welfare reform strategies the findings from which then 'played an important part in shaping social policy and programme practice' (Gueron, 1997, p. 79).

In trying to classify the different types of local welfare-to-work programmes that emerged through local flexibility and experimentation it helps to see them falling at 'various points on a continuum' (Bloom, 1998, p. 40). At one end, were 'labour force attachment' models that aimed to move participants into jobs quickly by requiring and/or helping them look for work. At the other end were 'human capital development' models that relied heavily on skill-building services, such as basic education or occupational skills training, to prepare participants for higher wage jobs. Between these two poles there were a variety of 'mixed' models that stressed elements of both approaches.

National welfare reform

The 1996 Personal Responsibility and Work Opportunities Act introduced fundamental change. The legislation cut or reduced a number of low-income programmes and replaced AFDC with Temporary Assistance for Needy Families (TANF). This ended automatic entitlement to cash benefits, and imposed strict time limits and requirements on those claiming support. Although States have some flexibility, federal TANF funding cannot be used to support a family for more than five years, and after two years the support must take the form of involvement in a work-related activity.

By removing minimum requirements from states, the legislation effectively ended the federal welfare 'safety net' that had been created in the 1930s. However, although states now have no federal obligation to provide assistance to any group of needy families, they are obliged to adhere to a set of rules imposed by the law, and face penalties if they fail to meet participation levels and targets set at federal level. In particular, states are required to ensure that a growing proportion of the eligible welfare population is involved in work related activities, increasing from 25% in 1997 to 50% in 2002. 'Work' must account for 20 hours of activity a week in 1997, increasing to 30 hours a week in 2002. The Act also favoured the 'work-first' labour market attachment model and severely limits the ability of states to count involvement in education and training as a relevant activity.

The legislation made major changes in the funding that states received. Whereas previously they received funding on a demand led basis; the TANF allocation is paid as a single block grant that the state can use for any reasonable purpose under the Act. Each state gets a fixed amount related to their levels of expenditure in 1994 and 1995, and the federal TANF budget is capped at US$16 billion until the financial year 2001.

135

In addition to TANF the federal government has also made available a specific US$3bn Welfare-to-Work block grant. This provides extra resources for active measures and has a partly competitive structure aimed at tapping into the expertise and innovation of more locally based groups and partnerships operating below State level. The block grant is divided into two streams. The 'formula' element accounts for 75% of the available funds and is allocated to States who are required to spend at least 85% of it through their local Workforce Development Boards, or an acceptable alternative. The other 25% is allocated thorough 'Competitive Grants to Local Communities', and is awarded directly to local governments, private entities or community based organisations. The funds have to be spent on employment and job search programmes that assist people to move from welfare to work.

What US welfare-to-work programmes look like

Across the US the new work based welfare system is being implemented in a number of ways, with increased variations both between and within individual states. According to one review of local implementation, programmes 'vary in terms of the amount of cash assistance they provide, the rules they set, and the services they offer'. Different government agencies may operate different parts of the system, and although federal law restricts privatisation of key eligibility functions the delivery of activities and services is being increasingly contracted out to a broad range of private firms or non-profit organisations. These range from large multinational corporations, such as Lockheed, through to small community based organisations (Baldwin, 1998, 59).

Although local variation is increasing, with markedly different systems emerging in States like Wisconsin or Vermont, most work focused welfare programs share the following features (Brown et al, 1998, p. 20):

- *Time limits*. Almost all states place limits on the amount of time that families can receive assistance, and about twenty have limits of less than five years. There are shorter limits on the amount of time that individuals can receive welfare without working or participating in welfare-to-work activities.

- *Welfare-to-work activities*. All state welfare programmes include activities designed to move recipients into employment. They are required to begin with an 'employability assessment', and this is followed by one or more of the following options:

- *Job search/job placement*. Welfare recipients are referred to job vacancies, learn job search skills and are assisted in conducting job search.

- *Job-readiness*. These activities provide preparation in basic work skills, such as punctuality, appropriate dress, and interacting with supervisors and co-workers.

- *Education and training*. Despite the move away from 'human capital' models, most States provide some opportunities for recipients to attend education or participate in training programmes to improve their skills and employment prospects.

- *Work programmes*. These can involve unpaid work experience or subsidised employment, or community service jobs.

– *Support services*. These include childcare, medical and transportation assistance, counselling, and access to work clothes. They assist welfare recipients participate in welfare-to-work activities and make the transition to employment.

– *Mandates and sanctions*. Almost all welfare programmes balance the services they provide with requirements that recipients either work or participate in activities designed to lead to employment. Different states apply different penalties to individuals who do not comply with programme requirements, ranging from partial grant reductions to ineligibility for assistance.

– *Financial incentives/Make work pay*. Most states offer 'earnings disregards' which discount a portion of earned income in calculating welfare benefits. The actual transition into regular work is also encouraged by US fiscal policy which 'makes work pay' for low earners through cash payments in the form of an Earned Income Tax Credit. The credit is usually paid in the form of an annual tax rebate. Over 15% of US taxpayers benefit and it raises the income of 4.3 million families above the official poverty line (SSC, 1998, p. 13).

Implementing welfare reform: local partnerships

The Clinton administration has put considerable effort into supporting welfare reform, and has called for a national broad-based and co-ordinated effort that utilises the resources of state and local governments, private employers and other organisations. Particular importance is attached to getting greater collaboration between welfare agencies and the emerging Workforce Development Boards.

Although there is no national model, the National Governors Association (1998) reports that states are building on interagency collaborations and public-private sector relationships that have developed over the years. Many welfare and workforce agencies are collaborating more than ever, especially to develop and operate integrated one-shop systems, but the extent of collaboration is uneven. Planning and applying the new welfare-to-work grants programme has intensified the dialogue between the welfare and workforce development systems and is helping redefine their respective roles and responsibilities.

Examples of where responsibility for welfare-to-work has been devolved in ways that enable it to be integrated with the emerging workforce development system include (Brown et al, 1998, p. 13):

- *The Local Investment Commission* (Kansas City, Missouri). This was established in 1992 to develop and oversee programmes in a variety of human services and is responsible for the implementation of welfare reform in the city. The Commission is managed by a 36-member citizen-board, and more than half the board's members come from the business community. LINC has authority to determine welfare policies, design welfare-to-work strategies, negotiate contacts with service providers, and monitor outcomes.

- *The Florida WAGES programme*. The state has delegated control of and responsibility for implementation of welfare reform to local boards, made up of over 50% business representatives, community leaders and local advocates. The local boards have freedom to design their own welfare-to-work programmes, contract with service providers, and prioritise spending of state and federal funds.

Other states, like Wisconsin and Texas, have already merged the agencies responsible for workforce development and welfare reform. In Wisconsin the welfare-to-work programme is run by officially designated agencies in each county, within the framework of a comprehensive system called 'Partnership for Full Employment' (PFE). This is an integrated, interdependent employment and training service delivery system which links services for job seekers with services for employers. Under the PFE model services for all job seekers, including TANF applicants and participants, veterans, displaced workers, people with disabilities, and others, are delivered through one-stop Job Centres (SSC, 1998, p. 9).

Although the logic of this integration is clear it seems that in practice there have been problems with weaving together 'the 'work-first' philosophy of many state welfare-reform initiatives and the 'customer-driven' philosophy guiding the one-stop initiative' (SPA, 1997, p. 1-10).

Pilot welfare-to-work initiatives in disadvantaged urban communities

Above all else, the greatest challenge to US welfare reform is in large urban areas, where poverty and long term dependence are concentrated. The Federal Government has encouraged Public Housing Authorities to become actively involved in efforts to get residents into work, and to forge links with workforce development systems. Links have also been made with urban policy in the form of the capacity and physical development that are being promoted in the recently created 'Empowerment Zones' and 'Enterprising Communities' established in some of the most deprived urban and rural areas in the US.

In many of these areas community based organisations are playing a crucial role in delivering a range of economic, employment and training programmes and services. These community associations or development corporations have grown at the same time as there has been what is described as the 'retreat' of government from deprived urban communities. Some are developing new jobs and community services; others are playing a crucial role as intermediaries with employers.

Of particular importance are some pilot 'Job-Plus' initiatives that attempt to harness the potential of local partnerships in inner city neighbourhoods with a work based welfare programme. According to MDRC the approach has been 'inspired in part by the growing number of community building initiatives across the country, spearheaded by new local partnerships among civic groups, community based organisations, government, private, philanthropies, businesses, religious institutions, and importantly, residents themselves' (1997, p. 17). The various projects include three components:

- an innovative package of employment and training services;

- new financial incentives to work created by changes in welfare rules and public housing rent-determination rules; and

- a community-support-for-work component which 'entails modifying and expanding residents social networks' so that in their efforts to find and retain work, 'residents are encouraged, supported, and assisted by family members, friends, mentors, and acquaintances, not just case workers'.

MDRC indicates that the approach being tested is based on the assumption that it is feasible to increase work dramatically across very diverse inner city neighbourhoods through a combination of strategies that local residents and institutions help to shape and come to 'own'. The aim is that the projects can take full advantage of the special opportunities, unique to place based interventions, to restructure the social environment and neighbourhood context within which residents live, which can profoundly influence their employment patterns. The interventions are also based on the view that reductions in joblessness and improvements in quality of life can be sustained over the long term 'only if the local collaborations formed for these projects among public and private social institutions and the poor people they serve evolve into enduring partnerships'.

The early impact of welfare reform

The proponents of the new US system argue that it will foster creativity and innovation, will save public money, and will send strong messages about the importance of work and the temporary nature of public assistance. By contrast, critics argue that the legal framework 'invites harsh and extreme state responses' and, because it removes state responsibility to assist poor families, will enable them to 'shift billions of dollars away from low-income programmes' (Greenberg, 1998, p. 5). Indeed, the new US welfare-to-work system is much harsher than was originally intended by President Clinton, and while it puts in place many new service possibilities it actually says nothing about the reduction of poverty, a key feature of the legislation it replaced (Handler, 1995, p. 125).

The clearest impact so far has been an acceleration in the decline in the numbers claiming welfare, which had already started to fall in 1994. Overall, states have experienced caseload reductions of between 30% and 40%, with some experiencing even greater reductions. By June 1998, according to the Vice

President, the numbers claiming benefits had declined by 5.2 million 'since the beginning of this administration'.

There is no comprehensive information about the circumstances of the families leaving assistance, but that which exists suggests that those who are getting jobs are receiving wages that are insufficient to raise their families above basic income levels. It is also a matter of considerable debate as to how much of the case load reduction is to do with the pull of an improved labour market, the impact of welfare-to-work programmes, or the 'go away' effect of tougher eligibility rules and sanctions (Greenberg, 1998).

The impact of a strong economy during the initial stages of implementation, coupled with levels of funding determined on a relatively generous bench mark, has also created a 'windfall' opportunity for those implementing reform. However, for many localities, the most difficult period is likely to arise when the economic cycle changes, with capped funding levels, and where large numbers of welfare recipients are both expected to be involved in programmes and are approaching the end of their entitlement periods.

United Kingdom: welfare-to-work and the New Deals

In the UK, the Labour Government has put welfare reform at the heart of its programme for modernisation. It has also placed particular emphasis on the creation of local partnerships that are seen to represent an alternative to simplistic free market solutions and the 'old centralised command and control systems, which stifled innovation'. The 'third way', favoured by the Prime Minister, involves creating 'partnerships at local level, with investment tied to targets and measured outcomes, with national standards but local freedom to manage and innovate' (Blair, 1998, p. 15).

This section describes the role played by national and local agencies, and by the comprehensive area based partnerships that have been used to implement local regeneration strategies. It then outlines the various welfare-to-work and New Deal programmes that are being introduced, and assesses the progress made by the new partnerships that are being created to implement them. Overall, the aim is to create a more flexible 'work based' and locally driven welfare state, which will eventually be delivered through a single employment focused 'gateway' to the benefit system.

Institutional arrangements and local partnerships

The British welfare state has undergone major transformations since the re-emergence of mass unemployment in the late 1970s. The structure and purpose of the benefit system, employment and training programmes, and the departments and agencies responsible for delivering them have been redefined, and the support system for those out of work has been more directly linked to the emerging flexible labour market. At local level new institutional arrangements and regeneration programmes have created a complex structure of public and private sector led partnerships which have, according to a recent comparative review, left Britain at the forefront in 'designing area-based programmes' aimed at tackling social exclusion (Parkinson, 1998).

The most significant employment and training institutions were created in the late 1980s. This was a period of major change involving the creation of semi-independent executive agencies and a wide range of private sector and employer led bodies which all delivered public services to specified national performance standards. In particular in 1987 the Government created a unified public Employment Service (PES) to bring together the previously separate network of Job Centres and Unemployment Benefit Offices. Shortly afterwards the Government created a national network of employer-led Training and Enterprise Councils (TECs) in England and Wales, and Local Enterprise Companies (LECs) in Scotland. These were modelled on US Private Industry Councils but were all established as private companies with a two thirds employer majority, designed to give employers a predominant role in the local design and delivery of training and enterprise programmes.

Although area based regeneration projects normally included employment and training programmes, and other services for those without work, the previous Conservative government made no significant attempt to integrate the national PES or its programmes into the local partnerships that were emerging. Institutionally, the PES maintained its independence and argued that it was 'a national organisation delivering standard products and services in all parts of the country'. It saw no 'scope for added value through separate product and service development in each region' (RPC, 1996, p. 119). The consequence was that PES programmes had little local flexibility, and the service was driven by nationally determined output targets.

There was also no effort to create direct links between the partnerships which were developed in local areas with the activities of the Department of Social Security and its service delivery 'Benefits Agency' (with about 500 local offices). The Benefits Agency is responsible for the assessment and delivery of most benefits but has little apparent flexibility about how they might apply their rules in ways that are better integrated with local employment development and training activities.

The national benefit legislation and the new welfare-to-work programmes cover the whole UK, but the PES and Benefits Agency only cover Great Britain, with different institutions responsible for delivering programmes and benefits in Northern Ireland. Scotland also enjoys considerable autonomy and the LECs are more powerful than TECs, as they are an integrated part of either Scottish Enterprise or Highlands and Island Enterprise which are responsible for many inward investment, development and regeneration programmes, that are delivered separately in England and Wales. These institutional differences are likely to increase following constitutional reform and local delivery and some programme elements may increasingly vary when the Scottish Government and Wales and Northern Ireland Assemblies are established.

Local experimentation and Intermediate Labour Market (ILM) projects

In contrast with the local experimentation that characterised welfare-to-work in the USA, the British system has been far less flexible. Although the PES could pilot new employment schemes and approaches, and did so with some success, social security legislation expressly prohibited initiatives which might involve people in identical circumstances being entitled to a different level of provision (Walker, 1997, p. 264). This changed in 1996 when the legislation which introduced the Job Seekers Allowance, which replaced other unemployment benefits, created new powers which allow for more experimentation.

Despite legislative inflexibility, and restrictive PES and TEC contractual requirements, over the past ten years a broad range of local and non-governmental organisations have developed their own smaller-scale local training and employment initiatives. Many were supported by Local Authorities, by regeneration partnerships, by TECs, and by the European Commission. Juggling with complex funding regimes and often inflexible benefit regulations, organisations working with women and lone parents, with refugees, with ethnic minorities, with the homeless and with the young and long term unemployed, created new advice, information and training services, many of which appeared to secure impressive job entry and progression rates. According to one review (Turok and Webster, 1998, p. 324):

> Many offer a wider range of support and better integrated provision, including independent guidance and counselling, personal development and vocational training in flexible packages, customised training for specific vacancies, work experience paying the rate for the

143

job and providing transferable skills, complementary childcare, intensive assistance with job-seeking, and progressive wage and training subsidies to private employers with some obligation to keep on recruits afterwards.

Of particular importance, and in a departure from national policies and practice at the time, non-profit organisations like the Wise Group of companies, Glasgow Works and CREATE in Liverpool, were able to pioneer the creation of what have been called 'intermediate' jobs which operate at the level of the local labour market (Bewick and Simmonds, 1997). This ILM approach represented a conscious attempt to develop local job creation initiatives that both provided for unmet local needs and offered the long term unemployed a bridge into the real labour market. They have the following characteristics (Finn, 1996):

- *intermediate*: because access to ILM jobs are limited to specific groups who, for whatever reason, have been socially excluded, and face particular problems in getting access to jobs;

- *waged or salaried jobs*: an ILM operates in the same way as the regular labour market. There is selection in jobs, work discipline, contracts of employment, and so on;

- *limited period of time*: the central purpose remains helping the unemployed move back into the regular labour market, secured through work experience, training and help with job search;

- *direct social purpose*: developing the provision of services and improving infrastructure for the benefit of the community in ways which facilitate local regeneration;

- *trading for a social purpose*: where, by establishing trading enterprises, local market failures can be overcome and services and goods provided at an affordable cost to local consumers who otherwise would not be able to afford them; and

- *work that would not normally be undertaken*: to encourage the development of additional activities and avoid substitution and displacement in the local labour market.

What is clear is that ILMs depend upon the twin goals of both providing support to unemployed people and providing socially useful work within a local economic framework. These twin goals have to be kept in balance otherwise there will be a tendency for ILMs to be perceived by employers and unemployed people as just another scheme.

Independent evaluations have shown these projects to be successful; both in getting the long term unemployed into work, and in generating socially useful services and products. The Wise Group, for example, which began working with the long term unemployed in 1983, delivers training and temporary work through projects involved in energy conservation, security, building and construction, environmental improvements, urban forestry, new technology and office administration. Its principal activities are in Glasgow, where it receives and combines funding from a wide range of sources, including Europe, local government and the local LEC. In 1995/96 it had a turnover of nearly £14m, and provided temporary jobs and training, for up to a year, to nearly 800 long term unemployed people, of whom around 60% gain a qualification and two-thirds find a job at some point in the six months after leaving (McGregor, 1998, p. 51).

Although the Wise Group consults with residents in the areas it works in, it is not a community-controlled organisation. It has a board largely made up of funders and key individuals, with professional and other expertise. Indeed, although the Group has consolidated on its local involvement in Glasgow it has a broader agenda and has worked hard to transfer its approach to different localities. One recent evaluation showed that they had succeeded in developing a model which was both transferable to other high unemployment areas and was also 'sufficiently robust to be adapted in a number of ways' (McGregor et al, 1998, p. 21).

Wise and other ILM projects have now been created in a range of urban areas, and the approach is seen as central to the development of the New Deals in areas of high unemployment. However, according to one parliamentary enquiry, the effective expansion of ILMs will require investment in local technical and organisational capacity. It will also be assisted if the Government is able to reduce administrative and legislative barriers to pooling funds from different budgets and allows for 'benefit transfer' where passive income support payments can be integrated directly into active measures – an approach now being tested in Employment Zones (ESC, 1997, Vol. 1).

Welfare-to-work and the New Deals

The Labour Government has put welfare reform at the top of its political agenda and since it came to power has put in place an ambitious agenda for transforming the prospects of those without work. The aim of the

Government's welfare-to-work strategy is to end what it has characterised as the 'dependency' culture that developed in the 1980s. New Deal's for the long term unemployed, for lone parents, and for people with disabilities are to provide routes into work for the 20% of working age 'workless' households where up to five million people now form what the Government describes as 'a workless class cut off from jobs and careers and fatalistic about their prospects' (DfEE, 1997, p. 9).

The 1997 welfare-to-work budget raised over £5 billion through the windfall tax on the profits of the privatised utilities. Most of this has been committed to finance the New Deal between 1998 and 2002. Although programmes have been introduced for the full range of working age people living on benefits, the bulk of the resources, just over £2.6bn, have been allocated to the young unemployed.

Since April 1998 all unemployed young people aged between 18 and 24 who have been out of work for over six months, who then numbered just over 136,000, have been guaranteed places on the New Deal. After a 'Gateway' period of up to four months, during which young unemployed people will have been given intensive job search support by a 'personal adviser', those who do not get work are offered a place on a New Deal option.

This can involve a subsidised job, normally in the private sector, where an employer receives a subsidy of £60 a week for up to six months (some will be able to try self employment). Alternatively young people may be offered six month placements on an Environmental Task Force or with a voluntary sector organisation where they are paid a wage or their benefit plus £15 a week. All the young people involved should receive either on-the-job or day-release education and training. The final option is full-time education for up to a year on 'an approved course' for young people with few or no qualifications.

The Government has emphasised that there is 'no fifth option of an inactive life on benefit' (PM, 1997, p. 7). If young people reject a New Deal option without 'good cause' they will be subject to a two-week benefit sanction. A second or any subsequent refusal will result in a four-week sanction. Hardship payments will only be available to specified 'vulnerable groups'.

Although there is less financial provision for the over 25-year old unemployed who have been out of work for over six months (of whom there were more than 700,000 in April 1998) major changes are taking place in the options available. In particular, the PES has developed new 'core values', is extending the role of personal advisers, and aims to deliver a more effective work focused service. One particular development has been the introduction of what are called

Programme Centres, operated through private and not-for-profit subcontractors. These have moved away from the previous generation of inflexible and unpopular compulsory courses and created a more imaginative client focused approach to the delivery of these job search and advice programmes. Training places will continue be available for some, through a revamped TEC programme called 'work based training for adults'.

More significantly, from June 1998 a New Deal for those out of work for over two years supplemented the compulsory courses and programmes of the previous Government with two new options: six-month wage subsidies of £75 a week for about 15% of the target group and full-time study opportunities for about 2,500 people a year (TEN, 1998, p. 10). These were followed in November by thirty New Deal pilot programmes aimed at those aged over 25 who have been out of work for over a year or over 18 months. Over a two-year period, these pilots are testing out less resource intensive versions of the 'Gateway' and options available to the younger age group, and after evaluation the more successful elements are likely to be extended.

There are also voluntary New Deals for lone parents and for people with disabilities. Since October 1998 lone parents who make their first claim for Income Support or whose youngest child starts school are now invited to their local Job Centre, to be given advice, directed as to where they might get jobs or upgrade their skills and be advised about any child-care support that can be obtained. The programme for people with disabilities has been less prescriptive, and between 1998 and 2002 organisations working with the target group will be testing new advisory services, and a limited range of more intensive support, aimed at enabling people claiming disability benefits to return to work.

The New Deal expansion of employment programmes and advice services is being matched by other major welfare-to-work reforms in the social security, tax and employment systems. In particular, work incentives are to be enhanced through the introduction of a national minimum wage in 1999 and through the introduction of a new Working Families Tax Credit (modelled on the US Earned Income Credit).

In effect, through the New Deals the Labour Government is integrating the active benefit regime it inherited into the broader process of welfare reform through which it intends to 'rebuild the welfare state around work'. In this new era 'it is the Government's responsibility to promote work opportunities' and 'the responsibility of those who can take them up to do so' (HMSO, 1998, p. 23 and 31). The critical assumption is that welfare dependency and unemployment can be substantially reduced by both improving the employability of working age benefit recipients and by connecting them more proactively to the labour market

Local partnerships: delivering the New Deal

Responsibility for implementing the New Deal has been given to the national PES. However, the Government recognised that the unpopularity of the 'schemes' the PES was associated with meant that it had a credibility problem with the unemployed, with employers, and with other local agencies, and from the outset it has been required to develop and work with new local partnerships. These are seen as crucial to avoid fragmentation, build legitimacy and ensure effective delivery. At the same time, it was hoped that these partnerships would be able to harness the good practice that had emerged in local employment and training initiatives.

As the details of the New Deal for the young unemployed were clarified, local PES managers were encouraged to consult widely and to form about 130 local strategic partnerships that would develop 'District Delivery Plans'. Although national guidelines were issued, PES managers had much discretion about the extent of consultation and the formation of their local partnerships. In most areas it seems that early broad based consultation was followed by the creation of a narrower group of key strategic partners, usually involving TECs, local government and, where they existed, regeneration partnerships.

Although some elements of the New Deal have to be delivered by the PES, there was no such requirement around much programme provision. Local partnerships were given a choice of three contracting models (ES, 1997, p2):

- – A series of individual contracts: the traditional contracting model where the PES delivers the District Plan through contracts with single organisations, or with consortia that form to deliver a specific New Deal option.

- – A Consortium led by a single organisation: where the PES has a single contract with either a legally constituted consortium or designated lead organisation.

- – A Joint Venture approach: where the PES works with a consortium to jointly develop the delivery plan 'and to implement the plan, once evaluated and approved, through a joint venture' agreement.

During the process of partnership formation, the Government announced that there was to be a departure from the proposed delivery model in ten districts. In these areas, private sector organisations, particularly private employment agencies, have been given the lead in delivering the New Deal.

District Plans were assessed by Regional Assessment Panels, which had Government and external representation. Although there was much diversity in the plans, the DfEE identified some common attributes that were shared by the 'best'. These included:

- a rigorous analysis of the area which defined priorities and shaped the services and provision on offer;

- the active participation of key partners, at senior level;

- the commitment by business of resources and expertise, in addition to offers of vacancies; and

- genuine innovation in the Gateway and each of the employment and training options.

Other positive features included the integration of the New Deal with existing job creation provision, and synergy with other funding streams, such as the European Social Fund, to extend help for young people before or beyond their time spent on the New Deal.

There were, however, significant weaknesses. There was 'confusion' about the contracting options and, apart from one region, most areas chose the least risky option and gave the PES the lead in contracting for all provision. Overall, there was also a 'lack of innovation', attributed to the short time-scales imposed, and a lack of direct business involvement in the design of the programme.

Despite the progress made in developing local partnerships the early evidence indicated some emerging problems. In particular, an independent evaluation of the first twelve 'pathfinder' areas found some significant tensions in the local delivery groups not least of which was 'partnership fatigue', where it was unclear how the New Deal for the young unemployed linked with a multiplicity of other local initiatives. There were also reservations about the ability of the PES to create effective partnerships or shake off its 'benefit policing' image. Concern was also expressed about potential conflicts of interest, and the review concluded that although local support for the New Deal partnerships was 'robust' there was little evidence of the 'shared risk' which they saw as the 'hallmark of true partnership'.

More critically, one assessment suggests that despite the rhetoric of partnership and consultation the New Deal remains very much a top-down and inflexible programme (Peck, 1998). The flexibility that exists has been in the delivery not the design of the programme, which has nationally standardised elements, allows little budgetary flexibility and permits very little scope for linking or re-sequencing the various options and processes.

Local delivery and area based initiatives

In the longer term, the UK Government's welfare-to-work strategy will involve further major organisational changes in the work of the PES and the Benefits Agency. In particular, both agencies are now expected to work more closely with local organisations and the private and voluntary sectors, and with the various partnerships that have been established. The long term aim, according to the Government, is to try to co-ordinate the relevant local activities into 'a single work-focused gateway into the benefit system for all those of working age who can work', in which personal advisers will help 'claimants develop a tailor made action plan for regaining their independence' (HMSO, 1998, p. 81). Pilot schemes started in 1999.

The welfare-to-work and New Deal strategies are seen, alongside new policies on education and health, as providing more effective national programmes for tackling unemployment and exclusion. However, area based initiatives are still seen as vital in meeting the special needs of areas facing multiple problems and a key role of the local partnerships established through the Single Regeneration Budget (SRB) and the European Union's Territorial Employment Pacts is to integrate these national programmes into their local strategies. These existing area programmes are now also being joined by other new 'zone' initiatives and by a specific New Deal for Communities.

Employment Zones and Personal Job Accounts

The Government is using a range of 'zone' initiatives to test new approaches to delivering public services in disadvantaged areas. Currently, there are 25 action zones for education, 26 for health, and fifteen have been created for employment.

The Employment Zones represent a different approach from the national New Deals. They are aimed at people who have been out of work for over a year, but can include lone parents and people with disabilities who are in receipt of benefits. The initial EZ budget, for the first five zones, was UK£58 million, to allow each of the five areas to recruit 1,000 participants, on a voluntary basis, over two years. Local partnerships have been expected to secure more effective co-ordination of local measures across agencies and funding streams. They have been given ownership of the programme, are allowed considerable flexibility in what they do and how they do it, and have been encouraged to develop innovative advice, learning, job creation and business support programmes (Jarvis, 1998).

All the zones are testing wage-based community jobs programmes, based on the ILM model. They have also been joined by New Deal partnerships in areas like Manchester, Southampton, Portsmouth and Nottingham, who have put together funding packages that enable them to develop ILM job opportunities which are seen as creating an innovative 'stepping stone' to mainstream employment (SEU, 1998, p. 60).

Most imaginatively the Liverpool zone and the Birmingham New Deal Partnership are developing the idea further and creating what are described as 'Jobs Pools' (partly modelled on the Danish and Dutch labour pools). These retain many of the features of the ILM but explicitly aim to develop 'intermediate jobs' across a number of sectors – small and medium enterprises, the domestic economy, large employers – and not just in the social economy. In Birmingham, the approach is to create a 'Managed Labour Market' where a co-ordinated set of local agencies manage a 'stock' of jobs which can be directed flexibly to meet:

- the recruitment needs of local employers;

- the needs of unemployed people by giving them the most appropriate experience which will secure lasting employment; and

- local regeneration by investing in those organisations that have the potential to create new jobs and meet the needs of local people.

The key to making this concept work on the ground 'is multi-agency co-ordination around a community regeneration strategy linked to existing employment and training programmes' (Bewick and Simmonds, 1997, p. 6).

One final dimension to the Employment Zones is the way in which the options they make available are testing what are described as 'Personal Job Accounts'. These aim to combine the 'money currently available for benefits and training'. If this idea of 'benefit transfer' is to be extended it will require primary legislation, but the aim is to create a mechanism that will allow what are currently passive benefits to be converted directly, on an individual basis, into active measures. If the zones are seen to succeed, and the legislation is passed, it is envisaged that up to 30 zones could be created in areas of high unemployment.

Single Regeneration Budget and the New Deal for Communities

The future of the zones will also be influenced by another separate area based initiative that was announced in the 1998 budget. The New Deal for Communities, which has been allocated £800 million over the next four years, aims to provide funding for the 'intensive regeneration of small neighbourhoods', typically consisting of between 1 to 4,000 household units. The programme starts with 17 'pathfinder' areas in 1999 and will support 'plans that bring together local people, community and voluntary organisations, public agencies, local authorities and business in an intensive local focus' to tackle 'poor job prospects, high levels of crime, and a rundown environment' (SEU, 1998).

Once chosen areas will be allowed 'enough time and money' to analyse what needs to be done, and to draw up a detailed plan involving local people. Each neighbourhood could receive up to UK£50m over a ten-year period, enabling it to make a substantial impact. The aim is to more effectively tackle 'social exclusion and (improve) the quality of life of some of the most rundown areas of the country'.

This New Deal links with and builds on the approach first introduced through the Single Regeneration Budget in 1994, which is being retained but restructured. The SRB initially integrated twenty separate programmes from a range of government departments, and introduced a major change in the approach to urban policy:

- the programme is based on the assumption that strategy should be defined locally rather than nationally, with government establishing overall guidelines;

- the bids from each area are competitive and applications must come from formal partnerships that include the community sector, who should be involved in the development of strategic plans and participate in implementation;

- projects usually last between three to five years and partnerships are expected to leverage in private sector finance of at least double the public sector commitment; and

- the range of possible projects that can be funded ranges from investment in training and employment projects, through to crime reduction, environmental improvement, and housing renewal.

In April 1999, responsibility for administration of SRB in England will pass to new Regional Development Agencies. Over the next three years, resources of some UK£1.3 billion will go to support over 500 existing local regeneration schemes, with an additional UK£700 million to support new activity. In 1998 the programme has been altered to concentrate more on areas of severe need, to give greater support to community development and involvement and to complement more effectively other initiatives such as the New Deal for Communities and Employment Zones (SEU, 1998, p. 55). Over the next few years, the Government has said that at least one major SRB programme will have been introduced in each of the 50 most deprived local authority districts.

The impact of welfare-to-work

The various New Deals are at an early stage of implementation, and there is little evaluation evidence available. However, despite disagreements about funding and the balance of options, they have won broad-based support amongst the organisations that will deliver the programme, and amongst many of the agencies working with the unemployed. The New Deals for the unemployed also build on the more positive features of UK experience, and there is credible evaluation evidence to show that many of the programmes that feature in local plans have delivered positive impacts, allowing for dead-weight, substitution and displacement (see, for example, White et al, 1997). It is also possible that the local flexibility that exists will enable them to draw on the approach of the smaller scale projects that seem to have performed so well.

However, there are forceful critics of the programme, many of whom suggest that its main weakness is the absence of a stronger commitment to direct job creation, especially in those areas that have highest long term unemployment. They fear that in these areas the New Deal will look very much like the failed programmes of the past and because there is a low employer base it could simply waste resources and merely churn 'people into and out of temporary projects and work placements, with no lasting reduction in unemployment' (Turock and Webster, 1998, p. 325; Peck, 1998). While this is a legitimate concern, it is somewhat exaggerated, and underestimates the potential links that can be made between the jobless and the existing concentrations of jobs. However, those links still have to be made and at the same time the New Deals will be more effective if local partnerships can ensure that the programmes are practically, rather than just rhetorically, linked to the job opportunities created through regeneration and local economic development strategies.

Finally, there have been criticisms of the potential incoherence that the various partnerships and zones are creating. In some areas, they join an already crowded local policy agenda with diverse and overlapping initiatives. However, it is too early to assess the 'added value' that the different partnership arrangements will bring to the delivery of the New Deal, or the extent to which they compliment rather than confuse existing partnership structures.

Welfare reform in the Netherlands

The welfare state in the Netherlands is undergoing radical reform. The Dutch have explicitly tried to create an alternative to what they describe as the 'Rhineland' and 'Anglo-Saxon' models. According to the most important advisory body, the Scientific Council for Government Policy (WRR), the former system is too bureaucratic, over regulated, and 'creates too much dependence'. Whereas the 'excessively low benefits' of the latter approach lead 'to risk-avoidance, immobility and poor allocation in the labour market' (WRR, 1998, para 4.2.1). The challenge has been not to recreate a dependency inducing 'social insurance entitlements policy' but to link social security, labour market programmes and education in a way that combines an individualised supply-side integration policy with a demand-side policy that increases the employability of those out of the labour market (ibid., par. 4.1). Increasing labour market participation is seen as essential to remaking an effective and affordable welfare state.

In the Netherlands the receipt of benefits for all people of working age is now subject to more scrutiny and verification and is conditional on more rigorous assessments of job search activity and capacity to work. This is linked with a range of measures aimed at improving the employability and job prospects of those out of work for long periods. In particular, significant changes are taking place in the tax, social security and benefit system, to improve work incentives and provide employers with incentives to take on the longer-term unemployed. In contrast with the USA and UK, the strategy also involves direct job creation in the public sector for the long term unemployed.

There have also been major changes in the organisation of the welfare system and the traditional relationship between central government and the social partners has been reshaped, and at local level resources have been transferred to the municipalities who have been given new responsibilities to reintegrate those receiving social assistance. The overall objective is to reduce the disproportionately high numbers of economically inactive working age people, especially amongst the long term unemployed and those receiving disability benefits. Locally, the government now requires much closer inter-agency collaboration and the aim is to build a new 'one counter' social assistance and benefit system. Recently this process has been paralleled by an emphasis on area based regeneration targeted at localities with high levels of unemployment.

Institutional arrangements: the PES, the social partners, municipalities and the private sector

In the Netherlands the key central government agency is the Ministry of Social Affairs and Employment (SZW), which is responsible for the vast majority of labour market policies. However, much of the benefit system and the actual delivery of programmes is organised through a complex network of tripartite bodies, regional and local governments and the social partners.

Historically, the social partners have administered and controlled a large part of the Dutch welfare system and, until recently, this was organised through 18 Industrial Insurance Boards (known as BVs). The 'employees insurance' schemes cover most people in employment, are strongly rights based and are funded through contributions paid by employers and employees. Until 1995, a federation of the BVs co-ordinated their activities on a voluntary basis, but they are now subject to more direct regulation. This is intended to create more coherence and co-ordination in the system and to restrict the ability of the 'social partners' to use unemployment and disability benefits to finance downsizing and early retirement. The BVs are now being abolished in their existing form to be replaced by employment based sector councils, with representation from the social partners, who have to negotiate their role and budget with a new co-ordinating institution, the National Institute for Social Insurance (LISV) (EO, 1997, p. 52).

The most significant tripartite body is the PES, which is run by a Central Employment Board (CBA). This is now formally independent from government, but subject to legal and financial controls. Although the CBA is responsible for general policy there are 18 tripartite Regional Boards (RBAs), which have a high degree of autonomy as long as they remain within central guidelines (de Konig, et al, 1997, p. 61). Each region has a network of local offices, which provide traditional labour exchange services, assess job seeking and availability for work rules, and are a key point of access to measures such as vocational training.

Alongside the insurance based welfare system there is the 'safety net' social assistance scheme, largely financed by central government but administered by municipalities. The local municipalities, of which there are over 600 in the Netherlands, deliver these benefits through their social services departments (GSD), and they also receive additional resources to fund job creation programmes and purchase services for the hard to place unemployed. Historically, central government has financed most of the costs of local social assistance payments, but this open-ended commitment has now been changed. From 1999, there will be a 'fixed budget for these payments based on historical expenditure figures'. Within this tighter budget local authorities are being given more discretion, but there are concerns about the capacity of the municipalities to continue to maintain the 'safety net' and manage the new services and active measures they are expected to deliver (Bolderson et al, 1997, p. 177/8).

As in the UK and the USA, a key part of the Dutch reform process has been to withdraw the public sector from the direct delivery of services, and to open up activities to competition from the private sector. One notable innovation was the creation of a tripartite organisation called START, which was once part of the PES, and now operates as an independent temporary employment agency which also places the long term unemployed. It now employs 3,500 people, places about 60,000 temporary workers a day, and is operating in Germany, the Czech Republic, Italy and Spain (InforMISEP, No. 62, p. 15).

Although the Dutch government has initially protected the role of the PES, in the delivery of services for the long term unemployed, it is anticipated that this market will be opened up to the private and non-profit sector and that over time the PES may itself evolve in the same way as START (de Konig et al, 1997, p. 142). Indeed, the WRR foresees a 'gradual interpenetration of the private and public employment agencies' which will in future allow certified private agencies to compete for and deliver a whole range of integration services (1998, par 4.2.2).

Welfare reform, disability benefits and work requirements

The Netherlands has been actively engaged in reforming its insurance and social assistance systems since the late 1980s. Benefit eligibility rules have been tightened and benefit levels (although still comparatively generous) have been reduced relative to wages. At the same time, a variety of labour market programmes have been introduced alongside the gradual creation of a more 'active' system.

The Dutch system of disability benefits has been a particular focus of reform. It has been described as the 'weak spot of the Dutch welfare system' and by 1993 nearly a million people were receiving disability payments, nearly one adult person in seven (OECD, 1998b, p. 82). The response was to begin to reduce the control of the social partners and to introduce extra inducements to employers to retain or hire the disabled. This was linked with a more stringent definition of disability coupled with a broader definition of the 'suitable' employment a person could be expected to undertake. The revised tests were applied to all new claimants, and those already receiving benefits are being reassessed. The impact was initially significant and the number receiving disability benefits fell to 850,000 in mid-1996, a fall of over 8%.

Another major change in the Dutch system has been in the approach to lone parents, who are now expected to actively look for work once their youngest child reaches the age of five (previously it was twelve). This reflects an important change in social attitudes, partly linked to the overall increase in part time work and in women's participation in the labour market. Lone parents are likely to receive their assistance payments through the municipalities, so local integration strategies now have to address their needs around childcare, flexible working hours, and so on.

The National Assistance Act was revised in 1996 and the different categories of social assistance recipients have now been replaced by an overall assumption that all those who need assistance who can work should seek to secure an income by participating in the labour market. Welfare benefits should only be provided for those who are unable to get jobs and benefit levels should be set at rates that are sufficient but which preserve incentives to work (OECD, 1998b, p. 80).

The legislation requires municipalities to focus on assisting eligible people by improving their employability and their access to the labour market. They are required to develop individual 'route plans' and work with the PES to implement them. This change in approach has been underpinned by a reform of labour market programmes and experimentation with new flexibilities in the tax and benefit system.

Labour market programmes, job creation and the activation of social benefits

The new strategy builds on the more individualised approach to the young and long term unemployed that emerged in the late 1980s and 1990s. This combined a process of action plans and reorientation or 'route placement' interviews, with various levels of programme support for both groups.

Traditionally, most of the direct assistance available - from help with information and advice, through to job search, training, and employment subsidies - was organised directly through the PES. For those still unable to get regular employment the municipalities were required to create jobs either for young people who were covered by a 'job guarantee', or for those out of work for over three years. As a last resort, they operated 'labour pools' which carried out a range of tasks, in the public and private sectors, and for the older long term unemployed the jobs were permanent. However, few participants made a transition to regular work and, because of cash limits, there were waiting lists for any labour pool jobs that did become available.

The emphasis has now changed. Municipalities are now responsible for reintegrating the unemployed. Resources have been transferred from the PES enabling the municipalities to tailor and purchase the services which they think are necessary. The approach to subsidised employment has also been changed by the 1997 Job Seekers Integration Act (WIW). In effect there is now a single 'Workfund' (amounting to about NLG 1.7 billion a year) which has replaced the separate funding for labour pools and the youth work guarantee. With this general fund, municipalities are expected to activate and offer 'tailor-made' training and/or work experience to the young and long term unemployed aimed at getting regular jobs. Young people are still covered by the existing 'comprehensive approach' and if they are not able to gain regular work within a year, the local authority will offer a subsidised job. There is no comprehensive guarantee for the older unemployed but the municipality will be able to offer some a permanent contract when it is clear there is no direct prospect of securing regular work (inforMISEP, No. 61, Spring 1998, p. 18-19).

The aim of WIW is to create a more coherent and flexible individual approach where the local authority will be able to provide the client with the most appropriate mix of support. This could cover 'social activation' (voluntary work), offering training and financial incentives, childcare support, and two different forms of subsidised employment which are the major WIW tools. This can involve either 'job experience places', aimed at getting the participant into work with a regular employer with the use of a wage subsidy, or 'employment contracts', which are similar to the jobs that were on offer in the earlier labour pools and youth guarantee. The main difference is that an employment contract can be combined with training and financial incentives to get early entry into regular work, or it can link into a longer term progression, for instance 'consisting of training, followed by an employment contract and finally a job experience placing and outflow into a regular job' (ibid., p. 19). The number of possible employment contracts under the WIW has been estimated at about 52,000 in 1998, rising to some 56,000 in 2001.

This reorganisation of labour market programmes is integrated with and consolidates the major drive to improve the employability of and opportunities for the long term unemployed that were initiated in 1995 and 1996. The so called 'Melkert' jobs, which were named after the then Dutch Minister of SZW, created three types of employment related opportunities.

One 'Melkert' strand involves the creation of 40,000 permanent jobs in the public sector by 1999. These can only be filled by people who have been unemployed for over a year and are aimed at increasing public safety, improving care for the disabled and elderly, environmental management, and services for groups such as the homeless or youth at risk. The jobs are concentrated in the areas of highest unemployment, especially the four largest cities. Little is known about the jobs created, but it seems that there have been difficulties in matching the target group with the demands of the jobs (de Konig et al, 1997, p. 121) Nevertheless, nearly 70% of those so far employed were previously receiving social assistance, and over one in five have been taken by workers from the labour pools.

The second 'Melkert' strand utilises the flexibilities created under the National Assistance Act where it became possible to transfer social assistance benefits directly into a fixed amount of employment subsidy, for a maximum of two years. The aim is to place 20,000 people who have been unemployed for over a year in the private sector through this 'benefit transfer'. A broad range of public and private organisations were invited to submit bids and initiatives, and a wide variety of projects have been approved. Some have permanent job guarantees, others, such as in Rotterdam, use the idea of the 'pool system'. All participants are employed by the 'pool' and employers hire them for a fee, with the element of subsidy decreasing over a two-year period, leading it is hoped to a permanent position. This initiative operates alongside other policies aimed at stimulating employment for the low skilled. These include a recent change in regulations aimed at broadening the market for domestic services, and the government has also introduced permanent tax relief for firms hiring low wage workers and temporary tax reductions for hiring the long term unemployed (OECD, 1998b, p. 69).

The final 'Melkert' strand involves the activation of social assistance itself. Municipalities have been allowed to experiment with schemes to provide socially useful and employment related activities for benefit recipients. Participants do not automatically receive additional payments and can have their assistance reduced or suspended if they refuse to take up a place. Over 160 experimental projects have been introduced in 25 cities, and until now, participants have received incentives and sanctions have not been deployed. Municipalities have either directly organised placements, worked with existing welfare and voluntary organisations or created partnerships. The aim of the experiments, which run until 2000, is to both help prepare people to return to work and/or to prevent social exclusion or isolation (inforMISEP, no. 60, Winter 1997, p. 23).

Collaboration, the 'one counter' service and area based regeneration

One of the key elements of Dutch welfare reform has been co-ordinating the complex range of agencies and institutions that work with the unemployed. The patterns of co-operation and partnership which central government has been fostering are now being consolidated through the 'Jobs and Income Collaboration Project' (SWI), which requires the PES to cooperage and enter agreements with the municipalities and insurance organisations. The aim is that all local or regional services responsible for the administration of benefits and for employment services should create a 'one counter system', creating a national network of SWI centres by the year 2000. This should lead to integrated 'intake and diagnosis, information exchange and client monitoring', enhance the enforcement of job search and availability rules and, it is anticipated, create greater competition in the provision of placement services (EO, 1997, p. 52).

Across the Netherlands, 'co-operation associations' have been established to build the new system. In Limburg, for example, a major conference was organised in April 1996 in order to define a plan of action to encourage the necessary collaboration. The responsibility for implementation has been devolved to five sub-regions, each of which has its own consultative structure. These are generally composed of a strategic steering group, with representation from the relevant agencies, with individual operational project groups.

Another example of partnership working was established in the Dutch region of Flevoland, an area of high unemployment. The *'Regionale Transfer Organisatie'* was created in 1995 through an agreement between the regional employment service, the social partners and the six local municipalities. It runs until 2000 and aims to facilitate the move from unemployment benefits into work through finding new jobs, developing new methods of work organisation, such as job sharing, and fully using the new employment programmes and benefit flexibilities created under recent legislation. It has been suggested that the direct involvement of the social partners reduces the risks associated with displacement and substitution.

The devolution of control to municipalities has enabled them to begin to integrate employment programmes with other regeneration initiatives, especially in the larger cities where issues of social exclusion, criminality, public safety and unemployment, have increased in significance. Particular concern has been expressed about the emergence of areas, in parts of the big cities, 'where being unemployed is the rule rather than the exception' with people 'reluctant to change their way of life for a paid job' (de Konig et al, 1997, p. 53).

Urban policy has gone through various phases in the Netherlands, but the most recent is described as the 'Major Cities Policy' (Parkinson, 1998). Although little new money was attached to the programme the aim is to give more local flexibility and control and, through partnership and performance targets, ensure that regeneration activity brings social as well as physical benefits. The policy is based on four key principles (Parkinson, 1998, p. 26):

- fragmentation should be reduced and deregulation and decentralisation promoted;

- the leadership capacity of local authorities should be increased to allow them to integrate the decentralised policy sectors;

- national government funds should be redeployed to increase local authorities' room for financial manoeuvre (as in the 'Workfund' reforms described above); and

- central government and the cities should forge a new alliance to form common ends and agree reciprocal obligations.

The government invited each major city to draw up integrated plans, specifying their approach to their urban problems, with a particular focus on three themes – employment and education; safety and quality of life. The Government agreed contracts with 26 cities which specify agreed targets on job creation, the reduction of unemployment, and so on, leaving the municipalities substantial freedom in how it will deliver them. In addition in each of the cities 'opportunity zones' have been created in particularly disadvantaged areas, with more relaxed administrative rules and some fiscal incentives, aimed at encouraging employment growth and complementing the broader area strategy (Parkinson, 1998, p. 27).

In a city like Rotterdam, which was in the forefront of the new urban policy, the authorities have moved beyond simple consultation and created 'public-private partnerships in which residents and firms participate from the beginning in the creation and implementation' of projects. In each of the five areas targeted for assistance, project groups have been created, involving politicians, civil servants, residents, the private sector, voluntary organisations and property owners. Unfortunately, there is little evaluation material at this stage, though it seems there have been problems in generating private sector involvement (ibid., p. 27).

The impact of welfare reform

In the Netherlands recent economic success and reductions in unemployment are not seen as a reason to slow reform, but as a 'breathing space' within which to further shift the emphasis of the social security system from one of 'sharing to earning' (WRR, 1998). Long term trends and an ageing population mean that the 'social security system cannot be sustained in its present form' and there will have to be an even stronger emphasis on promoting labour market participation with social security acting as a lubricant in a more mobile, differentiated and volatile labour market.

Apart from the formidable organisational problems that confront reform the Netherlands, like other countries, also faces a major labour market challenge, especially in generating enough job opportunities of the right type for the individuals who are now being expected to take up employment. For example, in 1995 an official survey found that of the 27,500 people who had their entitlement to disability benefits reduced or withdrawn during 1994, over a third (10,000) were receiving another social security benefit, usually unemployment assistance; another third were not working more but were receiving no other benefit; and less than a fifth (some 6,000 people) were working more (OECD, 1998b, p. 86). By the end of 1996 the numbers receiving disability benefit had again started to increase and it looked as if the decline in recipients may have been a 'one-off' factor, related to the early phase of the reassessment process which had been targeted at those aged under fifty.

Also while the Dutch have directly stimulated employment activities and created jobs for the long term unemployed, there is a danger that a new secondary labour market could be emerging with only tenuous links to more regular jobs. This is perhaps the greatest challenge to be faced by the new case management and 'one counter' system.

Conclusion

The countries reviewed in this paper are currently engaged in major organisational and programme reforms aimed at activating previously passive benefit systems. In response to major changes in labour markets, in social attitudes and in the structure of families, there is now a common assumption that people of working age who receive benefits should take jobs if they are able to do so. Increasing participation in the labour market is seen as an essential way of tackling welfare dependency and social exclusion, and reducing costs and caseloads.

However, there are major differences in emphasis and approach. In the USA, social assistance entitlement has been replaced by time limits and welfare-to-work programmes. In the UK and the Netherlands, a social assistance safety net has been maintained, but people receiving benefits have new rights and responsibilities. In the UK the unemployed now have to participate in New Deal employment and training programmes or lose benefits, but lone parents and people on disability benefits can choose to participate in active measures. In the Netherlands, which retains a strong work based insurance system, all those who have to claim social assistance are expected, and should be assisted, to get jobs.

In this process, the era of large scale, uniform and relatively inflexible national benefit systems and employment and training programmes, seems to be ending. Each country is creating a new balance between national and local delivery and welfare agencies and employment service bureaucracies are being radically reorganised and reshaped. New forms of co-operation and competition are being created to help both develop integrated 'one counter' or 'single gateway' front line services, and at the same time release and harness the contributions that can be made by non-profit and private organisations and by local initiatives.

Evaluations of national and local programmes

OECD governments have now experimented with a vast array of active labour market programmes, ranging from direct public sector job creation, through to stricter job search requirements, to assistance with job search, and the costs of taking up work, through to work experience programmes, employment subsidies, help with starting small businesses and training and education schemes. However, the evaluation evidence on their impact sheds little light on the extent of the contribution they make to reducing overall unemployment and stimulating employment growth. It also tells us little about which types of programmes are likely to work most effectively, with what client groups and in what circumstances.

Although specialist labour market economists have produced complex statistical and macro economic evaluations about the links between unemployment duration, benefit levels and various active or passive regimes, the results and their interpretation have often been heavily qualified and contentious. At the same time more focused micro economic evaluation evidence on European programmes is weak. Even more technically rigorous evaluations of training and job placement programmes in Britain, for example, have generated positive but tentative findings of small net impacts, usually reporting on programmes that by the time of publication have changed dramatically (Robinson, 1996, pp 71-77; Gardiner, 1997). In the US, which has produced by far the most focused evaluations, the actual interpretation of the results has been controversial and contested (Greenberg, 1998).

Nevertheless, according to the Director of the Manpower Demonstration Research Corporation (MDRC), which developed high quality control group studies through the use of random assignment techniques, the evaluation evidence that has been accumulated from the experimental programmes that have operated in the USA for over ten years, point to four broad conclusions (Gueron, 1997, p. 84):

- the results were positive, with many studies showing that programmes that required people to participate in welfare-to-work activities increased employment, reduced dependency on public assistance and ultimately saved taxpayers money;

- there were clear limitations to what could be achieved. Though some experiments produced substantial changes the gains were typically more modest, with many people remaining on welfare and many of those who increased their earnings being no better off because of corresponding reductions in their benefit payments;

- different approaches produced different results, with widely varying results from approaches that used job search assistance, job clubs, basic education and training, and so on; and

- management and resources matter, and the quality of implementation was vital.

164

By contrast, in a review of mainly European evidence, Calmfors concludes that 'despite an impressive amount of research' we 'know very little' (1994, p. 17). The variations in results, often between evaluations of the same programme, make it virtually impossible to generalise. However, he was able to point to a 'broad consensus between most studies' that intensified counselling and job search assistance do raise re-employment probabilities … especially for the long term unemployed' (p. 17). However, much of the gain involved substitution, where the jobs were gained at the expense of other job seekers. He also made the point that all types of active labour market programmes were 'subject to decreasing marginal returns' (p. 18). The larger the programmes the more they 'stretch institutional capacity' and 'lose focus'. Subsequently, the European Commission has pointed out that the 'systematic evaluation' of labour market programmes 'is still in its infancy', and that the existing literature 'tends to be highly heterogeneous and disparate in scope and method' (DGV, 1996, p. 127).

By contrast with the equivocal or limited findings of many national programme evaluations there are many evaluations of local projects that highlight the impact of innovative programmes with often comparatively impressive outcomes. The local experimentation that was used in the USA was technically sophisticated, and had widespread impacts. By contrast, the technical rigor of many of the European local evaluations is more limited, with many simply relying on provider records of job entry and progression rates. Whatever the technical rigor the evidence subsequently shows that it is very difficult to simply replicate these successes elsewhere, or to maintain the gains in larger versions of the programme (Peck, 1998). However, while diagnosing and then reproducing the success of these innovative local responses has proved difficult, pioneering private and non-profit organisations (like the Wise Group) have shown it is possible, and the US government and the European Commission have sponsored increasingly sophisticated ways of making this, and other, best practice, more widely available.

The accumulation of this highly disparate evidence seems to indicate that the best results from welfare-to-work strategies can be secured if policy makers maintain a flexible mix of programmes which can be adjusted to suit local and regional circumstances, particular client groups and the various stages of the economic cycle. It seems that the art of delivering an effective strategy, of creating new bridges between welfare and work, is to build in flexibility, to avoid excessive swings in policy, and to make the necessary long term investment in building the capacity and credibility of those organisations who work directly with the unemployed. In this context local partnerships and inter-agency collaboration seem to offer the best way of delivering the types of flexible provision that will be necessary over the longer term.

The role and management of local inter-agency collaboration and of partnerships

In the USA, the UK and the Netherlands there is a common recognition that there are no simple national, bureaucratic or market based welfare-to-work solutions and that better local co-ordination and integration of services and agencies is required. This is because policy-makers recognise that the diversity of local areas - in the structure and development of their labour markets and their patterns of employment, in their welfare populations, and in their institutions and the ways they do or do not work together – play a significant role in the delivery of effective programmes. In this sense local flexibility is 'not so much a political choice as a practical necessity' (Peck, 1998, p. 9).

In each country inter-agency and partnership arrangements are being put in place to deliver the new welfare services and programmes in ways that enable them to respond to the particular problems posed by local diversity. Increasingly funding mechanisms are being used to promote and require these new forms of collaboration. However, there are significant variations in how much programme and budgetary flexibility to give in these arrangements, and about how to set, monitor and assess performance targets. For example, the simple local application of rigid national performance targets can easily distort priorities and lead either to 'creaming', the selection of the more easier to place, or result in people being referred to programmes which do little to improve their situation.

Although the development of more accurate measures of performance is a complex and demanding management task, especially in decentralised systems, it is crucial that there is not only local variation but that local agencies and partnerships have more input into developing the measures against which they will be judged. If local organisations are to improve the service they deliver, they need to have more confidence that the performance targets they work to are useful and relevant. In 'Reinventing Government' Osborne and Gaebler expressed the point bluntly: 'saddling people with inappropriate measures in whose development they have had no input is a sure way to create resistance, destroy morale and encourage cheating' (1993, p. 358).

In the USA, individual states now have enormous discretion in how they construct their work based welfare and workforce development systems. Some have integrated both systems and created legal partnership entities that have their own budgets and are able to set strategies and performance standards and award contracts. Some have established state-wide arrangements; others have devolved powers to lower levels of government.

In the UK, New Deal partnerships have been established to bring the key local players together to develop strategic plans and create more locally coherent services. These partnerships have been given much flexibility to determine their own constitution and while most simply act as forums which facilitate co-ordination and co-operation, others are formally constituted with the power to set a strategic framework and award contracts. In the Netherlands, with a stronger tradition and system of social partnership and municipal government, agencies are being required to collaborate and co-ordinate, rather than constitute formal partnerships.

Across all three countries links are being established between welfare-to-work agencies and the more formally constituted area based partnerships that have been established to tackle the complex problems faced by inner-city neighbourhoods and peripheral estates, and by the towns and rural communities that are still dependent on declining industries, such as agriculture or mining. However, in contrast with these smaller area based partnerships, there has been less emphasis in welfare-to-work on securing direct representation from the communities most affected. Nevertheless, non-profit and advocacy organisations are often directly involved in welfare-to-work strategies, as providers and as partners. Equally, the development of the local strategic plans that are usually required normally involve at least some element of public consultation, feedback and accountability.

The welfare-to-work partnerships and inter-agency networks emerging in the USA, the UK and the Netherlands, are very different, in their legal status, their formal powers, their modes of operation, and in the programmes they operate. However, they share certain common objectives. They are intended to overcome the fragmentation and incoherence between different agencies and programmes. They provide a forum that can allow groups to combine their resources to develop complementary projects that provide multi-dimensional responses to complex individual and collective problems. They can allow a more extensive and accessible range of services to be provided through the creation of 'one-stop shops' and integrated back to work strategies.

Potentially, the establishment of common goals and the interaction between the key local players also improves the effectiveness of programmes by, for example, providing better matching between training for the unemployed and the needs of local employers. The collective scrutiny of partnerships can also allow them to minimise waste, duplication, and dead-weight and substitution. These positive attributes not only improve effectiveness; they can also help build legitimacy and popular support in the often highly controversial debates about welfare reform.

However, although it is clear that partnership arrangements, local flexibility and collaboration offer great potential, they can also have drawbacks. They require the development of new, often sophisticated skills from the agencies involved. If they are not focused and well-managed inter-agency partnerships can become 'talking shops' that waste time and resources. They may create yet another tier of unwanted bureaucracy or, as is a danger in the UK, lead to 'partnership fatigue', where conflicting and confusing local demands are created through a plethora of initiatives with different Departmental sponsors, budgets, priorities, timetables and spatial remits.

Partnership working could also divert some agencies from their core objectives, and others may see the arrangement as an opportunity to shift their costs and most complex problems onto other providers. While some areas are able to draw on a strong and diverse network of local agencies and projects, and/or a local tradition of collaboration, others may have few of these resources. Care must also be taken to ensure transparency and accountability so that in the context of performance and outcome driven funding regimes 'double counting' of job entries and other outcomes is minimised. Equally, while a collaborative approach may appear to reduce the direct costs for an agency to get someone into a job, collectively the costs may be greater.

Overall, across the countries examined, there was actually little external or systematic evaluation of the new institutional arrangements or partnership approaches that were being created, or of the value-added impact they have had. The assumptions about the gains of partnership working may seem evident, but they have rarely been tested (DGV, 1997, p. 46). Although reform is at an early stage it is essential that government's sponsor the development of evaluation methodologies which adequately test many of the new arrangements and assumptions, and do not have to rely on locally driven reports or simple outcome data. The future results of higher quality evaluations will be vital in establishing an evidential base that identifies best local practice and informs future policy developments.

The challenges ahead for welfare-to-work

Although evaluation evidence may not yet be available it does seem that local partnership and inter-agency approaches may be best placed to tackle some of the formidable problems that are beginning to emerge as individual countries implement their welfare-to-work strategies. These challenges include:

Support services: As welfare agencies and employment services attempt to assist the groups at most distance from the labour market, they are encountering barriers and revealing weaknesses in other services which, unless tackled, limit the potential for individuals to both take and retain jobs. For example, case managers and advisers often find that necessary and appropriate services do not exist. Public transportation systems frequently cannot get people from their homes to the places where there are jobs. Childcare may not be available, or may not be available during non-traditional hours or when children are sick. Few substance abuse or rehabilitation programmes have a strong employment focus. Work based learning opportunities for low wage entry-level workers are limited. In the USA, UK and the Netherlands, links with transportation, housing, economic development, and other systems are only starting to emerge.

Job retention, follow through and progression: The countries examined have enjoyed strong employment growth, but one result is that casual and temporary jobs make up a large proportion of the entry level jobs available to those making a transition from benefits. In combination with the domestic and personal circumstances of many of those who are long term unemployed this means that job turnover is high.

Job retention is a particular problem in the USA where strict time limits to entitlement mean that attention is turning to the 'job-keeping' challenge, and a range of local initiatives and projects, in the private, public and community sectors, are devising and testing new strategies that enable people not only to find but to keep jobs (Hershey and Pavetti, 1997). In the UK, there is much concern about 'churning', where New Deal participants experience participation as a 'revolving door' with a return to unemployment, and local partnerships are facing the challenge of building 'follow through' strategies for those affected. The Netherlands also faces these problems which ironically are exacerbated by the risk aversion of employers who are reluctant to extend the employment security enjoyed by regular workers. In all three countries, there is also concern about progression, where skill training and follow up support can assist those who do take entry level jobs to be able to make progress to higher paid and more secure employment.

Job creation: The main objective of welfare-to-work strategies is to integrate people into the regular labour market. However, as the welfare systems in each of the countries requires those receiving support to look for and accept work, considerable attention is now being given to how to create appropriate job opportunities in those areas where the local labour market does not have the capacity to absorb them.

In the USA some cities and states have introduced highly controversial 'workfare' employment programmes, where participants are used as cheap labour and forced to work in community service jobs for their benefits, with few employment rights (Baldwin, 1998). By contrast, in some areas the use of public resources to fund jobs addressing community needs is pointing the way to delivering worthwhile opportunities when no other jobs are available. As in the very different projects promoted by the European Commission, innovative community based organisations in the USA are in the forefront of these developments. According to one analysis it is these groups 'who are able to identify pressing needs in the neighbourhoods or areas in which they work' and who have the capacity 'to develop creative, highly visible projects that address these needs while tailoring individual job assignments to participants' skill levels, interests and needs'. They can also act as 'the crucial links to diverse segments of the community, raising awareness and fostering communication in ways that engender broader community support' (Johnson, 1997, p. 6).

In the UK much of the emphasis has been placed on employability rather than job creation drawing on the potential of the social economy and of ILM projects to generate worthwhile, albeit temporary employment opportunities. As in the USA it is now being stressed that in urban regeneration projects not only should local people get access to employment and training programmes but they should be given access to some of the jobs being directly created through physical renewal.

The Netherlands is also encouraging the emergence of jobs in the social economy and in ILM type projects, but it is also using voluntary work and is directly creating permanent jobs in the public sector. Although the emphasis is now on integrated support leading to a progression into regular work, the municipalities are also expected to find jobs for at least some of those who face the most difficulty. The Dutch have also decided, in a way that does not seem politically feasible in the USA, to create regular jobs for at least some long term unemployed people with low skills who are now being employed by municipalities to deliver new and improved public services. It will be interesting to see whether devolved Assemblies and the Scottish Parliament choose to add this element to an overall UK approach where central government has so far avoided any commitment to direct job creation.

References

Baldwin M. (1998)
    Welfare and Jobs: Rebuilding the Labor Market from the Bottom Down, *Working USA*, January/February, AFL/CIO, pp. 57-62.

Barbier J. and Theret B. (1998)
Welfare to Work or Work to Welfare: The French Case, in Gilbert N. (ed.), *Comparative Study of Evaluations on Welfare-to-Work Policies in Social Assistance*, forthcoming 1999.

Bewick T. and Simmonds D. (1997)
Employability in the Local Economy, in *Local Work*, No. 1, Centre for Local and Economic Strategies, Manchester.

Blair T. (1998)
The Third Way: New Politics for the New Century, Fabian Society, Pamphlet No. 588, London

Bloom D. (1997)
After AFDC: Welfare-to-Work Choices and Challenges for States, Manpower Demonstration Research Corporation, New York.

Bolderson H., Mabbett D., Hudson J., Rowe M. and Spicker P. (1997)
Delivering Social Security: A Cross-National Study, Department of Social Security, Research Report No. 59, HMSO, London.

Brown A., Buck M. and Skinner E. (1998)
Business Partnerships: How to Involve Employers in Welfare Reform, MDRC, New York.

Calmfors L. (1994)
Active Labour Market Policy and Unemployment: A Framework for the Analysis of Crucial Design Features, *Labour Market and Social Policy Occasional Paper*, No. 15, OECD, Paris.

Campbell M. (1994)
Strategic Approach to the Local Labour Market in Campbell M. and Duffy K., *Local Labour Markets: Problems and Policies*, Longman.

de Konig (1997)
'Netherlands: Labour Market Studies', a report by the Netherlands Economic Institute, Department of Labour and Education, DGV, European Commission, Brussels.

DfEE (1997)
Learning and Working Together for the Future, Department for Education and Employment, London.

DGV (1996)
'Employment in Europe', Directorate General V, European Commission, Brussels.

DGV (1997)
'Commission Draft for the Joint Employment Report', Directorate General V, European Commission, Brussels.

DHSS and DOE (1997)
National Evaluation of Welfare-to-Work Strategies, Executive Summary, US Department of Health and Human Services and US Department of Education, MDRC, Washington.

EAP (1998)
United Kingdom Employment Action Plan, HMSO.

EC (1995)
'Local Development and Employment Initiatives: An Investigation in the European Union', Internal Document, DGV, European Commission, Brussels.

EC (1997)
First Report on Local Development and Employment Initiatives: Lessons for Territorial and Local Employment Pacts, DGV, European Commission, Brussels.

EO (1997)
'Activation of Labour Market Policy in the European Union', *Trends* No. 8, SYSDEM, European Employment Observatory, Employment Commission DGV, Institute for Applied Socio-Economics, Berlin.

ERGO (1992)
ERGO Programme Phase One Final Report, DGV, European Commission, Brussels.

ESC (1997)
The New Deal, Second Report, Education and Employment Select Committee, House of Commons, Volume 1, HMSO.

ES (1997)
New Deal Procurement and Contracting Guide, Employment Service, London.

Finn D. (1996)
>
> *Making Benefits Work: Employment Programmes and Job Creation Measures*, Centre for Local and Economic Strategies, Manchester.

Gardiner K. (1997)
>
> *Bridges from Benefit to Work: a Review*, Joseph Rowntree Foundation, York.

Geddes M. (1998)
>
> *Partnership against Poverty and Exclusion? Local Regeneration Strategies and Excluded Communities in the UK*, Policy Press, Bristol

Greenberg M. (1998)
>
> 'US Welfare Reform', unpublished paper given at the Policy Studies Institute, 20 January, London.

Gueron J. M. (1997)
>
> 'Learning about Welfare Reform: Lessons from State Based Evaluations', *New Directions for Evaluation*, No 76, Winter 1997, Jossey Bass Publishers.

Handler J. (1995)
>
> *The Poverty of Welfare Reform*, Yale University Press, New Haven.

Hershey A. and Pavetti L. (1997)
>
> 'Turning Job Finders into Job Keepers', *The Future of Children in Welfare-to-Work*, Vol. 7 No. 1, Spring.

HMSO (1998)
>
> *New Ambitions for our Country: A New Contract for Welfare*, Cm 3805, London.

InforMISEP (1997 and 1998)
>
> *Policies,* Journal of European Employment Observatory, Employment Commission DGV, various issues.

Jarvis T. (1998)
>
> 'Innovation the Key in New Employment Zones', Working Brief No. 96, Unemployment Unit, London, pp. 14-18.

Johnson C. (1997)
>
> *Toward a New Generation of Community Jobs Programmes*, Center on Budget and Policy Priorities, Washington (www.cbpp.org).

Lloyd P., et al (1998)
Local Enterprises in Enterprising Localities: Best Practice in Area Based Policy in the UK, forthcoming.

McGregor A., Ferguson, Z., McConnachie, M. and Richmond, K. (1997)
Bridging the Jobs Gap: An Evaluation of the Wise Group and the Intermediate Labour Market, Joseph Rowntree Foundation, York.

MDRC (1997)
Biannual Report, Manpower Research Demonstration Corporation, 1996/97, New York.

Mead L. (1997)
From Welfare to Work: Lessons from America, Institute for Economic Affairs, London.

NGA (1997)
'Current Trends and Emerging Issues in Welfare-to-Work', NGA Issues Brief, National Governors Association, Washington.

OECD (1998a)
Local Management for More Effective Employment Policies, OECD publication, Paris.

OECD (1998b)
Netherlands, *OECD Economic Surveys* 1997-1998, OECD publication, Paris.

Osborne D. and Gaebler T. (1993)
Reinventing Government, Plume Books, New York.

Parkinson M. (1998)
Combating Social Exclusion: Lessons from Area-Based Programmes in Europe, Policy Press, Bristol.

Peck J. (1998)
'New Labourers: Making a New Deal for the 'Workless Class', paper presented at the Annual Conference of the Royal Geographical Society/Institute of British Geographers, Guildford, 5-8 January, 1998.

PM (1997)
>Speech by the Prime Minister the Rt. Hon. Tony Blair MP at the Aylesbury Estate, Southwark, on Monday 2 June, London.

Robinson, P. (1996)
>*Labour Market Studies - United Kingdom*, Directorate-General for Employment, Industrial Relations and Social Affairs, European Commission, Brussels.

RPC (1996)
>*Renewing the Regions, Regional Policy Commission*, PAVIC Publication, Sheffield Hallam University.

Schwanse P. (1998)
>'Activating the Unemployed', *The OECD Observer*, No. 209, December 1997/January 1998, pp. 10-12, Paris.

SEU (1998)
>'Bringing Britain Together: A National Strategy for Neighbourhood Renewal', report by the Social Exclusion Unit, HMSO.

SPA (1997)
>'Creating Workforce Development Systems that Work: An Evaluation of the Initial One-Stop Implementation Experience', Final Report, Social Policy Research Associates, Washington DC.

SSC (1998)
>'Social Security Reforms: Lessons from the United States of America, Second Report', Social Security Select Committee, House of Commons, HMSO.

TEN (1998)
>*The Next Stages of New Deal*, Briefing, Training and Employment Network, London.

Turok I. and Webster D. (1998)
>'The New Deal: Jeopardised by the Geography of Unemployment?', *Local Economy*, Vol. 12, No. 4, Longmans.

Walker R. (1997)
>'Public Policy Evaluation in a Centralised State: A Case Study of Social Assistance in the United Kingdom', *Evaluation, the International Journal of Theory, Research and Practice*, Vol. 5, No. 5, Sage Publications, London.

White M., Lissenburgh S. and Bryson A. (1997)
The Impact of Public Job Placing Programmes, Policy Studies Institute.

WRR (1998)
From Sharing to Earning: Considerations for Social Security in the 21st Century, Wetenschappelijke Raad voor het Regeringsbeleid, Netherlands Scientific Council for Government Policy.

CHAPTER 7
ISSUES RAISED BY WELFARE REFORM IN THE UNITED STATES

By Robert Straits, W. J. Upjohn Institute for Employment Research, United States of America

Introduction

This chapter offers an overview on the evolution of welfare-to-work in the United States, identifies the key issues for local programme administrators and advisory boards, and concludes with some suggestions on next steps that should be considered.

The chapter provides a summary of the major United States welfare-to-work initiatives during the past thirty years and a description of the primary provisions in the current programme. It is not intended to be all-inclusive but rather suggests some of the policies and perspectives that led us to the current programme. The current programme is described in some detail to demonstrate how the regulations guide and limit local options.

The discussion of key issues is intended to be critical as well as to give credit to what appears to assist in moving some recipients off of welfare. Perhaps what is most apparent is the need for further research and study of the current approach. Hopefully what is also clear is the need for programmes that recognise the barriers welfare recipients face individually in finding and retaining jobs; as well as concern with a 'one size fits all' approach to eradicating welfare.

In some ways, welfare-to-work policy has evolved in the United States by making significant policy shifts about every ten years. It can be argued that the evolution is not completely progressive and some fundamental issues are elusive; such as, flexible case management and a political focus on the longer term.

Approaches to moving people from welfare to work

Welfare policy in the United States has been significantly influenced by political debate since the War on Poverty began in 1964 (Clague, et al, 1976). Throughout this debate, two opposing views have prevailed. One side believes that government has a responsibility to assist individuals who cannot support themselves and who are 'entitled' to assistance. The other side contends that public assistance obligates the recipient to work ('there is no free lunch') in exchange for government support.

Conservative and liberal thinkers may consider the resulting legislation of the past four decades as, at best, 'trade-offs', but more likely 'sell outs'. Moderates would consider the resulting legislation as a compromise. Alternatively, practitioners would most likely appreciate it if programmes were isolated from the political process.

In the mid-1960s with the civil rights movement mushrooming, and the welfare roles expanding, the unemployed became a focal point. Women workers, blacks, and the young all continued to experience high unemployment rates despite continuing improvements in the economy. The Johnson Administration launched the War on Poverty in an attempt to combat the problems of the nation's indigent, particularly minorities and youth. A major objective of the resulting legislation was to help the most disadvantaged achieve employability and obtain jobs that would provide them with a level of income that would make a decent lifestyle possible. The belief was that the major employment problem of the disadvantaged was rooted in their own limitations as workers. Many individuals lacked prior work experience, and often social services were needed to assist in obtaining and retaining employment. Consequently it was agreed that the federal government needed to provide a full range of services for the poor including remedial education, vocational training, work experience, and counselling.

A centralised approach to welfare

The federal government took a centralised and categorical approach in an attempt to eradicate poverty. Funding from the federal government was targeted to specific groups of individuals. Funds were made available on a formula basis to communities based on size and estimates of the numbers of individuals below the poverty line. Community and neighbourhood agencies often competed for funding by submitting proposals to regional federal offices where a review team would evaluate the proposals against a set of pre-established criteria that included ensuring a 'geographical and equitable'

178

distribution of the available funds. The Congress and President determined the total amount of funds in their annual budget.

The federal effort during these years developed into a piecemeal approach, which reflected the belief that there were divergent needs among the individual groups who were the expected beneficiaries of the myriad of policies. In addition, the political reality resulted in the spreading of functions among many different departments and agencies in the federal government. Each department involved in the distribution received directives from a different piece of legislation. The grants did not interrelate with one another and often were a duplication of effort. The need for co-ordination at the highest levels became painfully obvious as early as the late 1960s and remains a problem today, evidenced by the inability of Congress to pass legislation that does little more than recognise the need for more collaboration.

During those early years, it was not unusual to find communities where similar programmes were located within blocks of one another, but could only serve individuals with certain characteristics. For example, a neighbourhood centre providing services to assist black youth in obtaining employment and a public school providing employment services to all minority youth could easily overlap and duplicate efforts. The more ingenious clients were often able to finagle between agencies when there was an incentive to do so.

An early model for 'work-first'

The Work Incentive Programmes (WIN I and WIN II) were the early model for 'work-first'. Congress began to react more forcibly to the dilemma of work and welfare and the increasing number of people on public assistance. In 1967, that attention resulted in the creation of a new training and job placement programme. This programme required mothers who did not have children under six years of age to be registered for employment and available for training. The ultimate objective was to reduce the number of welfare recipients and the amount of federal funds being spent to support these families. The major flaw identified in the Work Incentive Programme was that it was administered from regional offices that often did not have a clue about the communities the programmes were operating in. Other issues surfaced later, such as the growing problem of single parents and high school drop-outs that the local operators considered high priorities, but these issues received little attention in the 1960s (Clague, et al, 1976).

The Job Opportunities in the Business Sector programme (JOBS) was described as a means to meet employment needs and diminish social unrest in the ghettos.

The business community was to provide entry-level jobs and receive wage subsidies and with minimum paper work in exchange for 'workers'. The lesson learned in this programme cut to the foundation of welfare programmes: training for the hard-core unemployed costs much more than for the average trainee because the task is difficult and complex. Yet every job programme for the poor was based on the premise that it was just a matter of matching the job seeker and the job.

According to studies by Mathematical Policy Research Inc. and others, even in the best of economic times job retention correlates highly with education level, training and prior experience. Low cost programmes can place participants in jobs. But, unless the participants have the foundation, they do not retain the jobs into which they are placed.

A systematic approach characterised the era as programmes were set up to address particular categories of people. For example, programmes were established that only served specific target groups, such as minorities, women or disabled individuals. There were nonetheless only a few treatments implemented, such as on-the-job training, classroom skill training, remedial education, work experience and public service employment. Consequently, the programmes were essentially the same although the characteristics of the clients may have differed, raising concerns that the job training environment did not assimilate an ideal work force.

Unemployment was considered to be caused by either labour market maladjustments or labour demand deficiencies. Cyclical and chronic unemployment were the result of labour demand being low. If labour demand was low for the short-term, or on a seasonal basis, it was believed that the best treatments were short-term public service employment, temporary wage subsidies and temporary reductions in the working week. Long term demand deficiencies called for longer term public service employment, wage subsidies and permanent restructuring of the work week, job-sharing or early retirements. Labour market deficiencies, classified as frictional or structural, also focused on the degree of the deficiency ranging from job matching, labour market information and recruiting efforts, to job training, tax credits, on-the-job training and apprenticeships.

This logical approach still has its advocates. Evidence is that these programmes were beneficial to individuals in need of a boost, but failed to address the critical problems of the long term unemployed and hard-to-employ. However, it was the inefficiency of an overlapping system administered by federal regional offices that was the death knell of the first phase of job programmes. It was also considered 'too easy' for public assistance recipients to be exempt from any training or work requirements and still receive aid.

Because cost has always been a primary consideration in the delivery of services, duplication was a concern for those who argued that the government was not doing enough and it was ripe for attack from those who believed government was doing too much. Advocates for more assistance noted that the cost of unemployment to a society has long term consequences and is not only measured in dollars. A common belief of the programme operators was that the government seeks out solutions, but has not placed the kinds of dollars into these programmes that will truly give them a chance to eradicate poverty. These advocates also concluded that our society does not recognise that there is a long term cost associated with individuals who will always, or at least for an extended period of time, be in some way a cost to the community. More pronounced was recognition at the local level that there were gross inefficiencies due to the categorical nature of programmes and the centralised control by federal government.

A comprehensive approach to welfare

The 1970s brought on a more comprehensive approach to addressing the problems of the economically disadvantaged. The bureaucratic words 'de-categorical' and 'de-centralisation' became the theme of the era (Clague, et al, 1976). Decentralisation was considered as the transition of authority to the state and local government. Authority given was defined in the legislation and regulations. It often included the responsibility for designing, implementing, and to some extent, evaluating programme activities. De-categorisation meant that federal appropriations were no longer earmarked for specific programmes. A local determination could be made after analysing the needs of the disadvantaged population.

In addition, the concept of a local advisory board was introduced to ensure that the public interest would guide local planning. The council membership and role were established in the regulations and for some areas representation was 'guaranteed,' such as education and labour. In retrospect, advisory councils evolved differently throughout the country. Some were merely 'rubber stamps' while others had a significant role that included on-site monitoring and local policy development. The worse case scenarios occurred when council members took advantage of their position on the council to direct funding to preferred organisations.

The classroom skill training provided was identified as a major weakness of these programmes, since it was not the kind of training desired by local employers. For example, training welders when there were not any job openings for welders was criticised. Historically, the type of training provided was determined by the client and was not always in occupational areas that had high demand and a career ladder in the local market. Legislation in 1982 proposed limiting choices to skills that were desired by local employers and increasing participation of private sector members on the advisory committees in order to ensure that their interests were taken into consideration. By 1982, the public service employment programmes of the 1970s were also considered inappropriate because they were expensive and because of the large number of abuses identified by the media. For example, a small-town Sheriff used subsidised workers to supplant funds normally set aside to hire custodians. In another community, a sailboat was purchased on the pretence that subsidised employees were being trained to be fishermen. These kinds of situations played into the hands of those who did not support decentralisation and did not trust that local communities would make the best use of the funds.

It was the involvement of the private sector that promised to make a major difference in the lives of the poor by providing access to jobs that existed at the local level. While there have been many employers who have hired clients from the programme, most individuals on these boards either have a personal commitment to helping the poor or their company considers it a corporate responsibility to volunteer. Seldom did we see members looking to the programme to provide them with workers.

The natural evolution of programmes seemed to call for a range of services based on individual needs. Careful assessment and a holistic, family-centred case management approach were the logical next steps, particularly if complemented by what we had learned about locally designed programmes, driven by the local labour market and supported by the local private sector. However, the economic conditions of the mid-1990s had improved to the point where full employment existed in most of the United States.

The current approach

The thirty or more years of testing ways to eradicate poverty have led to the evolution of a new approach that shifts responsibility from government to the individual, divests the federal government and places unprecedented authority with the states. It exchanges an emphasis on skill training that will lead a family out of poverty for an emphasis on job placement that will immediately reduce the cost of welfare.

On August 22, 1996, the President signed the Personal Responsibility and Work Opportunity Reconciliation Act (PRWORA) which reformed the nation's welfare laws. A new system of block grants to states named Temporary Assistance for Needy Families (TANF) was created, changing the nature and provision of welfare benefits in America. This fundamental reform commits states to design welfare systems requiring most recipients to be in work within two years of first receiving benefits. In general, the law stipulates that adults must be working in no fewer than 25 percent of the families on welfare, or else states are subject to financial penalties. This figure rises by 5 percentage points a year, to 50 percent in 2002.

Also, under the law states can get credit for reducing the number of people on welfare. The federal work requirements are reduced, or liberalised, for states that have reduced their welfare roles since the base year (1995), as almost all states have. Nation-wide, the number of people on welfare has dropped by nearly one-third since August 1996. According to the Department of Health and Human Services Report to Congress almost all states have moved to 'work-first' models in their welfare programmes, requiring welfare recipients to move quickly into available jobs. Nearly every state has instituted 'social contracts' or other personal responsibility agreements in which recipients agree to specific steps towards self-sufficiency. States are enforcing these agreements, sanctioning people who fail to sign or live up to their agreements. States include sanctions that can remove the entire family from assistance where a parent refuses to co-operate with work requirements.

As is the case of previous legislation, the Personal Responsibility and Work Opportunity Reconciliation Act was a compromised legislation. This time the mood of the country was that entitlement programmes were not working, taxes were too high, and with low unemployment many believed that anyone who really wanted to work could find a job. In addition, a certain morality slipped into the preamble of the Act, capturing the political bias on marriage, families and the interest of children.

Funds are allocated to states with governors enjoying much more discretion than they had in prior legislation. This is the devolution of the federal role. Although a more direct relationship between taxpayers and tax-supported programmes has not yet materialised, a shift to the states is expected to lead towards an eventual shift to local governments. If the taxpayers want these programmes they will have the opportunity to vote themselves a tax increase.

Thirty-seven states enacted welfare reform programmes before the federal Temporary Assistance to Needy Families programme was approved (Report to Congress, 1999). In fact, at the end of 1998 all states and the District of

Columbia had enacted welfare reform activities, although, four states (Connecticut, Idaho, Louisiana and New Mexico) had not reported out a work activities component. These reforms represent a shift from the skill development approach of previous programmes to a 'work-first' approach that makes quick job placement the top priority. This transformation to a temporary and work based system assumes that families who cannot support themselves will be able to receive cash assistance and the training and the services they need to find work, quickly.

Not unlike earlier policy-makers, many of the current legislators apparently believe that moving people from welfare to work is only a matter of getting the right match in the labour market. However, the opinion that a good match and work place experience will result in jobs that will be retained has little support from the field. Studies are just now beginning to validate that low-wage jobs with few fringe benefits and no career path, in fact have high turnover (Strawn, 1998)·

Greater co-ordination between federal programmes is also the intent of the new legislation. Unfortunately, the federal government has not taken the critical step of incorporating related programmes under a single administration with common definitions and common reporting requirements. At the sub-state levels, a reduction in funding and the anticipated problems that will result when clients begin exhausting their time limits has resulted in a new urgency for collaboration. There have been movements toward 'one-stop centres' where clients can receive a comprehensive list of services available and access to these programmes, although these efforts are threaded with 'self-help' and minimal intervention. Establishing 'one-stop centres' as the access point for employment and training services is mandated in the Workforce Investment Act (Employment Services); welfare-to-work vocational and rehabilitation services must be available at least at one physical site.

In a typical state-administered welfare-to-work programme the primary eligibility requirement is that participants are receiving Temporary Assistance To Needy families (TANF) (www.acf.dhhs.gov). The components may vary between states, or within states, but the desired outcome is clear. 'Work-first' emphasises work as the focus for all individuals receiving public assistance, except for the following exempt classifications:

- Individuals can be temporarily exempt from the work requirement for medical reasons or pregnancy.

- Individuals 7-9 months pregnant, or who have a child less than three months old are exempt from the work requirement.

- Short-term medical exemption for 30 days can also be provided if there is sufficient reason. Applicants with apparent long term disabilities can be referred to a separate system (Social Security Insurance) and be temporarily exempt from the work requirement while their application for long term assistance is being processed.

Longer term exemptions include Social Security Insurance, Social Security Disability Insurance and State Disability Insurance. Each of these programmes has a different set of eligibility criteria, but in all cases a physical or mental disability has been diagnosed.

In general, new applicants for public assistance and all current recipients are assessed to determine if any of the exempt classifications apply. If not, the individual is referred to a 'work-first' or 'job first' component *or* service provider. Once referred, the individual must participate in job seeking activities until they become employed. If employed part-time, the hours worked can count towards the work requirements. Failure to participate in job seeking activity or work can be grounds for reduction in or loss of aid.

There are some subgroups of people within the overall umbrella of public assistance that receive special attention. They include non-custodial parents, food stamp only individuals and two-parent households.

A non-custodial parent is eligible if, through the action of the court, custody of children is awarded to the custodial parent and the custodial parent is receiving public assistance. If the non-custodial parent is in arrears in their child support they may qualify for special job search assistance. In 1992, only 54 percent of single-parent families with children had a child support order established and, of that 54 percent, only about half received the full amount due. Of the cases enforced through the public child support enforcement system, only 18 percent of the caseload had a collection according to the findings in the Act.

A food stamp only client does not receive direct cash assistance, but in order to receive food stamps they must perform a minimum of 12 hours job searching in addition to 'workfare' hours. Workfare is defined as performing work in public or private non-profit agencies as a condition of eligibility to receive services. Participation is intended to improve employability skills and move individuals into regular employment.

Only nine percent of married couple families with children under 18 years of age have income below the poverty level. In contrast, 46 percent of female-headed households with children under 18 years of age are below the national poverty level. Under 'work-first', when there are two parents in a household, the weekly minimum participation rate increases from 25 hours to 35 hours for the head of the household. If they receive federal child support the second parent must participate 20 hours a week.

The administration and service delivery arrangements have been complicated by various different ways through which individuals can be eligible for assistance. States are required to match federal funding (one dollar for two) but may introduce different eligibility criteria when state funding is used. For the federal share there is a 70/30 eligibility which requires that at least 70 percent of the funding be expended on the most in need. The term 'most in need' is defined as:

- The individual is receiving TANF assistance (or a former TANF recipient who would otherwise be eligible but has reached the federal or state lifetime time limit on receipt of TANF).

- The individual must be a long term TANF recipient and will become ineligible for assistance within 12 months due to either federal or state imposed time limits on receipt of TANF assistance.

- The individual has at least two of the three following employment barriers as determined through an assessment:

  - Has not completed secondary school or obtained a certificate of general equivalency and has low skills in reading or mathematics.

  - Requires substance abuse treatment for employment.

  - Has a poor work history. At least 90 percent of individuals determined to have a poor work history must have worked no more than three consecutive months in the past 12 calendar months. The remaining 10 percent can meet a local definition of poor work history as long as there is documentation that the individual's eligibility is consistent with the barriers identified by the local community.

Once eligibility is satisfied, the regulations establish the activities that are allowable. These activities are:

- **Unsubsidised Employment** - Employment not supported by TANF funds.

- **Subsidised Private Sector Employment** - The individual is an employee of a private sector employer. The wages are supported by TANF funds.

- **Subsidised Public Sector Employment** - The individual is an employee of a public sector employer. The wages are supported by TANF funds.

- **Work Experience Programme** - An unpaid training assignment for individuals who lack previous employment experience and/or job readiness and who are therefore, difficult to place in unsubsidised employment. The goal of work experience is to improve the skills, attitudes, and general employability of these individuals.

- **On-the-Job Training** - The individual is an employee of the employer and training is conducted on the job. Reimbursement of the training cost is provided to the employer with TANF funds. The employee is expected to retain employment with the employer.

- **Job Search and Job Readiness Assistance** - Activities that help participants become familiar with general workplace expectations and learn behaviour and attitudes necessary to compete successfully in the labour market. Job search includes job clubs, counselling and job seeking skills training.

- **Community Service Programme** - Community Service Programmes are projects which serve a useful purpose for the community or the public interest in fields such as health, education, urban and rural development, welfare, recreation, public facilities, public safety, and other purposes identified by the State. The Community Service Programme must comply with the minimum wage requirements and other laws related to employment.

The following activities are allowable under welfare-to-work as Post-Employment Services only:

- **Post-Employment Training (Vocational Education)** - Post-employment training is defined as an occupational training component which may combine classroom, laboratory and other related activities, and which is directly related to a specific occupational field or specific job.

187

- **Job Skills Training** - This is a classroom activity (a non-occupational training activity) for recipients who have a specific barrier to employment opportunities. This is only for recipients who have received a high school diploma or equivalent, for example English as a second language, remedial education or basic maths.

- **Education Directly Related to Employment** - This is a classroom activity (a non- occupational training activity) for recipients who have received a high school diploma.

In order to further emphasise employment, some programmes withhold 50 percent of the cost of job placement from the providers until the individual has been placed into unsubsidised employment for at least six months.

Funds cannot be substituted for services that are available or already provided through other sources. Services such as transportation assistance, substance abuse treatment of a non-medical nature, childcare assistance, emergency or short-term housing assistance, and other supportive services can be provided for job retention and support if they are not otherwise available.

According to a study completed by the Michigan League for Human Services, many recipients with skills and job experience could move back into the labour market fairly quickly because they need minimal levels of assistance. However, other groups will require more intensive services including, but not limited to, education and training. Four out of every ten participants exit the programme in two years. They tend to have more education and work experience compared to participants that stay on long term. For example, in 1992, high school graduates headed 65 percent of families staying on welfare for less than 25 months, but only 37 percent of families receiving welfare for more than 60 months (Herr, et al, 1991)

As the United States economy continues to expand, and as more jobs require higher and more sophisticated skills, education and training will become increasingly important. Time limits do increase the sense of urgency felt by recipients and programme staff alike. Recipients are therefore more likely to move ahead in searching for and preparing for work and programme staff are less likely to leave recipients waiting for long periods for services. Also, time limits are likely to increase the degree of co-ordination between welfare and employment and training departments. However, it is being argued that time limits do nothing to remove the barriers recipients have in finding jobs.

188

The legislation requires that in measuring programme outcomes, states will, at a minimum, need to demonstrate their success in serving eligible individuals in terms of:

- – Placements in unsubsidised jobs.

- – Duration of such placements.

- – Increases in earnings.

States may qualify for a performance bonus based on a formula for measuring performance. Michigan's performance standards are:

- – Number who arrive and receive services.

- – Number placed in employment **expected** 90 days at 25/35hours a week.

- – Number **retained** 90 days at 25/35 hours a week.

- – Cost per placement.

- – TANF case closures.

- – Two-parent work participation rate.

The Act states that grants cannot be used to provide assistance to a family that includes an adult who has received assistance under any state programme funded by the federal government for 60 months (whether or not consecutive). Months considered exceptions to the 60-month clock are: any month assistance was provided during which the individual was a minor and any month the individual was not the head of household or married to the head of household.

The states may also exempt a family from the 60-month limit if the family includes an individual who has been battered or subjected to extreme cruelty. However, the exception for hardship is limited to 20 percent of the average monthly number of families to which assistance is provided. Battered, or subjected to extreme cruelty, is defined to include acts resulting in physical injury, mental abuse, sexual abuse and neglect or deprivation of medical care.

The TANF legislation envisions a lifetime limit of assistance that provides a definite end to benefits unless the recipient family meets a definition of hardship. It is anticipated that this may apply to about 20 percent of the families receiving assistance after their five-year limit expires. About six states have authorised limits of less than five years.

An underpinning of the PRWORA Act is the devolution of control and funding from the federal government to the states and in some cases to the local level. Presently most states have low unemployment rates (below 5%) and 44 states have lower welfare caseloads than they had in 1994. Even states that have not implemented the 'work-first' approach have reduced caseloads. But, the rather favourable context in which welfare reform has been launched is not likely to last forever.

A substantial portion of the welfare-to-work programme was implemented in some states as early as 1994. Michigan's welfare caseloads have dropped by 261,000 individuals between October 1, 1995 and May 31, 1998 (Seefeldt, et al, 1998). In a sub-state area like Kalamazoo-St. Joseph Counties (population of approximately 300,000), the caseload dropped 42 percent from 13,106 recipients to 7,509 recipients during the same 32- month period. In fact, in all states that adopted this 'work-first' approach during the past three years, there has been a significant reduction of people on welfare. The Michigan Jobs Commission acknowledges that a sustained healthy economy has been a positive contributor, but does not believe that the improved economy is the only explanation for the reduced welfare caseloads.

Within the parameters established by the federal legislation, states have employed a mixed strategy approach in which job search is combined with training and other services. For example, in the Portland, Oregon, programme most people participated in job search, but many also participated in short term education, vocational training, work experience and life skill training. Although Portland aims to move people into the labour market, at one-on-one meetings directly following orientation, case managers evaluated some people as not ready to go immediately into job search. Initially about half of the first activity assignments were in job search activity; the other half were enrolled in education or job training activities. Over time an increasing proportion of people have been first assigned to job search and subsequently enrolled in education or training if they do not find a job.

The Michigan 'work-first' model requires a single parent to participate in job search for 25 hours a week in order to receive welfare benefits. Up to five hours of the 25 can be applied towards attaining a high school diploma. However, training vouchers are only available for welfare recipients who are employed and wish to upgrade their skills to improve their income in order to leave the welfare roles.

The Connecticut 'work-first' programme is called 'Jobs First'. It limits temporary cash assistance to 21 months, in which time individuals must find a job and become financially independent. The major part of the job search is the client's responsibility. The client must make a good faith effort to find a job and go to work as soon as possible. A failure to meet the requirements is met with severe sanctions. The first time a requirement is violated benefits are reduced by 20% for three months. The second time a violation occurs benefits are reduced by 35% for 6 months. Three or more violations result in benefits being discontinued (www.acf.dhhs.gov/news/welfare). Training and education are at the discretion of programme administration.

The State of Wisconsin emphasises that 'Wisconsin Works' is a welfare replacement programme based on work participation. Furthermore, Wisconsin says its programme is available to all parents with minor children, low assets and low income. However, it is not an entitlement programme and each recipient is placed in one of four tiers:

- **Unsubsidised Employment** - Individuals entering are guided first to the best available immediate job opportunity. Persons in unsubsidised employment may also be eligible for earned income credits, food stamps, medical assistance, childcare and job access loan.

- **Trial Jobs (subsidised employment)** - For those individuals who are unable to locate subsidised work but have a willing attitude, subsidised employment is explored. These trial jobs are a way to help the employer cover the costs of training a person on the job who might need extra support in the first three to six months.

- **Community Service Jobs** - For those who need to practice the work habits and skills necessary to be hired by a regular employer, jobs are developed in the community. Participants receive a monthly grant for working up to 30 hours per week and 10 hours per week in education or classroom training.

- **Transition** - Transition is reserved for those who are unable to perform independent, self-sustaining work. Participants spend up to 28 hours a week in work training or other developmental activities and up to 12 hours a week in education or classroom skill training.

The theme in the State of New York is 'Temporary Assistance for Permanent Jobs' and the State of Florida has the theme 'Work and Gain Economic Self-sufficiency (WAGES)'. Each state has its own way of marketing and taking credit for lower numbers on welfare, but the designs are all basically similar with the emphasis on working first as opposed to education or skill training.

Issues and next steps for local programmes

Recognise welfare recipients are individuals

The single focus approach of 'work-first' does not allow for individual variation, which would recognise that welfare recipients are people with all the variations that exist in any group. It is estimated that half of the families on welfare prior to 'work-first' would have benefited from an improved economy and greater access to jobs. The other half are challenged by a range of barriers as unique as the individuals themselves. There has never been adequate funding to fully assess and work with each individual applying for public aid and consequently expedient solutions continue to be sought. It would be more appropriate to provide a range of services and training to address the various needs identified during an initial assessment than a narrowly focused programme. Welfare recipients vary widely in their job readiness skills, ranging from those who are ready to work to those who face significant barriers to employment. A challenge is to target services to those who need it the most (Palmer, 1998). Yet, most programmes provide the same services to all participants, regardless of their past work history or skills.

Next Step: Develop and continue to refine *profiling* as a management tool that statistically identifies the probability that individuals will obtain employment. This raises the possibility of both potential cost savings and more appropriate services. Assessment is a process that could be enhanced by early profiling of applicants applying for assistance, but profiling should not be the only tool relied upon. There should be a range of services to select from that address individual needs.

Accept a long term commitment

We observe that the jobs many welfare recipients are entering are low paid and provide limited fringe benefits. To a large extent this is due to the limited skills and education of many of the welfare recipients. It is also the result of changes in the way many businesses hire employees through temporary agencies. By hiring through temporary agencies, businesses can avoid exposure to perceived unemployment insurance and workers compensation liabilities. Many

192

businesses face critical labour shortages and are anxious to hire welfare recipients *who are prepared to work*. But, because of intense competition in today's global economy, businesses will not hire people who are not qualified. Nor would it serve the best interests of the welfare recipients to be hired for jobs they cannot perform or in which they cannot advance.

According to previous studies, few families are long term welfare recipients. Rather they tend to move off welfare after short periods but return when they quit or lose their jobs (Rangarajan, 1998). Because the work readiness levels of welfare recipients are varied, so the training that they receive must begin at their point of readiness. At the same time, the training must also address the real world workforce needs of the employers.

Next Step: Basic education, including life skills, and occupational skill training need to be available to former welfare recipients for an extended period of time. There also needs to be financial assistance for individuals who have been long term recipients and the possibility of financial assistance needs to continue after a person leaves welfare (e.g. four years). Programmes that continue to offer services long after job placement, whenever the participant is in need, make sense. However, a component that assists welfare recipients into the labour market and then stays with them providing ancillary support and encouraging further training is lacking in most programmes. Currently, programmes are designed to move people out into employment and to open slots for new candidates who have not had any assistance. Support systems, including the holding of meetings of former recipients, need to be encouraged after an individual is working in an effort to break a recycling of clients.

Address the cause - not the symptoms

If poverty is the problem, what are the impacts of a 'work-first' approach going to have on the psychological, social and economic conditions of the poor and their families? The economic gap between poor and rich is now greater than ever. In 1993, the top 20 percent of American households received 48.9 percent of the income and those in the bottom 20 percent shared only 3.6 percent. Wage growth for unskilled welfare recipients, particularly female-headed households, does not keep up with the cost of living. If there is no wage growth without improving skills there is no chance of getting out of the poverty cycle. In many states the economy is booming, jobs are abundant, and employers are increasing wages to attract qualified employees. Labour shortages stem not from the lack of people, but from a lack of people with the necessary skills for the jobs available. It is these higher paying jobs that families will need to access in order to achieve a level of self-sufficiency and move out of poverty.

It is also a concern when poor families obtain entry-level jobs that are short in duration for any number of reasons. The poor seldom have an opportunity to establish a savings account affording them protection from periods of short-term joblessness and whilst it takes only one day to be terminated from public assistance, it takes forty-five days to be re-enrolled. The gap in family income over this period is met by local human service agencies (where they exist), or friends of the family. In either case, the system appears strained even at a time when the economy is healthy, which raises fears of what will happen when unemployment goes up and the least skilled are laid off.

Approximately 40 percent of families on welfare today have some earnings, but not a sufficient amount to support their family (Palmer, 1998). The other 60 percent are solely dependent on pubic assistance. However, cash assistance levels are currently set at more than 50 percent below the federal poverty level. The maximum a family of three can receive in Detroit Michigan is $459 a month.

Next Step: A thoughtful exploration is required of how to link public service employment, at a wage level that will sustain a family, with skill training for those welfare recipients who do not have the basic entry level skills to compete in today's labour market. The likelihood of achieving the desired result of moving families out of welfare by this means also needs to be examined objectively. This is an expensive approach, but for some long term recipients it may be the only approach that can lift them out of poverty.

Develop and appreciate qualified staff

The value of the relationship between the counsellor (educator, mentor) and the client's success has never been adequately determined. Programme operators believe that special training and the intuition of staff make a difference in a client's success. Role models and mentors who nurture and even demand when appropriate, are characterisations that participants have used in referring to the staff who had made a difference in their lives. There probably is not one particular type of person who can make a difference to everyone, but too often qualifications and experience of staff are under rated.

Next Step: Establish standards and competencies, including the continuous professional development of staff. We should learn from the private sector by ensuring staff are licensed and required to renew their credentials periodically.

Conclusion

In conclusion, strategies for alleviating poverty and decisions about government spending continue to be closely linked to the perceived causes of poverty. Poverty has historically been looked upon in the United States as an individual problem, or as a social issue rather than an economic issue. Current legislation plays to the myths and prejudices of the general population rather than the facts. The 'work-first' approach focuses on an individual's lack of personal responsibility as the principle cause of poverty. There seems to be a belief that poverty is a choice; that if the poor would only take responsibility for their own behaviour, and go to work, poverty would be eradicated. However, since much of the recent legislation has emphasised sanctions and compulsion, securing the support of some recipients to help themselves can be challenging. This is particularly difficult to deal with for staff who have selected a career in assisting the poor and now find themselves attempting to make the most out of a philosophy they do not consider beneficial to all the people they wish to assist.

The indications are that even with a sustained healthy economy most welfare recipients are faced with numerous barriers to gainful employment and economic independence and these must be recognised. Education, mental health, physical health, discrimination and childcare have all been identified as obstacles to moving individuals off of aid. Michigan and some other states have taken a systematic approach to addressing these issues by attempting to isolate problems. In some situations, such as mental health, once the barrier is identified assistance is shifted to another programme that may not carry as negative a stigma. Although there is a reduction in expenditure in what is considered welfare, there is often greater public expense for people receiving Social Security Insurance, with lower expectations of moving these people towards independence. A more direct confrontation of the myths and misunderstandings regarding welfare dependency and welfare recipients could substantially improve the general public receptiveness to expensive approaches such as childcare, wage sufficient public service employment and skill training.

Because one size does not fit all, experience tells us a long term financial and community commitment to individuals is essential to moving some of the chronically unemployed out of poverty. Others may never be gainfully employed and are likely to continue to be a burden to society. There may not be a way of determining who needs only minor intervention and who will require longer term support. However, we can apply criteria from past experience that will increase the efficiency of assessment, by integrating profiling into local welfare-to-work programmes.

A thriving economy and a 'work-first' approach have been successful in moving many people off the roles and establishing a vehicle for them to enter the labour force. The focus on work as a responsibility for the able, particularly when linked with skill training and support systems, is in keeping with the work ethic in the United States. Welfare recipients who become contributing members of society rather than a burden on society are testimonials to this approach.

References

Clague, Ewan and Kramer, Leo (1976)
    Manpower Policies and Programmes: A Review, 1935 - 75, W. E.
    Upjohn Institute.

Palmer, John L. (1998)
    'The Next Decade: The Economic, Political and Social Context of
    Employment and Training Policies', The Partnership for Training and
    Employment Careers and The Thomas M. Bradley Centre for
    Employment and Training Education and Research, pp. 9-18.

Herr, Toby, Halpern, Robert and Conrad, Aimee (1991)
    Changing What Counts: Rethinking The Journey Out of Welfare, Centre
    for Urban Affairs and Policy Research, Northwestern University, April.

Rangarajan, Anu, (1998)
    Keeping Welfare Recipients Employed, Mathematical Policy Research
    Inc., June.

Seefeldt, Kristin S., Pavetti, LaDonna, Maquire, Karen and Kirby, Gretchen
    (1998)
    Income Support and Social Services for Low Income People in Michigan,
    Urban Institute, July, pp. 11-16.

Strawn, Julie (1998)
    *Beyond Job Search or Basic Education: Rethinking the Role of Skills in
    Welfare Reform*, Centre for Law and Social Policy, April, pp. 4-9.

US Department of Health and Human Services (1999)
    'Early Implementation of the Welfare-to-Work Grants Programme',
    Report to Congress, March.

US Department of Health and Human Services web page:
    Http/www.acf.dhhs.gov

CHAPTER 8
WELFARE-TO-WORK PARTNERSHIPS:
LESSONS FROM THE UNITED KINGDOM

By Professor Mike Campbell, Simon Foy and Jo Hutchinson,
Leeds Metropolitan University, United Kingdom

This chapter examines the importance of local partnerships in securing the effectiveness of UK welfare-to-work policies and in particular of the New Deal programme. It aims to be useful to those, in the UK and elsewhere in the OECD, who are actively pursuing welfare-to-work policies, or active labour market policies as they are often known, which have a local design or delivery component. In developing and implementing such policies it will be valuable to learn the lessons from the literature and practice of local partnerships to maximise policy effectiveness.

The next section outlines the nature of UK welfare-to-work programmes, focusing on the New Deal and Employment Zones, and assesses the importance of the local dimension in such policies and the need for local partnerships. Then, in the core of the chapter, key lessons are set out from local partnership practice and research, which can be used to inform partnership formation, management and development, together with their implications for welfare-to-work programmes in the UK and other countries. The following two sections contain reflections on the UK New Deal local partnerships based on their early experience so far and conclusions on the future development of welfare-to-work partnerships in the light of the issues discussed.

UK welfare-to-work programmes and the value of local partnerships

New Deal

The New Deal 'family' of policies incorporates a range of actions: New Deal for Young People, New Deal for Adults, New Deal for people with a Disability,

New Deal for Lone Parents and the New Deal for Communities. In parallel, there is the pilot Employment Zones programme. We focus here on the first and last of these because New Deal for Young People has both the largest resource devoted to it and has been in operation for the longest period, whilst Employment Zones offer the greatest scope for local policy design. Neither is a long running programme. The New Deal for Young People has been in operation nationally since April 1998 whilst Employment Zones have been running in pilot areas since January 1998.

The New Deal for Young People involves a commitment to help 250,000 young people aged 18-24 into work in the period up to 2002. The total cost of the programme is estimated at UK£2.65 billion. People aged 18-24 who have been unemployed, and claiming Job Seekers Allowance (JSA), for six months are offered four options:

- A job with an employer 'subsidised' by UK£60 per week for six months. A contribution of UK£750 is also made to education/training costs. Jobs can be taken in both the private and public sectors.

- Work experience with a voluntary sector organisation for six months. A UK£750 contribution to education/training is provided as above. Participants receive an allowance, equivalent to benefit, retain entitlement to passported benefits and receive a grant of up to UK£400. There is a particular emphasis on placements to provide 50,000 new trained childcarers.

- Work experience with the Environmental Task Force for six months. A UK£750 contribution to education/training is provided as above. Allowance, benefits and grant are the same as in the voluntary sector option.

- Full time education/training in relation to basic skills for up to 12 months, for those with current qualifications levels below National Vocational Qualification level 2 (NVQ2). The allowance for the participant is equivalent to income benefits plus passported benefits.

Each of the first three options include one day per week of education/training. Help with childcare is available on all options and a self-employment option has also been developed.

'Gateway' provision where clients are allocated a personal advisor to assist with job search, careers advice, guidance assistance with exceptional problems (e.g. homelessness or drugs) and preparation for an option, is an essential element of the New Deal. So is effective 'follow through' to ensure clients are assisted during their time on the option and beyond. There is no 'fifth' option of remaining on JSA: the sanction of loss of JSA can be imposed for failure to take up offered places.

Some young people, who find it particularly difficult to find work but who have not been unemployed for six months are eligible from day one of unemployment e.g. ex offenders; lone parents; people whose first language is not English; those with literacy/numeracy problems; those leaving local authority care; and those with a disability.

The government's Employment Service (ES) has lead responsibility for delivering New Deal but local delivery arrangements vary considerably. A range of partners can be involved: Training and Enterprise Councils (in England and Wales); Local Enterprise Companies (in Scotland); Careers Service Partnerships; Local Authorities; employers; Chambers of Commerce; colleges; training providers; and voluntary organisations. In some areas lead responsibility has been given to a private sector organisation (usually a private employment agency) and in some areas the partnerships are more 'inclusive' than others. The precise configuration is up to the locality to decide. Each region has produced a strategic plan for delivering New Deal and each local area has produced a delivery plan to a common format. Local areas are defined on the basis of the pre-existing ES districts, which often cover more than one local authority or Training and Enterprise Council area.

The total number of 18-24 year olds unemployed at the end of 1998 was around 120,000, a sharp fall from its peak of 403,000 in 1994. The monthly 'flow' into this 'long term' unemployed stock was around 10,000. The largest numbers of eligible young people were in Birmingham, Liverpool, Glasgow, Manchester, Sheffield, Leeds, Hackney, Bradford, Lambeth, Newham, Nottingham, Wirral, Haringey, Newcastle and Hull.

Twelve 'Pathfinder' areas went into operation in January 1998, and the programme then went national in April 1998. The Pathfinder areas were Tayside; Swansea; Sheffield/Rotherham; Eastbourne; Lambeth; Harlow and Stevenage; Cumbria; Wirral; South Derbyshire; the Black Country; Newcastle/Gateshead; and Cornwall. A sympathetic, but critical review of New Deal for Young People in a local context can be found in Finn (1997).

Employment Zones were established in the five pilot areas of Glasgow, Liverpool, South Teesside, North West Wales and Plymouth in January 1998. The government has since extended the programme to cover fifteen areas. The focus is on local flexibility and innovation in tailoring provision to match local need using a 'cocktail' of funding sources to create a range of appropriate pathways from long term unemployment into jobs. Such a cocktail may include, in addition to Employment Zone funding itself, national government Single Regeneration Budget (SRB) funds and European Union funding (especially from the European Social Fund). It is also hoped to add funding from 'benefit transfers', i.e. funds currently spent on welfare payments to the individuals while unemployed. It is hoped that it will be possible to develop a 'Personal Job Account' (PJA) which will act as a means for the individual to purchase the most appropriate mix of services to meet his/her particular needs, as jointly agreed between them and their personal adviser. The focus is on those aged over 25 who have been out of work for more than one year as well as on others at a 'special disadvantage' in the labour market (for whom there is no duration eligibility), including those with a disability, basic skills deficiencies, women 'returners', lone parents, ex-offenders and those affected by large scale redundancies.

The approach to Employment Zone design and delivery is a matter for each local partnership, which should be set up on an inclusive and extensive basis. They are charged with developing an integrated and strategic approach. The key objective is to develop 'local solutions to individual needs' and to develop whatever mix of actions is required to meet specified local job opportunities, therefore overcoming the problems of lack of flexibility that can be experienced through a national 'programme' driven approach. Though its hallmark is local design and delivery, in general there are three main elements to Employment Zones:

- Learning for Work - a focus on skills/qualifications.

- Neighbourhood Match - a focus on intermediate labour market initiatives.

- Business Enterprise - a focus on self-employment.

The importance of the local dimension in welfare-to-work policy

It is essential that labour markets adjust to changing economic conditions. Where they fail to do so the result is structural, often long term, unemployment as the nature of labour supply does not adapt effectively to evolving labour demand patterns. In tight labour markets this unemployment can also coexist with skill shortages. There are considerable variations in local labour market conditions in the UK and also in most OECD countries. *A priori*, these will require locally differentiated management. Moreover such local management aims not only to tackle local labour market problems but the consequent national problem as well, which is, in effect, the national aggregation of local labour market adjustment problems.

Most labour market adjustments actually take place at the local level. For example, closures, openings, expansions, redundancies, labour force entry and exit, job search and recruitment. All these adjustments are primarily local in nature because of the nature of travel to work patterns and the relatively close proximity of most job seekers to potential workplaces. Thus, structural adjustment, local development and active labour market policy are all intimately connected (Davies, 1995). Actions to improve the adjustment process and help people from welfare to work therefore necessarily have a specific local dimension.

What are the main ways in which action at the local level can add value to national policies (OECD, 1998, Campbell, 1996b, 1997)? First, because of considerable local differences in the character, nature and extent of labour market problems, in particular unemployment, it is essential that national policy should take these into account and ensure that its application is appropriate to the needs of the local labour market. In other words policies need, at a minimum, to be locally 'sensitive'.

Second, policy designed at a local level is likely to be able to pursue a more refined, focused, targeted and flexible approach to labour market problems (Greffe, 1996). It is easier to identify and tackle problems where they arise and, as most adjustments take place locally (this is where most workers actually look for jobs and most firms look for workers), this is often at the local level.

Third, in order to ensure that such sensitivity is possible, it is vital that local labour market intelligence is utilised in the tailoring of policies to meet the needs of any specific local labour market (Campbell, 1996a). In this way, resulting actions will be based more closely on local knowledge. Mis-specification of problems or policies will lead to a reduction in policy effectiveness.

Fourth, the involvement of local actors (employers, workers and local agencies) can be a powerful instrument in: assessing local needs effectively; adapting policy, programme and project design; and, critically, securing increased ownership of, and legitimacy for, local actions. Particularly in localities which hitherto have been on the 'receiving end' of more costs than benefits of the labour market adjustment process, where communities feel marginalised or excluded, such participation can be a crucial factor in enhancing policy effectiveness. 'Proximity' of agencies and their 'closeness' to the problem are crucial here.

Fifth, there is a range of implementation benefits of localised policy to tackle long term unemployment. It brings the relevant labour market agencies closer to the 'grassroots', increasing information exchange, dialogue and access between them and the sites of labour market policy implementation. Also, given the relatively large number of agencies tackling labour market problems, the risk of fragmentation can be reduced by dialogue between them to enhance co-ordination. This is most easily done at a local level where 'networking' and the building of partnerships can be maximised.

Sixth, the tendency for labour market agencies to 'contract out' or delegate functions to local actors at the same time increases local responsibility and legitimacy and makes it desirable, in the control, regulation and administering of these contracts, to be physically close to them.

Seventh, because of the multi-dimensional nature of the barriers facing the long term unemployed and the multi-agency approach necessary to tackle them on a co-ordinated and comprehensive basis the mobilisation of relevant actors into a partnership becomes crucial to effective policy and delivery (Hutchinson and Campbell, 1998).

Finally, practically speaking, labour market policy in many OECD countries is in the process of being devolved to agencies at the local level, for example in the UK, Denmark and Netherlands, and thus considerable opportunity exists to tailor policy more closely to local needs. More generally too it has been argued that a return to the 'local level' is desirable (Demos, 1996).

In summary, a range of considerations assert the importance of the local level, as synthesised in the recent work of the OECD's Local Economic and Employment Development (LEED) programme (see for example OECD, 1998). First, there is the considerable and growing diversity of unemployment across local labour markets. Second, there is the proximity afforded by local action both to the problems and the stakeholders. Third, the local level is conducive to policy co-ordination and integration.

National policies predicated on the basis that labour markets are broadly geographically homogenous when, in practice, they are heterogeneous, segmented and connected only very imperfectly to each other are unlikely to be very effective in meeting local needs (for a critique see, Campbell, Sanderson and Walton, 1998). Characterising the labour market instead from the 'bottom up' and viewing the national labour market as a set of partially connected, differentiated, local labour markets, could alter the 'mindset' of policy makers considerably. As the OECD has concluded, 'many factors favour the increasing decentralisation of employment policy' (OECD, 1998: 22). Localised policies 'bring policy closer to people and their needs' (Campbell, 1997). The 'territorialisation' of policy can in practice vary from the geographical targeting of national measures to full devolution of responsibilities to local agencies. A 'flexible territorialisation' (OECD, 1998) of policy, based on local partnerships, which maintains a contractual relation with central (or regional) authorities within a national strategic framework, yet which has the capacity to design as well implement policy, is perhaps the most promising approach.

Partnerships

In recent years there has been increasing interest in the use of a partnership approach in tackling a range of problems. Partnerships have been promoted as an effective response to, *inter alia*, issues of urban regeneration, education, health care, rural issues and, of course, unemployment in the UK. For example, the government's Single Regeneration Budget arrangements require local partnerships to design and deliver the programmes; European Union Structural Fund actions supported under Objectives 1, 2 and 5b require local partnerships and under objectives 3 and 4 at least regional partnership working is required.

The interest in partnership in the UK has increased following the election of the Labour government in May 1997. For example, the White Paper proposing the establishment of 9 new Regional Development Agencies in England is called 'Partnerships for Prosperity'. Similarly, the new strategic framework for the Department for Education and Employment (DfEE) identifies partnership development as one of its six key challenges: 'creating and sustaining partnerships - both in developing and delivering policy' (DfEE, 1997). The need to work in partnership has, for many public sector agents become an imperative in the UK and the New Deal and Employment Zones are form part of a series of policy initiatives which rely on partnership approaches for their effective design and/or implementation.

The primary rationale for partnership based activities is that the multi-dimensional nature of the problems, in this case assisting people's reintegration into the labour market and connecting them to employment opportunities, requires an integrated approach to their resolution. The need for 'joined up' thinking and action, focusing on the needs of the target group rather than the current responsibilities of individual agencies, requires the agencies to collaborate in order to devise and deliver effective solutions. Thus a 'partnership' approach is required. This involves more than co-operation (informal arrangements focusing on sharing information) and even more than the co-ordination of existing actions, as we shall see.

It will be important to ensure that the new partnerships 'connect' effectively to existing partnerships to ensure effective synergy and value added.

Lessons from UK welfare-to-work partnerships

The authors have recently completed a review of the available literature on partnerships that has been published over the last 10 years, primarily though not exclusively from the UK, for the UK's Department for Education and Employment (Hutchinson and Campbell, 1998). This section seeks to distil the key lessons from the literature and to identify their implications for UK New Deal and Employment Zone partnerships and for welfare-to-work programmes elsewhere. We have sought to do this here by identifying eight key sets of messages which can be regarded in a number of ways:

- As a set of principles of good practice against which welfare-to-work partnerships could consider their own practices.

- As a set of 'critical success factors' which will influence the effectiveness of local partnerships.

- As a set of evaluation criteria against which to assess local partnership behaviour.

Partnership is a way of working

How should we characterise a partnership? Partnerships are more than a structure or a form of organisation. They are also a method of working (Hutchinson, 1994). Partnerships are created and, as such, are as much a process of building relationships as a structure identified by organisational form, membership structure and 'paper' statements of operation. Through this process, partners come to share 'risk, resources and skills' (Stratton, 1991) and work towards common goals through an agreed strategy (Bailey et al, 1995). Thus the process of collaboration itself, the negotiation, the compromise, the forging of agreements and search for common purpose are in themselves important aspects of the partnership building process and the degree to which they are taken seriously and addressed is likely to influence outcomes.

Partners represent different interests, have different organisational objectives, different systems of accountability, and different values. Partnership working requires that these, which are sometimes complementary, sometimes in tension, be harnessed in pursuit of the objectives for which the partnership was established. The partnership is, above all, a means to an end.

The range of organisational structures that have been established to deliver the UK New Deal and Employment Zone programmes is therefore of interest, because it may well be that different organisational forms, membership and leadership influence outcomes. However, it would also be useful to examine relationships, perceptions of actors and styles of working. Above all, the implication of regarding partnerships as a way of working is that it means that partnerships cannot be effectively fully assessed in the very short term. They will grow, develop and change as the 'partnership process' becomes more deeply embedded. This is, of course, only likely if the partners themselves in the localities treat partnership as a method of working as well as an organisational form. We would expect therefore some variation in local performance to be, in part, a function of what we will call the 'style of engagement' between the parties.

Partnerships should generate synergy

The foundation stone of partnership activity is the creation and generation of change. Partnerships are seeking to do more than could be done by the organisations working separately. They are trying to create 'added value'. By combining resources and skills to tackle multidimensional problems they should be able to create 'synergy', a phenomenon often captured in the phrase '2+2=5'. Mackintosh (1992) finds that such synergy arises from the use of the different but complementary resources and skills that partners bring.

The idea has been further developed by Hastings (1996) who found that synergy can be created in two ways. The first is resource synergy, which essentially means that better communication and co-ordination between partners generates a more efficient use of resources. The second is policy synergy, which refers to a partnership's ability to forge an innovative set of policies and solutions. This type of synergy can only take place when the partners value their differences and are willing to consider new approaches. Policy synergy is the result of a joint approach to issues and results from a process of constructive interaction of different cultures and styles.

Resource synergy is essentially about co-operation and co-ordination. Yet partnership is about more than co-operation and co-ordination (Winer-Cyr, 1992) and will generate policy synergy. In terms of the UK welfare-to-work programmes, whilst resource synergy is likely to be experienced under New Deal for Young People, policy synergy is more likely in Employment Zones. Policy synergy will, however, have been created in the former case to the extent that local partnerships have been able to influence policy design, in particular through the extensive consultative process undertaken in many localities.

The drivers of partnership creation

Developing partnerships takes considerable time and effort and their formation tends to be driven by several catalysts:

- *The policy environment.* In the UK, government policy has had a strong influence on partnership formation. For example, there has been a 'flurry' of partnership development as a consequence of SRB (Tilson et al, 1997) and New Deal also requires the establishment of local partnerships. In many areas of the UK, partners are therefore used to working together, although in others there may be a more limited experience of partnerships.

- *The existence of a 'public problem'* (Bryson and Crosby, 1992). Difficulties affecting communities can be a catalyst, where members of the community are aware of the problems, where they are important, where they are actionable and where the consequences of not dealing with them are serious. There has been widespread agreement that long term, especially youth, unemployment is a serious problem conforming to these characteristics. However the rapid decline in the numbers 'at risk' over the last 2 years because of rapid employment growth has, to an extent, diminished this perception in some areas.

- *A catalytic event* (Roberts et al, 1995). This can, for example, be a dramatic local event, or the arrival of a new player or a recognition that previous approaches have not worked. The election of the new government and its announcement of the New Deal programme and resource provided this in the UK.

- *Funding.* This can be an important stimulus where it is tied to the need to demonstrate partnership working. In the UK the resources provided are extremely large in volume terms.

– *Synergy*. There has to be recognition that no single organisation can deal with the issue alone, and that by working together synergies can be created.

The balance between the autonomous, organic, locally driven type of partnership and those being driven by 'external' forces depends in part on the configuration of the above factors and the alignment between them. For example, where external and local dimensions are similar and well connected the foundations of a local partnership are likely to be strong. Moreover, the greater the number of these drivers in place, the greater is the likely commitment to local partnership. In UK welfare-to-work programmes both alignment and the extent of drivers are likely to be strong, although again more so in some areas than others.

Partnerships, people and organisations

Partnerships that seek to develop a holistic response need to include organisations within whose remit the solution to the problem is perceived to lie. For problems and solutions with wide ranging objectives there is a tendency to wish to include a wide and inclusive range of representation (Geddes, 1997), as those with an 'interest' may be extensive in number. Yet it is probably better to 'consult' intensively in relation to these groups without necessarily involving them in the partnership *per se*, unless it is believed that local ownership and legitimacy would be enhanced by so doing. There is a danger of wanting to include everyone as a partner, when partner status is not really necessary, and therefore creating unwieldy structures.

However it is important to ensure that those with power, perhaps even more than those with an interest, are represented. It is necessary, in other words, to get the right organisations involved (Hambleton et al, 1995) in terms of their capacity to tackle the problem. For example, employers are crucial in the UK New Deal as it is they who ultimately will, or will not, take on New Deal leavers.

Partnership is also about relationships between people, a particularly important insight when partnership is almost an entrepreneurial activity. From this perspective, it is necessary to get people with the right skills, resources and contacts to participate (Kanter, 1994; Shaw, 1993). Partnership then becomes a process of relationship building between people from different sectors or organisations, and from different levels of hierarchies within organisations. Here, 'interpersonal' and 'cultural' integration are important.

Indeed the 'networks' of relations between people as individuals play a crucial role in establishing, developing and sustaining partnerships (Lowndes et al, 1997). The process of getting to know each other, understanding what people do and working with them can already be well developed where such networks pre-exist and are 'dense'. However such networks can be exclusive and maintaining them it can be costly in terms of people's time.

The kinds of relations, between organisations and individuals, that will develop are also partly a function of the structure and style of partnership working that is adopted. 'Federation' structures are those where relations between the organisations are relatively equal and extensive connections exist between all the parties. They also tend to exist where the partnership is created and sustained by a pre-existing network, or even a pre-existing partnership. Their operation and success is likely to be based on the strength of 'relational' contracts irrespective of the existence of 'transactional' contracts (Darwin, n.d.).

'Hub' structures are those where relations are uneven and unequal, with one 'core' partner who co-ordinates and integrates the activities of others whilst, often, exercising leadership or even executive control over the partnership. Here a greater emphasis on contractual (legal and binding) relations is likely.

The implications these insights for welfare-to-work partnerships are that programmes should seek to ensure that the 'right' organisations are involved in terms of their ability to assist in connecting the long term unemployed to job opportunities, that all key stakeholders are well consulted and that the locality 'owns' the resulting strategy and actions. However, the 'right' people are important too. Ensuring good inter personal relations and 'selecting' the right people to participate as individuals is important. It may well be that welfare-to-work partnerships will be more effective where strong local partnership and networks pre-existed in the locality.

In the case of the UK New Deal, the leadership role given to the public Employment Service, its orientation to accountability to government ministers and its previously limited role in local partnerships, may often lead to a more 'hub' than' federal' structure of partnership working. However, this may change over time as partnerships develop.

Agreed strategies and clear objectives

A strategic approach is widely seen as critical to the effectiveness of partnerships. Such an approach requires the establishment of a vision and mission, which can provide an enduring reference point for the partnership, and a set of core values; a sound understanding of the problem to be addressed; clearly defined (preferably SMART) objectives; agreed policies and actions appropriate to the task; resource deployment and identification of roles/responsibilities; the development of a sound monitoring and evaluating framework; and a commitment to adjust strategy in light of its findings (Campbell, 1992). Such an approach also encourages 'learning' from what works and what does not and minimises the risk of 'failure'.

In partnerships all this has to be achieved, of course, through a process of dialogue, agreement and consensus across the partner organisations in order to ensure commitment and ownership. Though difficult and time consuming, the long term benefits of a strategic approach are considerable.

Research into education-business partnerships (Wilson et al, 1995), for example, stressed the need for an overarching strategic vision with clear targets expressed in action plans. Research into local development partnerships (Field et al, 1995) stressed the need to have strong commitment among the partners to achieve these shared objectives. Roberts and Hart (1996) went further and found that success was most likely where partners not only had commitment to the strategy, but put those strategic interests above other local or sectional interests.

Strategy development is, in itself, a complex process particularly in a partnership context. It is important to develop an understanding of the problem from a number of perspectives (GFA Consulting, 1997), including from each other (Blamires et al, 1997), before an effective strategy (which embodies policy synergy) is generated. A good strategy also needs to strike a balance between what is needed and what is achievable. It has to be robust enough to guide action for a number of years, and yet flexible enough to respond to changing circumstances (Kintrea et al, 1996).

Local areas which have engaged in a prior process of strategy development will endow the partnership with a valuable 'strategic inheritance' but where this is absent the strategy may suffer with a tendency to focus on: the components of the programme, or even projects; internal issues, to the exclusion of a changing external environment; limited data/information to inform strategy; and a focus on getting a strategy 'done' than getting it 'right', especially in tight time frames.

In the UK, local New Deal partnerships, however, have a limited capacity to adopt a strategic approach to the basic design of their programmes, since the essential characteristics and contours of New Deal are nationally designed. Local adaptations and linkage arrangements with other programmes are nonetheless possible and some of the stages of the strategic planning process and the issues they raise remain locally relevant. Moreover, a strategic approach can be taken to implementation. Strategy development skills can, and should, be developed in the local partnership.

Results oriented practice

A strategic approach puts a premium on a clear focus on results. The setting of targets is integral to the strategy process and it is widely recognised that 'what gets measured gets done'. Effective management information, sound monitoring and its use in review systems are essential components of a results oriented practice. However the results, and the information and measurement systems to which they relate, need to be appropriate to the policy's objectives. Some of the information required will be quantitative and some will be qualitative, from partners and clients.

Furthermore, a results oriented 'culture' also requires a 'blame free' culture of continuous learning and continuous improvement, where mistakes are learnt from, where individuals and teams communicate and share, honestly, their failures as well as successes.

In order to secure the continued commitment of partners 'early success' is also important. Moreover this early success needs to be communicated back through the partner organisations and to the wider public. On the other hand there can be a tendency to set unrealistically high targets and to have unrealistically high expectations in the 'heady rush of the development' phase. Failure to achieve such targets, together with the possible public relations implications, make this a high risk strategy for fledgling partnerships or policies (GHK, n.d.).

For the UK New Deal, the local partnerships have set out clear targets. Regular monitoring against these will be crucial as will the need to develop an understanding of why targets were not met, if/when this is the case, and what arrangements can be put in place to either amend the targets or take appropriate action. Developing the appropriate culture is more difficult given the wide range of partners involved but all the more important.

Effective management

Partnerships need a leader or a champion. Leaders can be thought of as initiators (Bennett and Krebs, 1994), people who drive the process forward - in collaboration with their partners. Leadership requires a combination of personal skills, plus the status that an individual's role within an organisation or sector lends to them. At various times private sector representatives have claimed to be the natural leaders of partnerships (CBI, 1988), while at others local government authorities have taken on this mantle (Roberts et al, 1995). Leaders do not necessarily have to be partnership managers. However research does suggest that different types of locality support different 'types' of leaders and so it may be appropriate in a given area to work with the grain of the 'dominant regime' to maximise the chances of success (Bennett and Krebs, 1994).

The partnership manager has an equally important and challenging role. They have been the focus of research which examines the skills which they need (Clark, 1993). These skills fall into four major categories: analytical skills; process and operational skills; communication and motivational skills; and a co-operative style of working. Thus the skills and abilities of the management team and their leader need to be developed and nurtured as do those of the partners. In relation to the UK New Deal and Employment Zones, effective capacity building programmes will be important especially in areas/organisations with relatively little experience of partnership working (Campbell, Sanderson and Walton 1998; Martinos 1996). Identification and dissemination of good practice will also be important.

Sustaining Progress

All partnerships need to maintain momentum and to 'embed' the partnership firmly in the locality. This involves spreading the partnership ethos throughout the parent organisations and developing a sense of ownership of the values of the partnership (Kanter, 1994).

Team building measures are also important to create opportunities for mutual understanding and fresh thinking as well as to increase openness and trust between the individuals and organisations involved. More generally, capacity building to continue to enhance technical and management skills in the partnership is important to bring the skills of all partners and partnerships across localities up to an acceptable or desirable standard (Martinos, 1996).

It will also be important to recognise, and respond to, 'threats', such as an economic downturn, where opportunities for the partnership may be diminished and, without action, the commitment of the partners may diminish. Shifts in government policy or negative media coverage may have similar effects (Parkinson, 1996).

Indeed even without external threats, partnerships may suffer from inertia or fatigue, especially if there are just 'too many' partnerships in the locality (Peck and Tickell, 1994), without some external stimulus or a system of motivation and reward. 'Turf wars' can develop as organisations may see 'their own' role being diminished or threatened by the actions of the partnership or one of the partners (Martin and Oztel, 1996). This may occur especially when difficult issues have been avoided or the real 'culture' of partnership has not been fully embedded.

Finally, funding issues may cause difficulties for the effective operation of the partnership if it is either insufficient to meet needs or if funding streams do not match the balance of policy actions required.

As far as UK welfare-to-work programmes are concerned, it will be important for local partnerships to 'embed' the partnership, build teams and capacity, prepare for the possibility of a 'recession' and make appropriate contingency plans, as well as to maximise local opportunities to obtain additional funding to enhance provision and link it to wider initiatives.

Reflections on the early stages of New Deal and Employment Zone partnerships

The previous section has identified a range of lessons from our understanding of local partnerships for the operation of welfare-to-work partnerships and for the New Deal and Employment Zone partnerships that have recently been introduced in the UK. In this section we briefly draw on the limited amount of material available so far on the early implementation experience of the UK New Deal and Employment Zone partnerships themselves. It is important to reiterate here the fact that New Deal for Young People, the most 'mature' activity of the new welfare-to-work partnerships, was only introduced nation-wide in April 1998.

Each region, *de facto* the regional office of the Employment Service (ES), produced a regional strategic plan for New Deal for Young People which was designed to assist the local partnerships to 'develop their district delivery plans'. This produced a 'template' within which each area drew up its delivery plans. One section of this relates to the partnership arrangements and has four components:

  – How partners have been involved in drawing up the delivery plans.

- Identification of the management and partnership structure to deliver New Deal.

- Details of who the key partners are.

- Plans to consult with the client group.

Part of the national evaluation of the New Deal involves case studies of six of the pathfinder areas and a private sector led partnership (undertaken by the Tavistock Institute). The key question which these studies, which are currently being undertaken, seek to address is 'how effective is the structure and delivery of New Deal?' In particular it includes: an assessment of which different partnership configurations provide the most positive New Deal outcomes; an identification of the benefits and costs of participation for the partners; and an assessment of the extent to which partners are satisfied with the delivery arrangements.

Emerging findings from the early part of this research include:

- A wide variety of different partnership configurations have developed including Joint Venture Partnership agreements (JVPs) (where the partnership *per se* is responsible for the programme and the ES contracts with the JVP which subsequently contracts with each partner); ES led partnerships; private sector led partnerships (indeed nation-wide 10 are led by the private sector); limited companies; and TEC or Local Authority led partnerships.

- Sustainability of partnerships and partner involvement may well depend on client flows across the options.

- Some new networks are already developing.

- The Employment Service is a 'new player' in most local partnerships.

An evaluation of Employment Zones is also being undertaken at Manchester University and Leeds Metropolitan University. A specific focus is the 'qualitative assessment of partnership arrangements', in particular the way in which Employment Zone funding has 'strengthened local partnership and the formulation of consensual strategies for reducing long term unemployment'. The research questions include:

- How are partnerships formed and expertise used in local policy development?

- What is the distinctive expertise that different agencies bring?

- To what extent do the partnerships reflect longer standing patterns of co-operation?

- Why do particular agencies emerge as lead partners?

- Are operational targets defined and agreed by all partners?

- How does ES fit within decentralised approaches to policy development?

Emerging findings from the early part of this research include:

- The partnerships have sought an inclusive approach to partner involvement though this has led to some 'overcrowding' and confusion with subsequent action needed to streamline management and working methods.

- Locality boundaries are important in that where Employment Zone boundaries coincide with previous institutional configurations, partnership has been easier to take forward.

Taken together these evaluations will shed considerable light on the role of local partnership in effective welfare-to-work actions. It would also be helpful, however, to identify a range of 'critical success factors', as we have sought to do above, and investigate the extent to which these are present in the partnerships, particularly at the strategic level. Some of these are covered in the Employment Zone evaluation and it will therefore be useful to reflect on New Deal for Young People partnerships using these results.

Prior to the availability of the official evaluations it is difficult to assess the extent to which the lessons from previous partnership practice as identified in the literature have been incorporated into the current welfare-to-work partnerships. However we draw brief attention to four sources of partial information. First, the Local Government Association (LGA, 1998) report the results of a survey conducted by the Local Government Management Board in the Pathfinder areas. A key finding is the wide range of 'quality' in the approaches to partnership in different areas. In some areas the development of relationships was found to be strong but in others, particularly were previous relations had been non-existent or poor, 'real' partnership working had not developed largely because of the lack of time available to put it in place because of the tight implementation time-scale. There is also some concern that the contracting process frustrated some efforts at partnership working.

It is important to point out that a number of national consultation workshops were held on the design of New Deal and that a large number were held at regional and local level. Moreover the local strategic partnerships often held their own consultation events and client focus groups.

Second, NCVO (1997 and 1998) have produced a guide for voluntary agencies to help them get involved in New Deal and a survey of voluntary sector involvement in the Pathfinder areas. The key points they make are that partnership, for them, is about more than consultation or receiving a contract to deliver a service and that, they find, most partnerships were based on existing partnerships with the added involvement of the ES. Third, the House of Commons Education and Employment Committee (August 1998) concentrated mainly on the options, the Gateway and the contracting process. However their main point in relation to local partnerships was a recognition that the Employment Service had made strenuous efforts to work with/in the new local partnerships. This is important as the Employment Service has a more limited experience of partnership working than other partners like local government authorities, TECs and voluntary organisations. The Committee also recommended that best practice guidelines be developed and disseminated.

Finally, the authors undertook a study of the issues arising in the early implementation process in the Yorkshire and Humber region for the Government Office for Yorkshire and Humberside in partnership with the Employment Service and the region's TECs. The study was undertaken in spring 1998 when the Pathfinder area had been running for four months and when the other areas were preparing for their launch.

The key issues arising were, firstly, a view that partners need to dovetail New Deal provision with existing programmes and will therefore need to engage in thorough partnership working to achieve integrated provision. Secondly, it was interesting to note that different partners were tending to take the lead responsibility for a range of areas of activity when, a priori, one might have expected the pattern to be broadly common across localities given agencies particular experience and expertise. Thirdly, relations between the partners, especially between the national lead agency, the Employment Service, and the local TECs varied considerably. A critical factor in determining these relations was previous experience i.e. in those areas where the ES had worked closely with local agencies previously the relationship was, generally, more favourable that were that had previously been, for whatever reason, little collaboration. Fourthly, there is a tension in a nationally designed, but locally delivered, programme between horizontal (local) linkages between agencies and vertical (national) linkages, particularly as the ES reports to ministers when, for example, TECs report to their local boards. Finally, most areas reported significant progress in partnership development as a result of New Deal, largely because of the commitment of the agencies to both client and employer needs as well as to the possibilities that New Deal offered. Progress was strongest at the strategic level whereas at the operational level it was considered desirable to share more information and expertise and to build the relationship between practitioners.

Concluding Remarks

This chapter has sought to draw out the lessons from the examination of previous local partnerships for welfare-to-work programmes, including New Deal and Employment Zones in the UK. It has outlined the importance of the local dimension of welfare-to-work policies and sought to identify a range of issues which local partnerships might reflect upon to further to inform their development and effectiveness. It has also briefly outlined the experience so far of the new partnerships established in the UK for the New Deal and Employment Zones.

We conclude by identifying a number of key issues for the future development of welfare-to-work partnerships:

- How much autonomy and discretion should local partnerships have in welfare-to-work policy? The full benefits of local partnerships are most likely to arise when policy discretion is considerable, yet the uneven experience and capacity of local partnerships raises concerns about local policy effectiveness in such localities.

- What is the most appropriate balance between the national and the local in terms of policy design and policy delivery/ implementation?

- How can the standards of all be brought up to the standards of the best?

- What mechanisms for capacity building, know how transfer, identification of best practice and dissemination are available and most likely to be effective?

- Can we develop a set of principles, criteria or 'critical success factors' which characterise successful local partnership working and which command common assent? How can we seek to most effectively embed these in local practice?

The effectiveness of local partnership working is a critical determinant of the success of the local dimension of welfare-to-work policies. It is hoped that the discussion in this chapter has provided a foundation on which to further develop their effectiveness in future years.

References

Bailey, N. Barker, A. and MacDonald, K. (1995)
Partnership Agencies in British Urban Policy, UCL Press, London.

Bennett ,R. and Krebs, G. (1994)
'Local Economic Development Partnerships: An Analysis of Policy Networks in EC-LEDA Local Employment Development Strategies', *Regional Studies*, Vol. 28 (2) pp. 119-140.

Blamires, M. Robertson, C. and Blamires, J. (1997)
Parent Teacher Partnership. Practical Approaches to Meet Special Educational Needs, David Fulton Publishers, London.

Bryson, J,M. and Crosby, B.C. (1992)
Leadership for the Common Good, Jossey-Bass, San Francisco.

Campbell, M. Sanderson, I. and Walton, F. (1998)
Local Responses to Long Term Unemployment, Joseph Rowntree Foundation, York.

Campbell, M. (1997)
'Local Developments', *New Economy*, pp. 30-33, IPPR, Bryden Press, London.

Campbell, M. (1996a)
'Local Labour Market Management: Definition, Concepts and Issues', OECD document [DT/LEED/RD(96)6], Paris.

Campbell, M. (1996b)
'A Labour Market and Training Needs Assessment System', in Percy-Smith J. (Ed.) *Needs Assessment and Public Policy*, Buckingham, Open University Press.

Campbell, M (1992)
'A Strategic Approach to the Labour Market' in Campbell M. and Duffy K. (Eds.), *Local Labour Markets: Problems and Policies*, Longman.

Confederation of British Industry (1988)
Initiatives Beyond Charity, CBI, London.

Clark, C. (1993)
Urban Regeneration Partnerships: an Analysis of the Knowledge, Skills and Attitudes Needed by the Managers of Partnerships, Civic Trust Regeneration Unit, London.

DfEE (1997)
Learning and Working Together for the Future, DfEE, London.

Darwin, J. (n.d)
Networks, Partnerships and Strategic Alliances, Sheffield Business School, Sheffield Hallam University.

Davies (1995)
'Local Economies and Globalisation', OECD document LEED Notebook No. 20, Paris.

Demos (1996)
'Return of the Local', *Demos Quarterly*, Issue 9.

Field, P., Moore, J., Dickinson, P., Elgar, J., and Gray, P. (1995)
Local Development Partnerships and Investments in People, Employment Department, Sheffield.

Finn, D. (1997)
'Labour's New Deal for the Unemployed: Making It Work Locally', *Local Economy*, pp. 247-258, November.

Greffe, X. (1996)
'Policy and Practice in Local Development', LEDA Programme Synthesis Report, LRDP, London.

Geddes, M. (1997)
  Partnership against Poverty and Exclusion? Local Regeneration Strategies and Excluded Communities in the UK, The Policy Press, Bristol.

GFA Consulting, (1997)
  Education Initiatives and Regeneration Strategies: A Guide to Good Practice, DETR.

GHK Economics and Management (n.d.)
  Learning from Experience: TECs and Local Economic Development Partnerships, for Department for Education and Employment.

Hastings, A. (1996)
  'Unravelling the Process of Partnership in Urban Regeneration Policy', *Urban Studies*, Vol. 33 (2), pp. 253-268.

Hambleton, R. et al (1995)
  The Collaborative Council, Joseph Rowntree Foundation and LGC Communications, London.

HoC Education and Employment Committee (1998)
  'The New Deal Pathfinders', HC paper 1059.

Hutchinson, J. (1994)
  'The Practice of Partnership in Local Economic Development', *Local Government Studies*, Vol. 20 (93), pp. 335-344.

Hutchinson, J. (1995)
  'Can Partnerships Which Fail Succeed? The Case of City Challenge', *Local Government Policy Making*, Vol. 22 (3)

Hutchinson, J. and Campbell, M. (1998)
  'Working in Partnership: Lessons from the Literature', DfEE Research Report No. 63, Sheffield.

Kanter, R. M. (1994)
  'Collaborative Advantage; the Art of Alliances', *Harvard Business Review*, Vol. 72 (4) pp. 96-108.

Kintrea, K. McGregor, A, McConnachie,M. and Urquhart, A. (1996)
  'Whitfield' in Scottish Office, Partnership in the Regeneration of Urban Scotland, HMSO, London.

Lowndes, V. et al (1997)
'Networks, Partnerships and Urban Regeneration', *Local Economy*, Vol. 11 (4), pp. 333-342.

LGA (1998)
'Developing the New Deal for Young People: Challenges and Opportunities', LGA, London.

Mackintosh, M. (1992)
'Partnerships: Issues of Policy and Negotiation', *Local Economy*, Vol. 7 (3), pp. 210 -224.

Martinos, H (1996)
Lessons from the LEDA Programme, LRDP, London.

Martin, S and Öztel, H. (1996)
'The Business of Partnership: Collaborative Competitive Partnerships in the Development of Business Links', *Local Economy*, pp. 131-142

NCVO (1997)
Partnerships for the New Deal: Playing An Active Role, NCVO, London.

NCVO (1998)
Voluntary Sector Involvement, A New Deal Pathfinder Areas, NCVO, London.

OECD (1998)
Local Management for More Effective Employment Policy, OECD publication, Paris.

Parkinson, M. (1996)
'Twenty-Five Years of Urban Policy in Britain - Partnership, Entrepreneurialism or Competition?', *Public Money and Management*, pp. 7-14.

Peck, J. and Tickell, A. (1994)
'Too Many Partners ... the Future for Regeneration Partnerships', *Local Economy*, Vol. 9 (3), pp. 251-265.

Roberts, P. and Hart, T. (1996)
Regional Strategy and Partnership in European Programmes, Joseph Rowntree Foundation, York.

Roberts, V. Russell, H. Harding, A. and Parkinson, M. (1995)
Public, Private, Voluntary Partnerships in Local Government, The Local Government Management Board, Luton.

Shaw, K. (1993)
'The Development of a New Urban Corporatism: the Politics of Urban Regeneration in the North East of England', *Regional Studies*, Vol. 27 (3), pp. 251-286.

Stratton, C. quoted in Askew, J. (1991)
'Public and Private Sector Partnership for Urban Regeneration in Sheffield and Wakefield', *Local Government Policy Making*, Vol. 17 (4) pp. 37-43.

Tilson, B., Mawson, J., Beazley, J., Burfitt, M., Collinge, C., Hall, S., Loftman, P., Nevin, B. and Srbljanin, A. (1997)
'Partnerships for Regeneration: the SRB Challenge Fund Round One', *Local Government Studies*, Vol. 23 (1), pp. 1-15.

Wilson, V. Pirrie, A. and McFall, E. (1995)
Focus on Partnership: An Evaluation of Education Business Partnership and Options for the Teacher Placement Service in Scotland, Scottish Council for Research in Education, Edinburgh.

Wilson, A. and Charlton, K. (1997)
Making Partnerships Work: A Practical Guide for the Public, Private, Voluntary and Community Sectors, Joseph Rowntree Foundation, York.

Winer-Cyr, M. in Mattesich, P.W. and Monsey, B.R. (1992)
Collaboration: What Makes it Work?, Amherst H. Wilder Foundation, Minnesota.

CHAPTER 9
UNITED STATES EXPERIENCE IN ENGAGING
THE BUSINESS SECTOR IN WELFARE-TO-WORK POLICIES

By Lyn Hogan, The Welfare-to-Work Partnership, United States of America

Introduction

On August 22, 1996, President William Jefferson Clinton signed a bipartisan bill, supported overwhelmingly by the American public, designed to radically reform the country's welfare system. The law, called the Personal Responsibility and Work Opportunity Reconciliation Act of 1996 (Government Printing Office, 1996) fundamentally redesigned the welfare system, shifting it from an income maintenance system to one requiring work. Furthermore, for the first time in the country's history, welfare recipients' benefits became subject to time limits.

Since the law was signed, welfare rolls have dropped by over four million people or 1.5 million families, leaving approximately three million families still receiving public assistance (U.S. Department of Health and Human Services, 1996). The majority of these potential wage earners will need to move off welfare and permanently into the labour market over the next several years. This represents a significant challenge, not just for welfare recipients, but for the country as a whole. The business community has a significant role in meeting this challenge.

For welfare recipients to successfully move into the workforce, they need jobs that allow them to contribute in the workplace. Public sector jobs and subsidised work experience are available, but these pursuits are limited and still paid for by the taxpayers. The biggest opportunity for jobs comes from the private sector.

This chapter aims to demonstrate how government and non-profit organisations can effectively engage the private sector in hiring welfare recipients and others who are disadvantaged. The American experience offers a model that any developed country can follow. The private business community in the United States has participated extensively in developing welfare-to-work programmes and hiring and retaining welfare recipients. Initially, businesses were sceptical. However, positive hiring experiences have motivated thousands of business to participate and the number of those involved keeps growing.

Even in times of economic downturn, welfare-to-work can still succeed. Businesses always need ready access to new workers as turnover inevitably occurs. The welfare rolls can provide businesses with a good source of workers. The key to engaging the business community is to break down existing stereotypes to show that welfare recipients can be good, productive workers if given the chance.

Engaging the business community and The Welfare-to-Work Partnership

When President William Jefferson Clinton signed the welfare reform legislation in the summer of 1996, he viewed it as a first step, not a final measure. At the bill signing he said: '...[E]very business person in America who has ever complained about the failure of the welfare system [should] try to hire somebody off welfare, and try hard.' (President Clinton, August 22, 1996, Rose Garden, The White House.) Shortly after the bill signing, the President travelled to Stamford, Connecticut where he issued another challenge directly to the American business community. He said: 'The welfare bill was just a first step. We now have to figure out how to reform welfare. That's very different than passing a bill. We actually have to go out and do it.' (President Clinton, speech, October 7, 1996, Stamford, Connecticut.)

'Work-first': a shift in 60 years of social policy

Implementing the new welfare legislation meant breaking away from 60 years of social policy. No longer would welfare recipients be eligible for a lifetime of public assistance. Instead, they would receive time-limited benefits and be required to go to work. Further, government from the federal level on down would have to stop simply signing welfare checks and, instead, start helping welfare recipients find work.

The new legislation implored the federal, state and local governments to begin to develop job readiness and job placement programmes, emphasising quick attachment to the labour market over long term education and training. The labour market attachment model, known as 'work-first' represented a radical departure from the long term education and training model that had dominated demonstration programmes prior to the new legislation.

'Work-first' relies on the premise that on-the-job work experience, not federally run job training programmes, provides the best opportunity to train welfare recipients and then connect them to the labour market, helping them move up the ladder of work while incrementally increasing responsibility and pay. Only after one has forged a connection to the labour market are federal job training programmes useful. There is a wide body of research available supporting this premise (Hogan, 1995, 1996).

Broad support for the 'work-first' model is necessary to engage the business community in welfare reform. Business requires a quick response to its hiring needs and prefers to train employees in-house rather than have them trained by an outside source unfamiliar with company norms. Extensive surveying by Wirthlin Worldwide, based in Arlington, VA, found that while companies universally prefer to hire welfare recipients who have received job readiness training (basics such as grooming, punctuality, and supervisor relations), few companies prefer government training programmes over their own (Wirthlin Worldwide, 1998).

The Welfare-to-Work Partnership

One important method of engaging employers in welfare-to-work programmes is to encourage the emergence of networks of businesses committed to hiring and retaining welfare recipients. In the United States, this role has been played by The Welfare-to-Work Partnership.

In May 1996 at the urging of President Clinton, Eli Segal, former President and CEO of the Corporation for National and Community Service, founded the private not-for-profit organisation, The Welfare-to-Work Partnership (The Partnership). The Partnership's mission simply stated is to organise the American business community around hiring and retaining welfare recipients without displacing existing workers. The Partnership designed its activities around four key components: 1) business outreach; 2) policy development and technical assistance; 3) community outreach and government relations; and 4) press and communications.

The Partnership helps businesses meet key challenges they face when creating welfare-to-work programmes. The key challenges are three-fold: first, the business must structure a hiring programme; second, the business must figure out where to hire work-ready welfare recipients; third, the business must learn how to successfully retain new welfare-to-work hires.

Generally, The Partnership also operates as an intermediary between the business community and those organisations (government, non-profit and for-profit) that prepare welfare recipients for work.

The Partnership operates in the following manner. Business outreach typically occurs across the country generally through secondary sources. The Partnership approaches businesses through existing associations (such as the Society of Human Resource Professionals, The Hotel and Motel Association, and the American Management Association, etc.); through local Chambers of Commerce, Private Industry Councils and other local business groups; by holding large events based in cities with especially high welfare populations; and through direct mail.

Once a business has pledged to hire and retain at least one welfare recipient, that business becomes a partner of The Partnership. Each business that becomes a partner has access to vast resources from how-to materials covering hiring and retention and tax credit hotlines, to how-to conferences, individual technical assistance structured to a particular business, a national database of service providers (those organisations that will connect businesses to work-ready welfare recipients) and other tools.

It is important to note that few if any businesses are engaged in the welfare-to-work movement for benevolent reasons. Business leaders have been clear that their involvement rests first on bottom line principles and only second as a community service.

The Welfare-to-Work Partnership's results

At the launch of The Partnership, 105 businesses, including Sprint, UPS, United Airlines, Burger King, and Monsanto, had pledged to hire welfare recipients without displacing existing workers. Since May 1996, over 6,500 businesses of all sizes and all industries and represented in every state in the country have joined the ranks of The Partnership, not only hiring and retaining welfare recipients, but working with other businesses to encourage them to hire and retain. To date, those 6,500 businesses have been responsible for hiring over 135,000 welfare recipients. The key to The Partnership's success has been understanding the needs of the private sector and responding to those needs.

Consider the following statistics compiled by an independent survey organisation outlining the business community experience with hiring (Wirthlin Worldwide, 1998):

- 79% (eight out of 10) of welfare recipients hired by Partnership businesses are seen as good, productive employees;

- 76% of Partnership businesses are hiring welfare recipients in full-time positions;

- 80% of Partnership companies are hiring welfare recipients for hourly wage positions at an average pay rate of US$7.20 an hour;

- 19% of member companies are hiring welfare recipients for salaried positions with an average starting annual salary of US$17,000;

- Positions offered to welfare recipients by Partner businesses are most likely to be general labour, clerical and service jobs;

- Roughly 31% of welfare recipients hired over the past year by Partnership companies have been promoted (compared to a 20% promotion rate for entry-level hires by non-Partnership businesses);

- 73% of partnership businesses provide full health care benefits; and

- 69% of Partnership businesses provide mentoring services.

The challenges still remaining for The Partnership and Partnership businesses are around providing childcare and transportation and improving job retention rates.

- Only 12% of Partnership businesses provide help with childcare;

- 17% of Partnership businesses provide help with transportation; and

- 53% of Partnership businesses claim that welfare hires show the same (39%) or higher (14%) retention rates when compared to employees hired through standard procedures.

227

The Welfare-to-Work Partnership model, while discussed just briefly in this chapter, can easily be emulated in any developed country. Whether as an independent non-profit or an arm of the government, an effort to organise the business community around common hiring goals is essential to a successful welfare-to-work effort.

Welfare-to-work: a smart solution for business

Finding workers to sustain a company's operations is one of the most crucial concerns of business owners and managers across the United States. The large pool of workers within the welfare system can be recruited and trained to fill many available entry-level jobs, as well as positions currently being created. Visible successes have been achieved by companies as diverse as United Airlines, Salomon Smith Barney, WalMart and Sprint.

Today, companies of all sizes, in all industries, and all parts of the country are becoming involved in the effort to hire people off public assistance. At the Welfare-to-Work Partnership, over 6,500 businesses have committed to hire and retain welfare recipients. These 6,500 companies are as small as two employees and as large as 300,000. Further they span very state in the country and cover all industries.

As numerous examples have shown us, employers can leverage real social policy changes to maximise potential for their company. This can be a positive net effect on the bottom line. It just takes a modest level of discovery, planning, and action. Government and non-profit organisations approaching businesses to engage them in welfare-to-work should follow several steps following to help a business ensure success.

Businesses getting started

Whether a company chooses to create an informal or formal programme, experience shows that success hinges on each company doing the following.

1. Find or assign a company champion;
2. Assess the company's internal situation;
3. Review the hiring models;
4. Understand the welfare population;
5. Develop a strategic plan for hiring.

Step One: Find or assign a company champion

This step is perhaps the easiest to explain but one of the toughest to implement. If a company is interested in recruiting employees from the welfare rolls, that company must choose to commit resources to hiring. The best way to ensure company commitment is through a 'champion.'

A champion is generally a company's high level decision-maker who can build support for a project at the top levels of that company, while organising those at other levels to carry out the project. In smaller companies, the champion may be the owner or another senior leader.

> 'The key to running a programme like this is to have complete support right from the top. If it is understood from the top down how critical the programme is, then it can be turned over to the employment department and the rest of the company to implement.'
>
> *Scott Gilday, United Airlines*
>
> 'We make every effort to help our managers understand through conferences and newsletter the potential that welfare-to-work offers. We want all of our store associates to be committed to the programme and believe that this has been a key to the programme's success.'
>
> *Pete Pedersen, TJX*

Step Two: Assess the company's internal situation

Each company will realistically assess its opportunities to integrate welfare recipients into its workforce and its ability to support and motivate these new employees.

Before hiring, a company will conduct an evaluation of its existing resources, labour needs, personnel practices, company culture, and level of commitment to creating and maintaining these hiring practices. An evaluation of these components will allow a company to decide how many people to hire, how to hire them, what services to offer, and whether or not outside services will bolster the employees' success. In other words, an honest evaluation will yield good decision-making.

For instance, if a company does not have established access to support systems such as childcare, health care, or employee counselling, a company might want to consider forming a partnership with a community-based non-profit organisation that would be willing to provide free-of-charge information and services to new employees.

Step Three: Review the hiring models

There are various ways to tap into welfare recipients as potential employees, and many methods to integrate those employees into the workforce. Further, public dollars indirectly or directly offset a portion of training and hiring costs in many cases. While no one company's welfare-to-work programme is exactly the same, there are three general hiring models businesses typically follow. They might:

- Build an in-house programme;

- Contract with an intermediary;

- Hire directly from the public sector.

Build an in-house hiring model:

Many businesses choose to build an in-house programme, doing everything themselves from recruiting and training to job placement and retention. Marriott Hotels offers a prime example of a company that has built an in-house programme from scratch, recruiting 'rough', that is untrained, welfare recipients directly from government programmes and providing those recipients everything from basic job readiness (work a Community Based Organisation or government agency often undertakes) to specific skills training and ready support services.

Contract with a Community-Based Organisation (CBO) or other similar entity:

Some businesses choose to work though a Community-Based Organisation – a private or public entity that acts as the broker between the public welfare system and the employer. CBOs recruit, train, and place recipients with businesses, and follow-up to make sure that job placements are successful. Small companies, in particular, find CBOs offer easy access to work-ready welfare recipients. In addition to CBOs, a host of other similar organisations might also reach out to businesses for the same purpose: for-profit companies such as America Works and temporary staffing organisations often provide similar services to business.

Some will charge a company for this service, while others may contract with the state and therefore offer training and placement free of charge. CBOs and similar organisations negate the need for an in-house programme.

It is also important to note that temporary service staffing organisations, such as Manpower, Kelly Services, Norrell Services, and Adecco Employment Services, are partnering with government offices and CBOs to train and place welfare recipients in temporary positions. Such temporary positions offer welfare recipients valuable work experience that can lead to the next and better job.

Hire Directly From the Public Sector:

Other companies choose to work directly with the public job training or welfare systems, creating public-private partnerships that allow the business and the public entity to jointly move welfare recipients into jobs. For example, some companies may go directly to the JTPA's private industry councils (PICs), Workforce Development Boards, Job Corps Centres, One Stop Career Centres, or other publicly run organisations to find work-ready welfare recipients.

Some companies might also go directly to local social service offices for recruitment referrals. Many states have adopted a wage-subsidy programme that gives a company the option to turn a welfare recipient's Temporary Assistance for Needy Families (TANF) and food stamp benefit into a temporary wage. In many cases, the company temporarily hires the welfare recipient and simply invoices the state for the wage subsidy.

Step Four: Understand the welfare population

Welfare recipients have diverse backgrounds. Some are ready to work while others may need short-term training, and still others, intensified crisis management or drug rehabilitation. *However, from an employer's viewpoint, only one category of welfare recipients is relevant – those who are ready to work.* An employer should expect that any welfare recipient sent to interview for a job be of the same quality as any other potential recruit who might come through the door.

A variety of public and private sector organisations receive funding to prepare welfare recipients for work. Those organisations work on a regular basis with welfare recipients of all backgrounds. Rather than lowering their own quality standards, an employer should demand prepared workers and interact with public and private sector service providers as much as possible to ensure that quality.

Businesses can work with CBOs and public organisations to better target training and service strategies. Public-Private partnerships are among the best methods for employers to ensure that they have access to a labour pool trained to the necessary specifications.

Step Five: Develop a strategic plan for hiring

Developing a strategic plan gives a company an excellent opportunity to evaluate all options and to offer internal and external stakeholders the option to craft plans to deliver results. There are at least four major activities associated with developing a quality plan as outlined below:

Delineate internal organisational expectations:

Spell out all of the desired outcomes and sequences of activity.

Select a model:

After assessing the company's resources, labour needs, internal personnel practices, company culture, and strength of commitment, arrive at a conscious 'make-or-buy' decision, meaning choose to:

– Create an in-house programme.

– Directly contract it out to a private for-profit or non-profit intermediary.

– Work with the public system to hire directly.

Establish and identify support services for employees:

Set forth objectives, specifications, and arrangements for support service requirements including transportation, childcare, health care, mentoring, and counselling.

Delineate external expectations and performance measures for partners:

Communicate frequently with the intermediary and/or public system responsible for providing work-ready beneficiaries to the company, and don't be afraid to expect and demand quality work from any vendor.

Whether a company chooses to hire one or one thousand welfare recipients, success has proved difficult without following the steps outlined above.

The next step - retaining new workers

Many companies involved in welfare-to-work have had success not only hiring, but especially in retaining welfare-to-work hires. While every company programme is different in its approach, there are several universal components that drive a company's retention rates. Companies with successful job retention usually:

- Enter into public/private partnerships with either a government agency, community-based organisation, or for-profit entity and set high expectations for those partnerships;

- Provide training, either in conjunction with an outside organisation or as an in-house training programme;

- Offer varied benefits, particularly those that address obstacles to retaining a job, including childcare subsidies or referrals, transportation, health care, and an employee hotline or employee assistance programme;

- Provide employees with career paths; and,

- Maintain high standards.

Public-Private partnerships

Most companies with successful retention rates cite strong partnerships with a service provider or government agency as the key to success. Whether small or large, companies have realised that to succeed at welfare-to-work, or with any entry-level or low-income employee, it is valuable to utilise all available resources, including those in the surrounding community. A service provider is typically a public, private non-profit or for-profit organisation that works with the unemployed or disadvantaged population to prepare them for work and place them in jobs.

Results are best when a service provider offers business all or most of the following services:

- Employer-centred training, that is, training based on needs expressed by employers.

- Job-readiness training, including skills refreshment, punctuality, dress, interviewing skills, attitudinal training, supervisor-supervisee relationships, life skills, and problem-solving including budgeting and conflict resolution.

- Job placement into unsubsidised, private sector work. (A business should also ask what percentage of people sent to interviews are actually hired.)

- Job retention services including direct or indirect contact with childcare, health care, transportation, counselling, and mentoring services over a period of at least six months to help a recipient keep a job once she is working.

- Strong and continuing relationships with employers in their surrounding communities.

- Paid via performance-based contracts or willing to be paid based on performance.

- Required to track success through the number of job placements and retention in those jobs. (A common measure of success can be job placement and job retention, but customer satisfaction – that of the welfare recipients and the business -- is also a good measure of success.)

Most good service providers will have established relationships with local employers. Most important, businesses should use intermediaries or service providers in the same way they would use any vendor: set high standards for quality and enforce them.

Many businesses develop long term relationships with several service providers, thereby ensuring a constant source of work-ready employees. Following are a few employer comments about service providers:

'Once I find what seems like a good provider, I ask [that provider] to learn Borg's standards and send me people that meet [those standards] and want to work.'

Christine Hirschl-Thayer, Borg-Warner Protective Services

'We work with a number of small service providers that help us identify potential employees.... I have my favourites. They are organisations that are willing to go the extra mile. They will work with our staff as well as their clients, and they help us understand the type of problems that former welfare recipients face'.

Tine Hanson-Turton, Rehab Options

'How the programme takes shape really depends on the type of relationship [the company has] forged with community-based organisations. When we started, we hoped to form relationships with one community-based organisation in each location. Now we realise that working with two or three quality organisations can serve our needs and the needs of our workers better.'

Joe Hammill, Xerox

Training: in-house or out

Companies with successful programmes typically provide training to welfare-to-work employees. Sometimes the welfare-to-work training comes before a formal offer of employment and sometimes after. The type of training also varies, ranging from basic job readiness to in-depth skills training based on company need. Some companies create training programmes themselves. Others partner with a community-based organisation or government office to create a training programme, thereby splitting the work and cost. As companies see job retention rates soar after creating welfare-to-work training programmes, many expand their training programmes to cover employees company-wide.

Why is training important? Welfare recipients want to work, but some lack the formal knowledge of the labour market or the basic skills necessary to perform on the job. Soft skills training—how to dress for the office, the importance of punctuality, managing supervisor/supervisee relationships, and the like—many times determine success on the job. Once given the opportunity, companies report that welfare recipients have little difficulty quickly learning the necessary skills to perform in the today's labour market. Likewise, receiving specific skills training increases the likelihood of success for any new employee. Several companies utilise tax credits to help offset the cost of training programmes.

Following are examples of various training programmes:

- **Borg-Warner Security Services** receives referrals from service providers then provides 26 weeks of industry-specific training plus an additional 24 hours of training needed to qualify new employees for a state licence.

- **Marriott International Hotels** created an in-house training programme, splitting the cost with Private Industry Councils and local community-based organisations such as Jewish Vocational Services, Goodwill and Job Corp. The training programme provides 60 hours of classroom training and 120 hours of occupational skills training.

- **Salomon-Smith Barney Financial Services** partnered with Wildcat Service Corporation to create a tailored training programme providing 16 weeks of skills training combined with on-the-job experience followed by a 16-week paid internship.

- **Sprint Telecommunications** partnered with the Full Employment Council, an organisation that screens recipients, and the Metropolitan Community College to provide six weeks of technical and life skills training. Sprint then provides its standard two-week customised technical training.

The type and length of training varies for each company. However the results are the same: improved employee retention and bottom line savings.

Benefits: The basics plus

As a cost saving measure, companies often shy away from offering new or entry-level employees benefits. However, with tight labour markets making it tougher to find and keep good employees, businesses are learning that providing benefits makes good bottom line sense. Companies with especially strong job retention figures are themselves examples of how the welfare-to-work investment is worth making. Moreover, many of these companies are offering non-traditional benefits ranging from childcare referral services and van pools to housing assistance for low-income employees purchasing their first homes.

This might seem expensive at first glance, but these benefits lead to higher employee retention and ultimately lower costs. Small businesses with less resources to invest in wide ranging benefit packages are finding creative ways to the road to retention.

Following are examples of companies providing not only health care and other basic benefits but also special programmes to enhance employee retention. In the end, managers are realising that they are improving their bottom line through welfare-to-work.

- **CVS Pharmacies** offers financial assistance for first home buyers and provides generous benefit packages including health and dental coverage, a 401(k) plan, and a 20 percent discount on all items in the store to all employees.

- **Hygienic Service Systems**, a small business, provides its employees access to 'The Ride', a private van line that picks up employees and drops them off at work. The company also contracts with an outside company to run its Employee Assistance Hotline. Finally, the company helps its employees access the Earned-Income Tax Credit (EITC), a tax rebate available to low-income workers with children.

- **Rehab Options**, a small business, utilises flex-time to allow employees with childcare or transportation issues to complete work on weekends or off hours if necessary.

- **United Airlines** has developed an in-house mentoring programme matching anyone from a senior vice president to a peer to new employees for 60 days. The mentoring programme helps welfare-to-work employees acclimate to their new jobs and address any issues that may arise. United also offers an Employee Assistance Programme and provides employees with good benefits. Finally, United worked with the Illinois Department of Human Services and the Regional Transit Authority to establish a bus route to service one of its harder to reach facilities.

Providing career paths

Not every company is able to offer career advancement or promotions from within because of the nature of a company's business. Some companies' jobs are primarily entry-level. Other companies are too small to promote from within. However, all companies with good retention rates believe that their welfare-to-work employees are receiving valuable work experience to prepare them for future jobs. Further, many of the companies actively promote former welfare recipients into positions with increased responsibility and pay.

Following are several examples of companies promoting welfare recipients:

- **Marriott International Hotels** encourages its trainees to view its Pathways programme as the start to a career with Marriott. Many Marriott employees who began as dishwashers, security guards, desk clerks, and other entry-level jobs have moved into management positions.

- **United Parcel Services (UPS)** has a history of promoting from within. Almost everyone in the company from the president on down began working for UPS as a part-time employee. UPS is proud to offer welfare recipients and other entry-level employees the opportunity to move up, oftentimes by helping employees further their education.

- **Xerox** encourages its welfare-to-work employees to develop new skills that will allow them to advance through the company and within the industry. Currently, the company is developing a curriculum with a local community-based college to teach employees advanced skills that can lead to a career in the document business.

Maintaining high standards

Perhaps the most pressing fear any company faces when considering whether or not to hire welfare recipients is that it will have to lower its hiring standards. Companies fear that welfare-to-work employees will perform poorly or will require different treatment than other entry-level hires. Companies with high retention rates say just the opposite. In fact, one key to success cited by many companies is maintaining and enforcing high performance standards.

Those running welfare-to-work programmes agree that performance standards should never be lowered for anyone. Employees are expected to rise to established standards. Companies with good retention rates not only insist that all employees, regardless of background, meet the same standards, but discovered that welfare-to-work employees often *surpass* their standards.

238

Following are a few comments about maintaining a quality workforce with welfare-to-work hires:

> 'We encourage companies to continue their quality hiring standards when employing people off of welfare. Xerox has long embraced quality as a basic principle. With this foundation, our commitment to welfare-to-work is grounded in the belief and confidence that our placements will meet and exceed high standards and expectations. We have clear examples of people from welfare who are experiencing success in their new careers and delivering value to our new customers.'

> *Joe Hammill, Xerox*

> 'I have kept the same high expectations I have for the rest of my staff. We have simply found people that want to succeed'.

> *Rick Kalina, Kirkwood Insurance Service Company*

> 'It has not been necessary to change our training at all [since hiring welfare recipients]. You get the same individuals from the welfare office as you get anywhere else.'

> *Jim Myrick, Manhattan Health Care*

A special note on small businesses

For many small businesses, starting a welfare-to-work programme seems daunting - it will take up too much time, cost too much money, or undermine employee morale. However, small business has had just the opposite experience.

Small businesses - even those with as few as five employees - have successful welfare-to-work programmes, boasting high retention rates and great satisfaction with those hired from welfare. None suggest that time or cost constraints hindered their welfare-to-work programmes.

For the most part, small businesses are successful for the same reasons large businesses are: A strong company commitment to becoming involved; a focus on public-private partnerships to hire and train employees; the creativity and vision to provide the necessary benefits; and a commitment to maintain high standards. A small business's programme may be less formal, but the key components are all the same. Small and large businesses adhering to these programme standards find higher retention leads to significant savings due to reduced employee turnover.

The one distinguishing factor noted by small business leaders is that everyone gives welfare-to-work hires personal, one-on-one attention. Each small business leader we have worked with stresses that 'personalised attention' and 'one-on-one relationships' are crucial elements to success. In fact, small companies have a clear advantage over large companies in this regard. Large companies struggle to offer the sort of personal attention more natural to small businesses. United Airlines and Giant Foods created mentoring programmes for employees to provide one-on-one attention to employees. Other large companies have done the same.

Following are comments from several small businesses that cite personal attention as a key to success.

> 'I try to stress that my door is always open. Personal attention is essential. I cannot stress that enough.'

> *Gwen Clemens, Hygienic Service Systems*

> 'We made it clear form the beginning that we were there to help them solve the problems they would encounter....Everyone became involved in helping them learn their jobs.'

> *Rick Kalina, Kirkwood Insurance Service Company*

Government incentives to encourage employers to hire welfare recipients

While American businesses have risen to meet the challenge of welfare-to-work and have done so in a way that helps their bottom line, business has succeeded with some help from government programmes.

Federal, state, and local governments have long used tax incentives to encourage specific business practices. More recently, new tax breaks have been created to entice businesses to operate in certain urban areas in need of revitalisation, and to encourage business to reduce pollution and other unwanted activities. Welfare reform is no exception: it comes with its own set of useful incentives for business.

Five key incentives are offered to businesses by the federal government to encourage them to hire welfare recipients: the Work Opportunity Tax Credit (WOTC); the Welfare-to-Work Tax Credit; the work supplementation programme offered under the new welfare law; On The Job Training (OJT) offered through the Federal Job Training and Partnership Act, and specific tax credits for hiring in federally designated Empowerment Zones and Enterprise Communities. In addition, every state offers its own tax incentives. Some companies find these incentives helpful in offsetting the initial costs associated with hiring.

The Work Opportunity Tax Credit (WOTC) and the Welfare-to-Work Tax Credit

Two federal income tax credits – the Work Opportunity Tax Credit (WOTC) and the Welfare-to-Work Tax Credit - have been created to encourage businesses to hire job seekers moving from welfare to work, and to encourage the hiring of other targeted groups that may experience barriers to employment. The WOTC is available to businesses that hire disadvantaged people from a variety of categories including welfare recipients. The maximum WOTC employer credit is US$2,400. The Welfare-to-Work Tax Credit is designed specifically for businesses that hire the harder to place welfare recipients (those recipients with more barriers to employment). The maximum Welfare-to-Work Tax Credit is US$8,500 if an employee is retained two years.

Work Supplementation

The new federal law gives states the option to create a work supplementation programme (also called wage subsidy and grant diversion). Work Supplementation allows an employer to receive a welfare recipient's cash benefits as a subsidy for wages to be paid to the welfare recipient for temporary work (six months to one year) performed. The employer by law is required to pay at least the minimum wage to any welfare recipient hired in a temporary position, so must add in additional funds to the welfare benefit necessary to bring the wage up to the minimum. For example:

Assume that a welfare recipient receives US$250 per month in TANF benefits and another US$350 a month in food stamps, bringing the available monthly subsidy to US$600. If that employee is working in a minimum wage position for 40 hours a week (160 hours a month), the employer would receive US$3.75 an hour from the state toward the employee's wage. The employer would make up the difference between the subsidy and the minimum wage

241

It is important to note that welfare recipients' benefits vary by state, therefore the available wage subsidy will vary by state.

On The Job Training (OJT)

On-the-Job Training (OJT) is a strategy that many states use to offset the cost of training people. Similar to Work Supplementation, employers receive a payment to offset part of the wages paid to welfare recipients for a limited period. However, while work supplementation is funded through welfare benefits that would have otherwise gone to a welfare recipient, OJT subsidies are paid through state labour department programme funds. OJT is used extensively in the public employment and training system under JTPA to increase participants' access to permanent employment. JTPA rules limit OJT subsidies to 50 percent of wages for up to six months and preclude using OJT for youth below age 22.

Empowerment Zones and Enterprise Communities

Empowerment Zones and Enterprise Communities (EZ/EC) are Clinton Administration initiatives designed to promote economic growth and physical revitalisation of urban and rural communities plagued by chronic poverty and unemployment. Businesses in EZ/EC communities are entitled to targeted tax incentives designed to foster job creation, stimulate investment, and attract new business development. For example, using the Wage Tax Credit employers can access tax credits equal to 20 percent of the first US$15,000 of wages or training expenses paid to qualified Empowerment Zone residents. Residence in an EZ/EC also qualifies certain new hires for the Work Opportunity Tax Credit.

The $3 billion Welfare-to-Work Grants Programme

The Balanced Budget Act, signed by President Clinton in August 1997, authorised the U.S. Department of Labor to provide US$3 billion in grants to states and local communities to create additional job opportunities for *hard-to-serve* recipients moving from welfare to work. The programme provides two types of grants: *formula* grants to the states and *competitive* grants to organisations in local communities. US$1.5 billion in grants will be awarded in fiscal year 1998 and US$1.5 billion in fiscal year 1999.

Twenty-five percent of the US$3 billion Welfare-to-Work Grant programme has been allocated by competitive grants to private industry councils, local governments, and private entities including community-based agencies, community development corporations, faith-based organisations, and colleges and universities, and can be in partnership with private sector businesses. The private entities must apply for the competitive grant in conjunction with the private industry council or local government. This competitive grant does not require a match. The competitive grants will give the private sector an opportunity to develop partnerships in the community with the private industry council or local government and other private entities to set up training programmes, support service programmes, or other programmes for the purpose of moving.

The Welfare-to-Work Grants must be used to move hard-to-place recipients into unsubsidised employment by providing job placement services, transitional employment, and job retention efforts.

State-Based Incentives

In addition to federal tax incentives, many states have also passed their own state-based tax incentive for employers and for employees. Examples of state incentives include tax credits to employers for hiring welfare recipients as well as state-based employee Earned-Income Tax Credits called EICs, and childcare tax credits.

Conclusion

For too long in the United States, those receiving welfare had been trapped in a system of dependence. Government programmes provided income maintenance indefinitely while offering little or no opportunities for unsubsidised employment. When President Clinton signed the landmark 1996 welfare reform legislation, he radically altered 60 years of social policy by mandating work in exchange for benefits and providing opportunities for all on welfare to enter the mainstream economy.

Today, two years since the legislation was passed, 1.5 million families have successfully exited the welfare rolls. Such numbers would not have been possible without the express involvement of the country's business community. However, to ensure the best results from business, an organised effort of the business community is essential. Further, government incentives and subsidies provide the additional funding to encourage companies to participate and to bolster internal training and job retention services.

Addendum: Business Case Histories

Marriott International

Janet Tully, the director of community employment and training for Marriott International, is adamant about two things regarding Marriott's welfare-to-work programme. First, operating the programme, called Pathways to Independence, is a great deal of work. Second, all of the effort is worth it. Not only has Marriott hired more than 1,000 dedicated and reliable employees since implementing Pathways, but it has retained 70 percent of its welfare-to-work hires after one year. That figure easily exceeds the 52 percent retention rate for other entry-level, non-welfare employees.

The welfare-to-work programme

Such impressive retention figures are the result of Marriott's commitment to tap a new source of workers. The Pathways training programme is in operation in about a dozen Marriott locations around the country. It lasts six weeks and normally trains between 12 and 18 participants. The programme combines a total of 60 hours of classroom training and 120 hours of occupational skills training. Marriott splits the cost of the training programme with Private Industry Councils (PICs) and with independent community-based organisations like Jewish Vocational Services, Goodwill and Job Corps. Marriott also accesses the Work Opportunity Tax Credit to help offset the cost of Pathways. Once on the job, former welfare recipients receive a full benefits package including health and dental insurance.

Keys to Success

The Pathways programme is designed to establish a relationship between the trainees and the company during the training. Marriott managers and supervisors conduct classes and skills training. Upon successful completion of the programme, participants are guaranteed job offers with Marriott or with another employer in the hospitality industry. From the beginning, participants are aware that they are being trained by a potential employer. Likewise, managers and supervisors are aware that they are training potential employees. Therefore, both the trainees and the company become invested in making the programme work.

Human resources professionals are assigned to supervise the programme at various locations. In addition, they serve as job counsellors during the transition into employment. 'When something goes wrong or there is a discipline issue and there always will be - a trained and experience job counsellor handles it,' says Tully. 'I wish we could offer this to all of our employees.'

Tully has been frustrated in the past by social service agencies that seem to cut off their clients as soon as they find work. 'There are still issues that need to be addressed after the person has found a job,' explains Tully. 'As an employer, we cannot get too involved in the personal lives of our employees.' Marriott succeeds in utilising the supportive services of local community-based organisations in their area to help welfare-to-work employees address issues like transportation and childcare. As part of the classroom training, participants are taught how to access the Earned Income Tax Credit and other available subsidies that can help an employee increase take-home pay and defer the cost of childcare and transportation. In addition, Marriott offers an associate resources line. Employees can speak to trained professionals about personal issues that could affect retention and job performance. For those employees who need an extra level of assistance, an Employee Assistance Programme allows them to access professional face-to-face counselling free of charge.

Marriott encourages its trainees to view Pathways as the start of a career with Marriott. Tully describes how the manager of the World Trade Centre Marriott, speaking to a group of trainees, explained how he had begun working for Marriott as a security guard. Another executive explained that he had begun as a dishwasher. 'Examples of people climbing our corporate ladder are all around,' says Tully. 'It makes our welfare-to-work employees realise that they can really get somewhere.'

In one Pathways location in New York, all 13 trainees who graduated the programme are still employed. Tully explains, 'It just goes to show you that just about any problem a former welfare recipient may have is solvable, but they need to know that the company is right there beside them. We have been able to get employees who hit the ground running. We knew that they would be well trained. That they have been so loyal is something we did not really expect. It really has been good for our business.'

Marriott's experience with Pathways has always been grounded in good business sense. 'Let's be honest,' says Tully. 'All the community involvement and personal gratification is great, but it wouldn't be good enough if it wasn't good for our bottom line.' Marriott's ability to retain its welfare-to-work employees has helped to insure that its bottom line has indeed been served.

Contact Person: Janet Tully, Tel. No: (301) 380-6896

Rehab Options

Rehab Options, located just outside of Philadelphia, is a growing provider of rehabilitation services, home healthcare and integrated health services to urban seniors. With only 50 employees, Rehab Options does not have the same resources as larger companies to invest in a successful welfare-to-work programme. However, according to Vice President of programme development Tine Hansen-Turton, it is Rehab Options' small size that gives it an inherent advantage in retaining its welfare-to-work employees. 'We might not have the most formalised welfare-to-work programme, but we provide the personal attention that makes the difference,' Says Hansen-Turton. Rehab does not formally track retention for its entire workforce, but for welfare-to-work hires, retention has been hard to ignore. Hansen-Turton is proud to report that Rehab's retention rate for former welfare recipients is a perfect 100 percent. Rehab Option has hired five welfare recipients in the past 18 months.

The welfare-to-work programme

Rehab Options employs welfare recipients in several positions including administrative, clerical and home health aide positions. Rehab offers a complete benefits package to all employees. Potential employees are identified through providers throughout Philadelphia. If a client has been selected to be a home health aide candidate, a comprehensive course is administered by a representative from Rehab Options. Clients must pass the course and complete mandatory hours of instruction and clinical expertise in order to get a certificate qualifying them as home health aides.

Once clients have been hired, they receive an evaluation during the first three months assessing their attitude, performance, appearance, competency and nursing care skills. Once they have passed a three-month probationary period, they receive a yearly performance evaluation. During the year, home health aides are supervised bi-weekly by registered nurses and therapists.

Prior to hiring any residents coming off welfare for any administrative or clerical jobs, clients must take a test to determine their skill levels and meet competency standards measured by regular supervisor evaluations.

Keys to success

While Hansen-Turton places a premium on forming supportive personal relationships with the former welfare recipients in her company, she also stresses the importance of searching out the resources available in the community. 'It is a real benefit knowing what support services are available in your area. We work with a number of small service providers that help us identify potential employees,' she explains. While there are many organisations out there working with welfare recipients, a company should search around for the organisation that meets its needs. 'I have my favourites,' says Hansen-Turton. 'They are the organisations that are willing to go the extra mile. They will work with our staff as well as their clients, and they help us to understand the type of problems that former welfare recipients face.'

Rehab Options allows employees to utilise flex-time so work can be completed on weekends and off-hours if the need arises. Flexible scheduling allows workers to develop networks of family and friends to help provide for childcare and transportation needs, according to Hansen-Turton.

While flexibility is crucial, discipline is just as important. Hansen-Turton has worked with welfare recipients for years. 'You will be tested,' she says, 'so you have to be firm about what the company will and will not accept. By making your expectations clear, you allow the worker to adapt to the demands of the workplace. By being flexible when problems arise, you demonstrate to the worker that they can overcome obstacles and that their employer is there to help.'

'There are always going to be personal problems,' adds Hansen-Turton. 'When an employee comes to you with a problem, you need to be able to sit down and talk it out with them.'

Hansen-Turton credits Rehab-Options' understanding staff with the success of their welfare-to-work programme. 'People here have made an effort to understand what it takes to get off of welfare,' says Hansen-Turton. 'From the owner of the company on down, our employees have developed one-on-one relationships that have been beneficial to everyone involved.'

Contact Person: Tine Hansen-Turton, Tel. No: (610) 617-775

Salomon Smith Barney

Entry-level jobs with salaries of US$24,000 a year may seem beyond the reach of welfare recipients, however, Salomon Smith Barney, a financial services company with more than 35,000 employees, is providing just those types of opportunities to welfare recipients in New York City. Since Salomon Smith Barney's programme started two years ago, 48 of the 52 welfare recipients hired by the company are still employed. The retention rate of 92 percent over two years has allowed Salomon Smith Barney to significantly reduce recruitment and hiring costs and to realise significant savings on expenditures for temporary help. The company normally expects 19 percent turnover for non-welfare hires in similar positions.

The welfare-to-work programme

Salomon Smith Barney works with Wildcat Service Corporation, a New York City service provider to help identify and train welfare recipients for positions with the company. Wildcat trainees participate in a 16-week work experience programme combining on-the-job experience with skills training tailored to Salomon Smith Barney's current needs. The training includes life skills, classes in business English, math and various software applications. Following the work experience, trainees begin a 16-week paid internship with Salomon Smith Barney. Upon completion of the internship, the company hires more than 90 percent of the interns. On the first official day of employment, former welfare recipients are eligible for benefits including medical, dental, and vision coverage, stock options and a retirement plan.

Wildcat helps its trainees develop skills in crisis management, according to Jeff Jablow, vice president of planning for Wildcat. 'Every worker is faced with difficulties, whether they are leaving welfare or not. We try and help people understand that they can have problems and work at the same time,' he explains. Wildcat encourages its trainees to build networks of family, friends and other resources to help when the car breaks down, the baby-sitter is sick or other problems arise.

Keys to success

Working with Wildcat is the main reason for the success at Salomon Smith Barney, according to Senior Vice President Barbara Silvan, who oversees the programme for Salomon Smith Barney. 'If these women walked in the door and left their resumes, we wouldn't even consider hiring them. But we know that Wildcat's people have been trained in the skills that we need,' says Silvan, who added that as a result of the extensive training by Wildcat, Salomon Smith Barney simply trains former welfare recipients as they would any other worker. 'We mainstream these employees immediately. Their confidence is low when they start, and we have found that treating them just like everyone else is the best way to build their self-esteem,' says Silvan.

Housing and childcare are the biggest retention obstacles for low-income workers in New York City, according to Silvan. The company's relationship with Wildcat has helped minimise these concerns, however. 'By the time they come to work for us, Wildcat has already helped them to resolve childcare and housing issues. I never have to deal with any of that,' says Silvan. Salomon Smith Barney provides an on-site emergency childcare facility that all employees can use if there is a problem with their primary provider. Additionally, Wildcat provides continuing follow-up with both the employee and the supervisor to help address workplace problems. 'We want to solve problems before they become problems,' says Jablow.

Silvan makes sure she explains to her supervisors why hiring a Wildcat trainee is a good idea. 'When we place a person with a supervisor who is new to the programme, I take 15 minutes to explain things,' says Silvan. 'I start by saying that they probably wouldn't hire this person if they saw a resume. Then I explain that the employee will have to miss some time to meet with case workers. Finally, I tell them all the reasons why I am sure this person will work out. Once they understand the success we have had with these employees, they are eager to help out.'

Silvan distributes performance appraisals to supervisors three times during the internship period. 'These workers consistently receive glowing reviews,' she says. When problems arise, Silvan works with the supervisor to help the employee. Recently a supervisor commented that a new employee was learning her responsibilities rather slowly. Silvan suggested a transfer to a department that is more process-oriented. The supervisor resisted, however, seeing that the worker had potential. She has since developed into a valuable member of the department.

> 'When we started this programme, I had no expectations,' says Silvan. 'Since then I have learned that there are no downsides to hiring welfare recipients. Not only have we benefited from the efforts of 48 dedicated employees, we can help members of the community earn a living and provide for their children. The programme has become a source of great pride for Salomon Smith Barney as well. We can act as role models to other financial services companies and encourage them to follow our lead.'

Contact Person: Barbara Silvan, Tel. No: (212) 816-2524

United Airlines

United Airlines is the largest majority employee-owned corporation in the world, with more than 92,000 employees. Of those employees, 550 are former welfare recipients. Since March 1997, when United's welfare-to-work programme began, United has retained 69 percent of its welfare-to-work employees. That retention rate is more than double that of all non-welfare hires. A key component to high retention is an innovative mentoring programme. In fact, the mentoring aspect is so successful that it was incorporated into United's training curriculum for all employees.

The welfare-to-work programme

United works with service providers to recruit welfare recipients to fill job openings. It encourages all agencies to customise training to match the skills needed at particular United locations. Agencies screen trainees and select ones whose skills best match United's needs. United provides on-the-job training to prepare former welfare recipients for the demands of their new jobs. For example, new reservations and customer service employees participate in a six-week training programme. Georgina Heard, manager of executive development and succession and an architect of United's welfare-to-work programme, stresses the importance of finding and working with quality service providers. 'The organisation needs to know the kind of people we are looking for,' says Heard who encourages agency representatives to shadow United employees on the job so that they become familiar with the positions and the skills necessary for success. She adds, 'They can help us select the right people without placing an additional burden on our staff.'

Once on the job, former welfare recipients are offered a full range of benefits including health and dental insurance and a retirement plan. United's mentoring programme is an additional benefit. Former welfare recipients are assigned a mentor for the next 60 days. Mentors range from senior vice presidents to peers. All mentors are volunteers and are expected to perform mentoring activities on their own time. Mentors participate in a brief training session to learn about their role, how to use the employee assistance programme, a hotline employees can access to address serious personal problems, and how to refer new employees to the benefits service centre. Mentors are also instructed on building a rapport with their 'mentee.' A 'location champion' is assigned to oversee the programme and assist both mentors and employees.

After years of struggling with low retention in entry-level positions, United seems to have found a solution that works. 'We have spent a lot of time and money hiring consultants to analyse our jobs and our processes,' says Heard. 'We finally realised that the bottom line is making people feel like they aren't lost.' In response, United developed a welfare-to-work programme containing a system for peer mentoring.

United's mentoring programme was created by a cross-functional design team consisting of union representatives, international employees, senior-level executives and former welfare recipients. Their goal was to create a peer-mentor support system that would boost retention while not interfering with employee-supervisor relationships. The team decided that flexibility was the key to functionality. 'We didn't want a cookie-cutter approach. We wanted different locations to actually use the programme,' says Heard, adding that the design team limited the programme to 60 days so mentors would not have to commit long term. 'We hoped relationships would develop and continue after their official time was up, and in many cases they have.'

United was so pleased with the results that they instituted the programme for all new hires in 1998. 'Not only did we improve retention, but a survey of mentors showed that the mentors actually felt better about their jobs and the company,' says Heard. 'I wouldn't be surprised if there has been a jump in mentor productivity as a result of this programme.' The fears of the design team, especially securing volunteers, never materialised. 'Our retired employee association really wants to get involved,' says Heard, 'but we already have enough mentors.'

Even the incredible success of the mentoring programme does not address all of the challenges former welfare recipients face. Transportation is a concern for many United facilities located in suburban locations. In one facility, which handles ticket stock sorting and distribution, turnover has been a major problem, partly because of lack of public transportation. In response, United has worked closely with Senator Carol Moseley Braun (D-IL) and Congressman Danny Davis (D-IL) to help pass the Jobs Access Act, to provide funding to states and localities to solve similar transportation problems. United also worked with the Illinois Department of Human Services and the Regional Transit Authority to establish a bus route to service the industrial park housing the United facility. 'Not only did this help us get workers to the job, it helped all of the other companies in the industrial park as well,' says Heard. 'We even heard of a number of mentors helping new employees join informal company car pools.'

United is not done building innovations into their welfare-to-work efforts. It is currently exploring flexible scheduling to help alleviate public transportation limitations. And United continues to set its sights high. By the end of the year 2000, United plans to have hired 2,000 welfare recipients.

Contact Person: Georgina Heard, Tel. No: (847) 700-7289

United Parcel Service

United Parcel Service is the world's largest package distribution company. It serves more than 200 countries and territories and delivers more than 12 million packages a day. UPS employs more than 339,000 worldwide. UPS also has one of the nation's largest, longest-running and most successful welfare-to-work efforts. Last year, UPS hired 8,268 former welfare recipients and plans to build on its success in the future.

At UPS's Philadelphia Air Hub, for example, welfare-to-work hires maintain an 88 percent retention rate through the first six weeks of employment. UPS normally expects only 60 percent retention after the first six weeks of employment. In fact, the welfare-to-work programme is so successful, UPS expects it to be completed by all entry level workers. UPS has also developed innovative solutions to transportation problems that push retention rates as high as Philadelphia's in many other locations.

The welfare-to-work programme

The UPS site at the Philadelphia Air Hub implemented an innovative system to address transportation challenges. Located far from downtown Philadelphia and needing workers around the clock, the facility faced a serious labour shortage. Division Manager Rodney Carroll saw welfare-to-work as a solution to labour needs. Carroll brought special insight into the needs of people moving from welfare-to-work. Growing up in Philadelphia, Carroll's family received public assistance.

Upon completing the UPS programme, trainees are guaranteed jobs at UPS, and perhaps more importantly, eligible to join the union. Instead of using supervisors to do the training, welfare-to-work employees are instructed by employees performing the jobs. '[These training co-ordinators] took it as their personal responsibility to make sure that the participants were taught well,' says Carroll. Many of the training co-ordinators developed relationships with trainees, and when possible, helped with personal barriers to employment.

The extended training programme is an important part of UPS's success in retaining former welfare recipients. 'We knew that the people we were reaching would need extra training and more time to learn about what we demand,' says Carroll. 'So we extended our normal five-day training programme to six weeks. The longer time period allows us to be patient with the trainees and give them some leeway with attendance if they have personal issues that need to be resolved.'

While UPS developed an excellent pool of trained workers, it was becoming readily apparent that many of them would have difficulty getting to work. To meet this challenge, UPS worked with the New Jersey Transit Authority to set up a bus line to transport workers from nearby Camden, New Jersey to the Philadelphia airport. UPS even agreed to fund the bus line if it failed to provide enough riders. As it turned out, getting enough riders was never a problem. 'It worked tremendously,' says Carroll. 'We eventually had three buses up and running.' In many cases, drivers made special stops closer to the employees' homes in Camden's more dangerous neighbourhoods.

UPS also offers tuition reimbursement at its Philadelphia facility and arranges for teachers from area community colleges, as well from Villanova and Temple Universities, to conduct classes on-site at the airport. 'If people think they are in a dead-end job they are going to leave,' says Carroll. 'Although we start people out part-time, we offer them the opportunity to move up, either with us or by furthering their education. At the very least, we help people gain credibility in the job market that can be used as a stepping stone to help get them wherever they want to be.' All UPS employees start as part-time employees, but Carroll makes arrangements with other employers at the airport to combine jobs so trainees could work full-time hours. In addition, all employees receive full-time health benefits. Six months after the first training class graduated, three trainees had been promoted to supervisor, four had earned significant raises by learning new skills, and 12 had begun teaching others as training co-ordinators.

Recognising the accomplishments of welfare-to-work employees can be a valuable retention tool, according to Carroll. Three weeks into the first training programme, Carroll congratulated all of the trainees for their hard work. He encouraged them to start making a guest list for the graduation ceremony at the end of the programme. The ceremony gives the trainees an opportunity to share their achievement with family and friends. Carroll later learned that a number of participants considered dropping out of the programme before he told them about the ceremony. 'When they realised that they were half-way there and that the company was eager to celebrate their success, they stuck it out,' he says.

Although Carroll was motivated to start the programme more by a need for workers and a desire to serve the community, tax incentives became a bonus for UPS. UPS actively accesses the Work Opportunity Tax Credit (WOTC) to help underwrite the cost of training. Additionally, many UPS human resources staff are adept at aiding employees in accessing the Earned Income Tax Credit (EITC). 'We didn't start the programme thinking about tax credits, but our knowledge of them has evolved,' says Carroll. 'That knowledge now serves to help both the company and the employee.'

UPS utilises similar solutions to transportation problems in Louisville, Kentucky and Schenectady, New York. It operates welfare-to-work programmes in several cities, including Chicago, New York, Dallas-Fort Worth, and Harrisburg, Pennsylvania. 'UPS doesn't just want to drive through the communities we serve,' says Carroll. 'We want to give something back to the community as well.'

Contact Person: Rodney Carroll, Tel. No: (202) 955-3005 x330

Xerox

Xerox Business Services (XBS) is the fastest growing division of Xerox Corporation. XBS is the world-wide leader in document outsourcing, providing a comprehensive portfolio of services to more than 4,000 client companies in 36 countries and up to four million people a day. The division employs 47,000 individuals in fifty locations nation-wide. XBS's welfare-to-work pilot programme, begun in 1997, has exceeded nearly all of the company's expectations. XBS operated welfare-to-work programmes in 13 different locations last year and hired 105 welfare recipients. The 91 percent retention rate, measured over nine months, exceeds the company's standard entry-level retention rate. Xerox prides itself on being an industry retention leader, easily surpassing the 60 to 70 percent industry average. The especially high retention rate of welfare-to-work hires insures that the company maintains its high standards.

The welfare-to-work programme

The pilot programme's success has encouraged XBS to roll out its welfare-to-work initiative, referred to as START, to all of its 50 locations nation-wide.

Each Xerox location has the flexibility to implement its own welfare-to-work programme. In Washington, D.C., for example, trainees complete a week of on-site orientation before six weeks of shadowing a seasoned account associate. Each Friday, the trainees meet with the local human resources supervisor to discuss progress and address any challenges that have arisen. In other locations, new hires immediately begin to work on accounts. 'How the programme takes shape really depends on the type of relationship they have forged with community based-organisations,' says Joe Hammill, manager of staffing and strategy, who oversees Xerox's welfare-to-work effort.

Most individuals hired through the START programme begin as account associates, earning US$7 to US$8 per hour. The results of Xerox's welfare-to-work programme have been so successful that additional locations are anxious to participate. 'We expected some hesitancy from our managers when we introduced the programme,' says Hammill 'Once they began to see its potential, they were coming to us and asking to be involved.' In 1998 Xerox plans to move more than 300 individuals – six to eight in each location -- from the welfare rolls and onto the Xerox payrolls.

Keys to success

XBS has an aggressive plan to insure that as its welfare-to-work programme expands, it maintains high retention rates. Hammill believes that a key element to success is establishing a strong working relationship with service providers and community-based organisations. These groups help teach the skills necessary to succeed in the workplace and often provide ongoing support to help a former recipient successfully transition into employment. 'When we started, we hoped to form relationships with one community-based organisation in each location. Now we realise that working with two or three quality organisations can serve our needs and the needs of our workers better,' says Hammill.

XBS believes an important part of employee retention is encouraging workers to develop new skills critical to advancement through the company and within the industry. Currently, the company is developing a curriculum with a local community college in Rochester, New York so employees can learn the advanced skills that can lead to a career in the document business.

In 1997, XBS created mentoring programmes for its welfare-to-work employees. After promising initial results, the company will expand its mentoring effort in 1998. XBS is working with Women in Community Services (WICS), a national organisation providing mentoring expertise, to insure that both mentors and new employees receive the most from the programme. 'In 1997 we didn't take the time to train mentors and 'mentees' on how to make the most of these relationships,' explains Hammill. 'Working with WICS will allow us to do a better job making sure that our mentors know what works.'

XBS is also developing a toll-free line that managers can use to assist employees in emergencies. This line will supplement the employee assistance programme already available to all Xerox employees. It will give workers faced with particularly serious personal problems a place to turn for professional outside assistance. In addition, XBS is partnering with the Xerox credit union to allow employees facing financial problems to qualify for loans. 'To an employee just leaving welfare, situations like car trouble and rent increases can place a tremendous burden on a family's finances,' says Hammill, who adds that all employees will benefit from the services. 'With these programmes in place, a problem that could force a person to return to welfare can be dealt with. This is a classic example of how the START programme has acted as a catalyst for new opportunities for all of our employees.'

The positive response flows through the entire company. Seeing XBS provide new opportunities to employment has boosted morale throughout the company. 'When our employees read about START in the company newsletter, they are interested and many want to know how they can help,' says Hammill.

Contact Person: Joe Hammill, Tel. No: (716) 264-5372

References

Brown, Amy, Buck, Maria and Skinner, Erik (1998)
> *Business Partnerships: How to Involve Employers in Welfare Reform*, Manpower Demonstration Research Corporation, New York, NY.

Hogan, Lyn A. (1998)
> *Blueprint for Business: Reaching A New Workforce*, The Welfare-to-Work Partnership, Washington, DC.

Hogan, Lyn A. (1995)
> 'Jobs, Not JOBS: What It Takes to Put Welfare Recipients to Work', Policy Briefing, July 17, The Progressive Policy Institute, Washington, DC.

Hogan, Lyn A. (1996)
'Work-first: A Progressive Strategy to Replace Welfare with a Competitive Employment System', The Democratic Leadership Council, June, Washington, DC.

Public Law 104-193 (1996)
'104th Congress, The Personal Responsibility and Work Opportunity Reconciliation Act', Government Printing Office, August 22, Washington, DC,.

US Department of Health and Human Services, Administration for Children and Families (1998)
'Change in AFDC/TANF Caseloads', June, Washington, DC.

Wirthlin Worldwide (1998)
Trends in Executive Opinion, No. 1, Wirthlin Worldwide, Arlington, VA.

Wirthlin Worldwide, (1998)
Trends in Executive Opinion, No. 2, Wirthlin Worldwide, Arlington, VA.

CHAPTER 10
SOCIAL ENTERPRISES: A LOCAL TOOL FOR WELFARE-TO-WORK POLICIES

By Professor Carlo Borzaga, University of Trento, Italy

Introduction

Over the last few years, the notion of 'social enterprise' has been coming into use both among researchers into the non-profit sector and among those involved in the sector, including practitioners and policy-makers. Although the attribution of the adjective 'social' to some entrepreneurial forms (for example, in some European countries, to co-operatives) is not a completely novel development, the two concepts of 'enterprise' and 'social' have never been systematically coupled to denote the birth of a new type of enterprise.

The progressive spread of this concept has accompanied the development – in European countries as well as in the United States – of organisations oriented to the production of social and community care services on a steady and permanent basis. The types of services produced by social enterprises vary from country to country, but almost everywhere one finds social enterprises which produce services intended to favour the employment of disadvantaged or hard-to-place groups of people (the long term unemployed, the disabled, etc.) either independently or in collaboration with public employment policies. The development of social enterprises, producing social services not normally provided by any other firm or organisation, has been closely tied to employment policies (and supported by public funds) in order to create (temporary) jobs for unemployed people. Two examples of these programmes are the 'Intermediate Labour Market' programmes in the United Kingdom and the 'Lavori Socialmente Utili' (socially useful works) in Italy.

In some countries, social enterprises have gained their own legal status, whereas in other countries they have adapted already existing legal forms to their needs, in some cases thereby obtaining explicit legal recognition. The granting of full legal recognition to social enterprises is currently under consideration in several countries.

However, the attitude of researchers, policy-makers and civil society (especially trade unions) towards these new forms of enterprise is still ambiguous. On the one hand, there is acknowledgement that these organisational forms are able to match the demand for social and community care services in an innovative way and to create new employment, and the collaboration between the employment services and social enterprises is growing. On the other hand, there is the suspicion that these new organisations are not enterprises in the strict sense, and they are sometimes regarded as devices to create a secondary labour market with scant employment and salary guarantees.

A thorough understanding of the actual and potential role of social enterprises is hampered by various factors:

a) A legal tradition, mainly European, which assigns a profit motive to any kind of enterprise;

b) The widespread conviction among economists that the maximisation of profits is a fundamental condition for the efficiency and success of any firm;

c) The prevalence of a political culture that assigns the role of producer of personal and community care services mainly to public units;

d) The close relations, mainly financial, between social enterprises and the public administration.

The intense development of these new organisational forms, however, can no longer be ignored. It requires explanation in order, amongst other things, to encourage a more efficient co-ordination with public policies, and this applies especially to social enterprises providing employment services and work integration for disadvantaged people.

The intention of this chapter is to begin such analysis, with particular attention paid to social enterprises that seek to integrate hard-to-place people into work. The chapter divides into four parts.

The first part provides an overview of the various types of social enterprises and of the services that they produce. The second part proposes an interpretation of the growth of social enterprises, attempts a definition of them, and analyses their economic rationality. The third part is entirely devoted to the subgroup of social enterprises which provide employment and work integration services. In order to interpret their role, the concept of 'disadvantaged' or 'hard-to-place' workers is firstly defined, with an analysis of the obstacles that they encounter in the work integration. After a brief review of the traditional policies adopted to favour the employability of these workers and their shortcomings, the specific advantages of work integration social enterprises are discussed. Then some figures are presented on the diffusion of this type of social enterprise and the results of a number of studies that have sought to assess their performance. The final section analyses the role of social enterprises as an active employment policy instrument and the possibilities for collaboration between work integration social enterprises and other employment policies, with particular reference to welfare-to-work programmes.[1]

A typology of social enterprises

Before defining and analysing social enterprises, it is useful to clarify their institutional setting. They are part of a broader set of organisations that pursue goals other than profit. Various terms reflecting the specific cultural and legal context of the country concerned are used to denote this set of organisations. Four of them are most widely employed: 'voluntary sector' (UK), 'non-profit sector' (USA), 'social economy' (France), 'third sector' (Italy, Germany). Each of these concepts emphasises a specific characteristic of the sector: the fact that the organisations of which it is composed are the outcome of voluntary action by private individuals and often use voluntary work (voluntary sector); the fact that they are not permitted (by statute or the law) to distribute profits to the owners or trustees (non-profit); the fact that they pursue or give priority to social goals (social economy); the fact that they cannot be defined either as public organisations or as ones which operate solely according to market principles (third sector).

Although often used as synonyms, these definitions do not all cover the same organisations. The broadest term is 'social economy', because it comprises both private organisations which do not distribute profits and/or benefits to their members and co-operative enterprises. The latter, however, are not covered by the other three definitions, with the exception, in some countries, of the new co-operatives (called 'social co-operatives') more oriented than traditional ones towards maximising the social utility of their activity.

---

[1] The paper draws on materials produced by the EMES group. The EMES (L'emergence des enterprises sociales. Response novatrice a l'exclusion sociale en Europe) group is a research network funded by the European Union and coordinated by Prof. J. Defourny, Université de Liege.

Although there is therefore no clear and shared definition, for a number of years scholars have principally employed the two concepts of 'non-profit' or 'third sector', giving them the same meaning and extending them to all private organisations which may not or do not distribute profits, as well as to some new organisational forms (like social co-operatives) which, although they are allowed to distribute some of their profits or to otherwise benefit their members, are constrained to the pursuit of goals in the public interest.

Social enterprises belong to this broader group of organisations and, in particular, constitute its productive part. In some countries their characteristics have been defined by specific legislation, while in others the law has modified already existing organisational forms. In the majority of the European countries, however, there is no legal definition of the 'social enterprise', but the term is increasingly used to denote organisations which pursue social goals as enterprises managing social and community care services independently of their legal form.

Social enterprises can be classified according to the type of services that they produce. The most widely used[2] typology distinguishes between:

a) social enterprises which provide social and community care services;

b) social enterprises aimed at the integration of disadvantaged people into work (work integration social enterprises).

The former are aimed at satisfying the need for social services especially among the most vulnerable and marginal groups. The social services provided may be either in the traditional domains (home help, care for the elderly, housing for the handicapped, etc.) or in new domains where creative solutions have been found to address more contemporary challenges: activities to fight failure in school, illiteracy or urban insecurity, the setting up of soup kitchens, social housing agencies, centres for giving help to drug-addicts, homeless people, etc.

The activities they develop and the range of services provided depend closely on the previous size and organisation of social services production (by public units or by third sector organisations). Some of them (the 'regies de quartier' in France and some 'social co-ops' in Italy) do not receive public subsidies, but the majority of them work in partnership with local government authorities, with a greater degree of autonomy than the traditional third sector organisations. To

---

[2] This is explicitly envisaged by the Italian law on social co-operatives.

enhance this autonomy they use volunteers, donations and resources from the users.

Work integration social enterprises provide employment services intended mainly to help hard-to-place or disadvantaged workers (people with disabilities or with social problems, the long term unemployed, the unskilled unemployed, etc.) to find and keep a job.

They provide a variety of services: some seek to restore work motivation to unemployed workers (especially in deprived urban areas), helping them to recover confidence in themselves and in their abilities; others provide vocational training; yet others organise the labour supply of groups of unemployed workers and help them to remain in contact with work through forms of temporary employment.

The most widespread category of work integration social enterprise comprises those that produce private goods and services[3] in order to create jobs for disadvantaged workers. This subgroup, however, is highly differentiated. For simplicity's sake it can be divided into three further types:

a) sheltered employment workshops: these are the most traditional type. Although they engage in productive activities, they usually do not intend to provide disadvantaged workers with permanent and regularly paid employment, but rather to use work activity for their social integration;

b) 'closed' work integration social enterprises which mainly seek to provide permanent and regularly paid employment for disadvantaged persons on their own premises;

c) 'open' work integration social enterprises which employ disadvantaged persons on a temporary basis, with the aim of increasing their employability by means of on-the-job training so that they can re-enter the open labour market.

Although it is not always easy to attribute an individual case to one or other of these categories, since the beginning of the 1990s one notes an evolution from the first (the most traditional) type towards the second and then the third. There is a constantly growing number of social enterprises that favour the transition of

---

[3] They can also produce public goods or social and community care services, especially if they are engaged in programmes financed by public funds (like the Intermediate Labour Market scheme).

disadvantaged workers to the open labour market, and which endow themselves with the necessary technologies and human resources in order to do this (personalised integration programmes, professionals employed for placement in the open labour market, etc.). The development of such 'open' work integration social enterprises has been (and will probably continue to be) favoured by employment policies aimed at creating specific but temporary jobs for the unemployed, like the UK 'Intermediate Labour Market' programmes. The aims of these enterprises are in fact consistent with those of such innovative employment policies.

Work integration social enterprises are in reality enterprises with a dual product: the private good or service which is sold according to market rules and contributes to the enterprise's income, and the work training (the human capital) of the disadvantaged people. However, this latter product is often not recognised as an economic outcome and therefore as part of the enterprise's income.

These work integration initiatives have evolved under different names: 'intermediary associations' or 'integration enterprises' in France, 'b)-type social co-operatives' in Italy, 'training-through-work enterprises' in Belgium, etc. Often the distinction between work integration and other social enterprises is not clear cut: many of them, in fact, simultaneously engage in the production of both social services and employment services.

Social enterprises: definition and explanation

In order to understand the development of social enterprises, the evolution of welfare systems during the last twenty years will be examined in this section together with the consequences of this evolution on the non-profit sector, especially in the European countries. Subsequently, a definition of social enterprise will be given. Finally, with reference to non-profit economic theory, the advantages and limitations of social enterprises will be analysed.

The evolution of the non-profit sector and welfare systems

Non-profit organisations may perform a variety of roles: advocacy, pioneering, resources distribution, services provision. In universal welfare systems, like those of most Western European countries, until the 1970s third-sector organisations were engaged mainly in the first two functions (advocacy and pioneering). When these organisations were also engaged in the provision of social services they tended to depend closely on public authorities as to decisions concerning the quantity and type of services to supply and for their financing.

During the 1980s, the situation changed substantially, and the European countries saw not only an increase in the number of non-profit organisations but also, and especially, the strengthening of their provision of social services and an increasing autonomy from public policies.

This was the outcome of:

a) the increased demand for community and personal services which accompanied the growth of income, the growth of female participation in the labour market, demographic changes, and the increased diversification of needs;

b) the financial difficulties of public welfare systems, especially in European countries, which gave rise to stationary or slowly growing spending on the provision, either direct or by private organisations, of social and community services.

The third sector's productive role and its autonomy therefore seems to have grown up in the gap between increasing needs and stationary or decreasing (public) supply and as a consequence of the demand for integration of socially excluded people at the local level. This has given rise to changes in the configuration of the third sector: many organisations created to undertake advocacy activities (consumer or user organisations, voluntary groups) transformed themselves into producers of services in order to accomplish the mission for which they had been founded. Simultaneously, other organisations, partly new in their characteristics and organisational framework, have been established with the aim of producing services. Most of these organisations have endeavoured to give support, in some cases innovative, to groups of people at high risk of social exclusion (handicapped, long term unemployed, and so forth), though some of them more generally provide services of collective interest for the benefit of people not at risk of exclusion.[4]

This evolution towards production has recently received a further impetus from privatisation policies and especially from the increasing contracting-out of social services by public agencies.

---

[4] An analysis of the evolution of the non-profit sector in the European countries is carried out in Borzaga and Santuari (Eds.) (1998).

However, the strengthening of the third sector's autonomous productive role has had a series of consequences, the most important of which has been the expansion of the range of organisations making up the sector and the change in the importance assigned to their various organisational forms. It is in this context that social enterprises have developed, as a consequence of the strengthening of the productive role of the association in some countries (France, Belgium), and of the social purpose of the co-operative in others (Italy, Spain). In many cases associations and co-operatives have changed from organisations with homogeneous memberships into multi-stakeholder ones: that is, organisations with memberships and administrative bodies consisting of various kinds of interest-holders (consumers, users, workers, volunteers, etc.) (see Borzaga and Mittone, 1997). These changes can be regarded as a worthwhile institutional innovation, towards the creation of new organisational structures able to provide incentives to agents to innovate in the field of the social and care community services (characterised by high rigidity and poor supply) and to reduce production costs.

The new 'social enterprises' organise and manage, with at least partial autonomy and following private rules, the provision of collective services by assuming characteristics that foster fiduciary relations between customers and enterprises, and between enterprises and workers.

The definition of social enterprise

It is not easy to define the social enterprise, due to the diversity of national contexts. The expression 'social enterprise' as such is still rarely, if ever, used in most countries. However, the idea of economic initiatives with social objectives is becoming more widespread and relates either to well-established experiences, or to embryonic or fast-developing ones.

In some countries, social enterprises are usually set up in an already-existing legal form, which may be an association (in France, Belgium and Finland) or a co-operative (in particular in Italy where a specific law on the 'social co-operative' was enacted in 1991). In other countries, social enterprises exist in various legal forms – ranging from the Swedish 'ideel' association, or the English 'friendly society', to more classical capital-based companies, with, somewhere in between, the Spanish 'sociedad anonyma laboral'. In some cases, new legal frameworks have been specifically created for economic initiatives with a social objective. As well as the Italian law of 1991 on social co-operatives, Belgian law - since 1996 - has allowed the adoption of any of the classical commercial forms with the addition of the qualifying term 'à finalité sociale', as long as a certain number of conditions are fulfilled (see Borzaga and Santurari (Eds.), 1998).

One of the main problems is distinguishing social enterprises from traditional non-profit organisations, which in some countries are well established and highly developed.

In trying to define the social enterprise, one must start from the twin characteristics of the initiative, that is, its entrepreneurial and social aspects.

As regards the entrepreneurial side, four elements are usually considered as the most relevant:

1. *A continuous activity producing goods and/or services*

Social enterprises, unlike traditional non-profit organisations, do not normally engage in advocacy, or in the redistribution of financial flows (like, for example, grant-giving foundations), but they are directly involved in the continuous production of goods and/or in the supply of services to people. The production of services is therefore the reason, or one of the main reasons, for the existence of social enterprises.

2. *A high degree of autonomy*

Social enterprises are voluntarily created by groups of people and are governed by them autonomously. Accordingly, they do not depend closely on the public authorities or on national organisations, and they have the right to both 'voice' (protest) and 'exit' (closing down).

3. *A significant level of economic risk*

Those establishing a social enterprise totally or partly assume the risk of the initiative, both by investing their own capital and by committing, in situations where results are uncertain, their own labour. Unlike most public institutions and most traditional third-sector organisations, their financial viability depends on the effort of their members and workers to secure enough resources.

4. *The presence of paid work*

As in the case of more traditional non-profit organisations, social enterprises may likewise combine monetary and non-monetary resources, volunteers and paid workers. However, the activities of social enterprises require the presence of a paid workforce.

On the basis of advances observed in Italy and in the United Kingdom, a possible fifth parameter might be added, without being deemed an essential criterion: a *market orientation*, which means that a significant part of the organisation's income has to be derived from the market (services sold directly to the user) or from contractual transactions with public authorities.

Five indicators encapsulate the social dimension of these organisations:

1. An initiative undertaken by a group of citizens

Social enterprises are the result of a 'collective' dynamic involving people belonging to a community or group that shares a certain need or aim, and they must involve and maintain relationships with the community.

2. Participation by the persons affected by the activity

Representation and participation of clients/customers, stakeholder orientation, and democratic management are distinctive features of social enterprises. In other words, one of the aims of a social enterprise is its desire to increase local-level democracy.

3. Power not based on capital ownership

This does not only signify the principle 'one head, one vote'; it also implies internal relations and a framework different from those characteristic of enterprises based on capital ownership. Capital owners are obviously important, but property rights are shared with other stakeholders.

4. Limited profit distribution

This feature intends to apply the definition of social enterprise not only to organisations characterised by a total non distribution constraint, but also to organisations (like co-ops in some countries) which can distribute profit only to a limited extent, thereby averting profit-maximising behaviour (if they have the other characteristics).

5. An explicit aim to benefit the community

One of the principal aims of social enterprises is to be of service to the community or to a specific group of people. This means that a feature of social enterprises is their desire to promote a sense of local-level social responsibility through economic activity.

The *innovativeness of the service produced*, with regard both to the typology of the services supplied (which also meet needs not traditionally addressed by the public welfare systems) and to the productive processes, can be seen as another specific, even if not essential, characteristic of these organisations.

This is a working definition intended to lay the basis for future analysis.

In many countries, non-profit organisations are changing. Consequently, it is not always possible to verify the evolution of all the characteristics described in the definition. Nevertheless, these characteristics can be used to distinguish between 'core' and 'periphery' social enterprises: whereas the former have all the characteristics described, the latter have only some of them but can move in the direction of the former.

The economic rationale of the 'social enterprise'

The idea that an enterprise may assume aims other than profit-making in the production of certain services conflicts with dominant economic theory. Should the enterprise pursue different goals, especially social ones, theory maintains that it has scant chance of surviving.

But economic theory has also demonstrated the existence of 'market failures', the most important reasons for which is the presence in markets of imperfect and asymmetric information.

It has long been supposed that market failures should be tackled by the state. The institutionalist branch of economic theory, however, has shown that these same failures may equally be tackled by other private organisational forms, which can overcome some of the limitations connected with asymmetric information (see Coase, 1974, and Grillo, 1995). The economic literature on non-profit organisations has long worked on this idea, although it has mainly been concerned with asymmetric information between producer and consumer.[5]

In interpreting the existence and development of social enterprises, one must take into account that they operate in areas, such as social services, in which the problems relating to imperfect and asymmetric information exist not only for consumers – because of the difficulty for them to evaluate and control the quality of the services supplied – but also for owners and managers in

---

[5] Starting from the seminal papers by Hansmann (1980) and Weisbrod (1977), the economic analysis of the non-profit sector has grown. For a summary of the development of this specific literature, see the review *Voluntas,* issue 8(2), 1997.

controlling the efforts of employees. Indeed, some of the characteristics of these enterprises (the non-distribution constraint and the participation of consumers in decisions concerning the characteristics of products and modes of production) may help to reduce information asymmetries between consumers and producers. Some other characteristics (such as worker participation) counteract imperfect information between management and workers, thus enabling the selection of workers with ethically-directed behaviour, willing to work for disadvantaged people. At the same time, the presence of volunteers reduces production costs and creates close links with the community and reputation. Moreover, it yields monetary free resources with which to create and finance the enterprise.

In this respect, the specific characteristics of social enterprise may be regarded as a particular mix which make it possible to produce social services in a private form, with specific advantages (see Borzaga and Mittone, 1997).

First, the social enterprise created in the interest - albeit not exclusive - of consumers/users, of the local community and of those who work in it, and catering to a mix of private and public demand, can guarantee the quality of the services supplied and help create a system of trust relations between consumers and producers. Due to the profit-distribution constraint, it has no incentive to reduce the quality of the services provided in order to increase its owners' earnings. If the social enterprise is a multi-stakeholder organisation, added to this form of indirect control is the direct control ensured by the fact that the consumers themselves, their representatives or representatives of the local community, are members of the organisation and participate in its management bodies.

Moreover, the establishment of trust relations between consumers and producers encourages the formation of demand and at the same time facilitates identification of demand and its quantity. In other words, the social enterprise allows for the joint construction of supply and demand. Distortions in consumption behaviour, in fact, make consumer preferences difficult to determine when most of the services in question are merit goods. Therefore, were it left to the market alone - that is, to the decisions of for-profit firms - these services would be produced in quantities smaller than those deemed socially desirable.

When compared with traditional non-profit organisations, other advantages of social enterprises are their ability to mobilise resources and their potentially greater efficiency. Since they are not wholly constrained in the distribution of profits (like co-operatives), and since in some cases they are able to remunerate capital (that provided by financier members or by members in the form of loans), social enterprises have greater opportunities compared with traditional non-profit organisations to finance not only their routine activities but also projects for development.

This ability to remunerate capital, albeit to a limited extent, has also favoured the growth in all the European countries of financial institutions specialised in the gathering of ethical savings and their investment in social initiatives. These are completely different from the Anglo-Saxon 'umbrella organisations': whereas the latter collect donations, the new institutions finance projects, at low interest rates, but on the undertaking that the loan will be repaid.

Although social enterprises are set up for purposes other than the maximisation of profits, they have features that suggest that, unlike traditional non-profit organisations, they may be no less efficient than for-profit firms. From the efficiency point of view, the advantages of social enterprises compared with for-profit firms and with public units derive from their ability to reduce the cost of producing services. This increases their capacity to produce both for public and private demand. The decisive factors in this ability to curb costs are the following:

a) The participation in management by interest groups, like consumers and voluntary workers, which differ from those that derive monetary benefits from belonging to the organisation, should guarantee operational control over costs. Moreover, the frequent involvement of consumers as co-producers reduces production costs and encourages their direct employment in production, by means of voluntary work as well, and reduces the temptations of opportunistic behaviour.

b) Social enterprises are able to attract human and economic resources at low cost: voluntary work, often highly specialised, which is especially important during the start-up phase; and donations, both to cover management costs and provide working capital.

c) Since social enterprises have been set up by groups of people who, although with diverse interests, all share the mission of the organisation, they guarantee a high level of effort, especially in the presence of incomplete work contracts. Controlling effort is of particular importance in the production of personal and community services, since these have high relational content. In a sector like this, where the quality of the product depends principally on worker commitment, it is more difficult, and therefore more costly, to control such commitment. It is precisely this difficulty, combined with opportunistic behaviour, that is one of the factors responsible for the low efficiency of public units of production and for the scant presence of for-profit firms in this sector.

d) Social enterprises seem to have high flexibility in the use of their workforces. This is a typical characteristic of organisations for social ends, but in the case of the social enterprise it is reinforced by the latter's better organisational capacity. This flexibility lies mainly in the structure of working hours, and therefore of delivery of services, in the greater variety of tasks that the workers can and are willing to perform. In general, flexibility in social enterprises entails not only lower costs but also better quality.

e) Social enterprises are often characterised by wages lower than those paid by public production units - that is, pay is fixed according to the budget available and not vice-versa - but off-set by other aspects of the work. Studies on labour cost in these organisations have shown, in fact, that pay levels are normally lower than those in public and for-profit units, but they are compensated by non-monetary benefits such as the sharing of the organisation's mission by the employees, greater flexibility, and a better work environment (see Soraruff, 1996, for Italy; and also: Mirvis and Hackett, 1983; Rudney and Weitzman, 1983; Johnston and Rudney, 1987; Mirvis, 1992; Preston, 1990, 1993).

These advantages overlap internally in social enterprises, often creating cumulative effects which offer significant opportunities for organisational and social innovation.

In short, the endeavour to combine social goals, user protection and entrepreneurial management enables the social enterprise to establish an equilibrium which both ordinary firms and traditional non-profit organisations find difficult to achieve.

The social enterprise has also disadvantages relative to other organisations, both for-profit firms and traditional non-profit organisations. The main disadvantage is the 'fragility' of the model. The social enterprise, as defined here, is an organisation which produces a certain amount of positive externalities, because at least part of the wealth produced benefits someone different from the enterprise's owners. Especially if the organisational forms are not clearly defined by the law and the members are able to modify them, and if the consciousness of their specificity declines, a social enterprise can easily transform itself into a normal for-profit enterprise. At the same time, if the contracting-out policy established by the public authorities seeks to exert full control of the social enterprises, the latter tend to transform themselves into public or quasi-public units. The fragility of the entrepreneurial model increases with the growth of the economic and occupational dimension of the social enterprise, because the local communities lose control over them. The transformation of social enterprises into for-profit or public organisations may be also the consequence of high management costs due to the greater complexity of the decision process resulting from the need to take account of different interests.

Work integration social enterprises

On the basis of the foregoing general analysis of the role of social enterprises, it may be stated that work integration social enterprises perform a specific function as institutions able to intervene in labour market failures. More than other markets, in fact, the labour market suffers from major problems of imperfect and asymmetric information, given the peculiar nature of the 'good' exchanged, namely work. The latter is normally difficult for the purchaser (the firm) to evaluate, and even more so when the worker concerned is a disadvantaged person. Work integration social enterprises intervene with diversified solutions precisely to solve the work integration problems of these kinds of workers.

Analysis of the role of social enterprises in this area therefore requires definition of the concept of labour market disadvantage and of the reasons why disadvantaged workers are discriminated against, and therefore penalised, by traditional (for-profit) firms. This topic is addressed in the next sub-section. The second sub-section analyses labour policy measures to encourage the full professional and social valorisation of disadvantaged persons, and the reasons why these measures have often proved ineffective and/or inefficient (these two sections summarise the contents of Borzaga, Gui and Povinelli, 1998). The third sub-section discusses the reasons why work integration social enterprises seem able to deal more effectively with the work integration difficulties of disadvantaged persons.

The 'disadvantaged worker' and his/her difficulties in the labour market

A worker may be defined as 'disadvantaged' (or 'less favoured', or 'hard-to-place' (see Erhel et al., 1996).in the labour market by virtue of any characteristic which, given the normal requirements of employers, places him/her at a disadvantage with respect to the majority of workers. The most common cause of disadvantage (or handicap) is some sort of disability: that is, 'any restriction on or lack of ability to perform an activity in the manner or within the range considered normal, which is due to physical or psychological infirmity or impairment' (see World Health Organisation, 1980). An infirmity or an impairment may therefore reduce the amount of work that an individual can perform and/or the range of tasks that s/he can satisfactorily accomplish, with respect to the abilities of a 'normal' worker. However, incapacity (or reduced capacity) to perform a given activity may also depend on a number of environmental and socio-cultural factors (poor education, lack of socialisation) which interact with the individual's functional limitations (see Berkowitz and Berkowitz, 1990); OECD, 1994). Often, these factors alone may restrict a worker's employment opportunities. We can thus use the wider concept of 'disadvantage' to cover not only 'disabled (or handicapped) people' in the traditional sense of the term but also all other people who encounter systematic limitations/difficulties in achieving acceptable working standards (from the firm's point of view): former drug addicts, ex-prisoners and individuals with poor or no work experience or with obsolete or no qualifications, such as many long term unemployed.

Worth noting is the fact that the presence of limitations, whatever they may be, do indeed create a worker's productivity gap, but in the majority of cases this is neither absolute (gaps in all possible work tasks) nor definitive (irremediable gaps). On this basis, two groups of disadvantaged people in the labour market may be distinguished:

a) on the one hand, there are those individuals whose productivity falls systematically below normal levels in any job, regardless of any training or adaptation of the job;

b) on the other hand, there is the majority, consisting of those people whose productivity is lower than that of other workers on average, but not in all jobs and/or not definitively.

Except for the individuals in group a), who would normally be excluded by the open labour market even when perfect information exists (except in case of perfect wage flexibility), the employment of the majority of other disadvantaged workers (group b) is principally hindered by imperfect and asymmetric information concerning their real capabilities, their effective productivity and the conditions required for the full realisation of that productivity. In fact, the main obstacle to overcome for satisfactory integration into work of these workers is identification of a suitable job, one which enables them to use their skills to the best advantage and/or provides the training indispensable for developing the abilities that they lack, thereby narrowing or even eliminating their productivity gap (see Erhel, et al., 1996).

The solution is thus a personalised selection and training process that in most cases requires a considerable amount of resources.

As for the selection process, the costs incurred in identifying the 'right' job for a disadvantaged worker are higher than the costs of identifying a position for a 'normal' employee. To reduce selection costs, firms generally rely on signals, i.e. on visible worker characteristics, since these are much cheaper to observe (see Spence, 1974). Statistical discrimination against the categories of disadvantaged workers is therefore very common.

Also the training process of a disadvantaged worker is usually more expensive for the firm (see Stern and Ritzen, 1991; Booth and Snower, 1996). First s/he needs additional general training, particularly in order to improve his/her relational skills; furthermore, in the majority of cases, this kind of worker will also need specific training for a longer period of time, or more intensively, in order to reach satisfactory productivity levels. In any event, once again a firm will try to reduce training costs by choosing workers from among those already with good levels of general human capital, since their training period is generally shorter and therefore cheaper (see Arulampalam, et al.,1996).

Such behaviour, which is rational from the firm's point of view, creates a fragmented labour market, with on the one hand educated and specialised workers able to profit from further training, and on the other an underclass of less-productive and ill-educated workers who find it very difficult to exit from the 'disadvantaged' pool (see OECD, 1994).

Moreover, institutional rigidities and social constraints often operate in a manner such that the benefits of the insertion of disadvantaged people into work are largely reaped by disadvantaged people themselves and by society as a whole, while the related costs and risks are essentially borne by the employer, thus further increasing the work integration difficulties of these people in traditional for-profit firms.

One may therefore sum up the analysis conducted so far in the statement that the employment difficulties of disadvantaged workers are caused principally by two interacting phenomena operating on the labour market, i.e. the lack of information and the presence of institutional rigidities, both of which stem from the wider range of market failures. It is here that intervene the various labour policy measures that have sought in different ways to counterbalance the market failures (and institutional factors) responsible for the exclusion of disadvantaged people from work.

The limitations of traditional labour policies for the work integration of disadvantaged people

Several kinds of labour policies have been designed by governments in order to favour the integration of the various categories of disadvantaged worker (see Haveman, et al., 1984; Schmid and Semlinger, 1984); OECD, 1990, 1992, 1994). These measures have, however, proved largely ineffective in many countries, and their failure can mainly be explained once again by asymmetry in the information available. Indeed, since only enterprises are able to assess the real productivity of disadvantaged workers (and only after they have hired them), on the one hand the authorities responsible for labour policy are reluctant to award them significant public incentives, and on the other the unions are unwilling to accept wide wage differentials.

The literature classifies measures to foster the work integration of disabled people into various categories. Both theoretically and practically, the classificatory criteria used can be extended to the broader group comprising all disadvantaged people. One of the most common classifications (see Schmid and Semlinger, 1984), which is also used here, distinguishes traditional labour policies in favour of disadvantaged people into the following categories: regulatory policies, substitution policies and compensatory policies.

Among regulatory policies, the imposition of quotas was the policy most widely adopted until the 1980s (see Emerson, 1988). However, it achieved unsatisfactory results, because of its difficult management, and because of the high costs that it imposed on firms, which in many cases tried to by-pass this obligation to recruit.

With substitution policies, the state directly promotes the work integration of targeted groups of disadvantaged workers in the public sector, in sheltered employment, or in *ad hoc* businesses; in other words, it creates a demand for labour 'outside the market', or a 'substitute labour market'. The main limitation of these policies is that often, instead of encouraging the real occupational (and social) integration of disadvantaged people, they may end up by creating ghettos, imprisoning individuals capable of playing an active part in even the normal labour market within closed production structures.

Compensatory policies, designed to compensate for the (real or presumed) productivity gap of disadvantaged workers, include both vocational training and/or vocational guidance, and wage subsidies paid to firms hiring these workers.

Vocational training has the following limitations: firstly, it is often structured solely in function of the characteristics of the people receiving the training, without taking sufficient account of labour demand; secondly, the most disadvantaged unemployed people are generally less inclined to take part in training programmes (see Raam, et al., 1993), and, even if they do take part, their employment prospect remain poor (see Pedersen et al., 1993); thirdly, in some cases, training and guidance programmes may even be counter-productive because employers interpret attendance on such a programme as a signal of low productivity potential (See Dolton, 1993); finally, in some countries, businesses often regard the public vocational training system as unreliable.

Wage subsidies encourage employers to hire disadvantaged workers by offering them money to compensate for low productivity and training costs. In this case, several effects (substitution, relocation, dead-weight, 'creaming off') combine to raise the cost to the public purse of every new job created for a disadvantaged person. The problem is thus one of assessing the unjustified payment of subsidies to unscrupulous or lucky employers (moral hazard problem) (see Gui, 1990); Gautié et al., 1993)

Recent years have seen the growth of new kinds of policies which differ from the traditional approaches: most notably, more personalised employment services and various forms of 'supported employment' (see Thornton and Maynard, 1986). Here, one of the most widely used measures is the employment of an assistant/tutor who gives specific support to the disadvantaged worker during his/her integration period, tailoring the help to his/her personal requirements, so that a normal level of productivity is assured to the firm. Often there is also intensive one-to-one training (on the job) with a qualified instructor. These new measures have proved more effective than traditional policies, but their principal shortcoming is their exceptionally high cost per person, which impedes their large-scale utilisation to deal with the huge number of disadvantaged (unemployed) workers.

Work integration social enterprises as a tool of active employment policies

Social enterprises aimed at the work integration of disadvantaged persons should be placed against the background just described, as an alternative to the failure of traditional employment policies. In some respects they replicate the solutions adopted by supported employment (such as the various kinds of assistance for training), but in others they are distinct from them, particularly as regards their specific institutional and/or organisational forms, and because their ultimate aim is precisely the work integration (temporary or permanent) of disadvantaged persons. These factors enable the work integration social enterprises to by-pass, to a certain extent, the obstacles against investment in the selection and training of disadvantaged workers, thereby meriting the confidence of public authorities, trade unions and the society as a whole. Furthermore if these bodies manage to achieve a certain degree of reputation, they may be in a position to supply other employers with credible information regarding the true abilities of trainees, thereby reducing both the costs and the risks that these employers would face when hiring them. Consequently, the presence of this particular type of enterprise improves the functioning of the labour market.

Moreover, work integration social enterprises, especially the 'open' ones, can be seen as an innovative response to the problem of the professional and social integration of disadvantaged people 'through work'. They can count on two advantages.

The first advantage is that they can select and train at a lower cost than other businesses, thanks to their freely available human and financial resources and to skills which have been developed through constant work with disadvantaged workers. Moreover, social enterprises can provide some sort of certification which vouches for the worker's skills acquired on the training programme, backing it with their reputation as reliable intermediate institutions. This comparative advantage thus enables them to act as privileged 'gateways' from welfare to (productive) work. Traditional for-profit enterprises, using the employment services of the social enterprises, will bear much lower selection and training costs when taking on a 'disadvantaged' worker.

The second advantage is that as a result of the profit-constraint feature, and of their participatory nature, social enterprises are able to demonstrate their reliability and credibility both to the public authorities, which are constantly preoccupied that incentives will prove no more than monetary gifts to employers, and to the trade unions, which for similar reasons are reluctant to accept exceptions to minimum pay levels in the form of entry or training wages. And a further guarantee that the organisation's stated objectives will be pursued is the presence in the membership, and/or in the management, of beneficiaries and volunteers, together with promoters and other traditional workers.

Thanks to this double advantage, social enterprises can devote themselves more efficiently to the training of disadvantaged people and to the more profitable work integration of the same workers. The increase in productivity thus achieved may then be utilised within the social enterprise itself or outside it in the open labour market.

If this is the case, social enterprises aimed at the integration of disadvantaged persons through work should not be seen as a fall-back solution after traditional employment policies in favour of this category have failed. Instead, they are a measure that warrants special consideration by policy-makers. Social enterprises, in fact, have special features that other measures cannot reproduce, and which increase their likelihood of success in the selection, training and occupational integration of disadvantaged workers. They are certainly incapable on their own of providing a solution to the huge problem of integrating disadvantaged workers, but they seem particularly suited to a co-ordinated use with other measures.

The diffusion of work integration social enterprises

There are no systematic analyses of the diffusion of work integration social enterprises,[6] except for a few local and, at best, national studies.

Information on social enterprises engaged in the integration to work of disadvantaged persons and in employment services is still fragmentary. It derives mainly from empirical research based on 'case studies' of community-based organisations aimed at combating social exclusion. This research has shown the existence of well-established organisations producing these kinds of services in the United Kingdom (see Amin, Cameron and Hudson, 1998) and in the United States (see Mayer, 1998).

More information is available on social enterprises that produce goods and services in order to create jobs for disadvantaged workers. Comparisons among the members of EMES has enabled construction of a preliminary and in many respects approximate estimation of the diffusion of this kind of social enterprise in many European countries (see Table 1).

---

[6] Two recently published books (Borzaga, Santuari (Eds.), 1998 and Defourny, Favreau, Laville (Eds.), 1998) present the evolution of social enterprises in different countries.

Table 1: Work integration social enterprises: organisational forms and countries

ORGANISATIONAL FORMS	COUNTRY	NUMBER
Social co-ops type b)	Italy	750
Co-ops of special purposes	Greece	20
Social solidarity co-ops	Portugal	50
Labour co-ops (transitional initiatives)	Finland	65
Social firms	Finland	20
Social enterprises for the long term unemployed	Spain	200
Special work centres for the disabled	Spain	Unknown
Workshops/new social enterprises (disabilities)	Ireland	26
Social firms for the long term unemployed (transitional)	Ireland	10
On the job training enterprises (unemployed)	Belgium	40
Social workshops (Flemish)	Belgium	100
Sheltered workshops	Belgium	400
Rehabilitation institutions	Denmark	50
Activation projects / work projects	Denmark	unknown
Mentally-ill co-ops	Sweden	50
Community business	UK	400
Enterprises d'insertion	France	750

In Italy, where work integration social enterprises coincide with b-type social co-operatives,[7] data from the Istituto di Previdenza Sociale have made it possible to reconstruct the evolution and size of the phenomenon until 1996. The figures are given in Table 2.

Table 2 – Italy: work integration social co-operatives 1993 – 1996

(October)	1993	1994	1995	1996
Number of co-operatives	287	518	705	754
Rate of growth (%)		80.5	36.1	6.9
Total employment	4501	7115	9837	11165
Rate of growth (%)		58.1	38.3	13.5
Disadvantaged workers employed	1675	3204	4686	5414
Rate of growth (%)		91.3	46.2	15.5
Employees by co-operative	15.7	13.7	13.9	14.8
Disadvantaged workers by co-operative	5.8	6.2	6.6	7.2
Percentage of disadvantaged workers in total workers (%)	37.2	45.0	47.6	48.5

Source: INPS

---

[7] For more information on the experience of work integration social co-operatives in Italy, see Borzaga (1996), (1998).

According to information provided by INPS, at the end of 1996 the number of work integration co-operatives in Italy amounted to 754[8] and employed 5414 disadvantaged workers out of a total labour force of 11,165 employees. Table 2 summarises the evolution of the number and employment levels of work integration co-operatives since 1993, i.e. two years after approval of law 381. However, one should not be misled by the rapid growth indicated for 1993 to 1994, given that the figures refer both to new co-operatives and to those which regularised their position in that period (by notifying INPS of disadvantaged workers hired or by separating work integration activity from the delivery of social services). More realistic is the growth registered between 1994 and 1996.

The figures on the number of disadvantaged employees set out in Table 2, however, do not account for all the work integration activity performed by the Italian co-operatives. The surveys conducted by the Consorzio Gino Mattarelli (1993 and 1996) have shown that, in fact, there are still co-operatives engaged in activity targeted both to work integration and the production of social services, and that many co-operatives train people who are not fully employed. Data regarding these co-operatives are not included in the set of INPS data on which Table 2 has been constructed.

According to the INPS data, the average size of work integration co-operatives is rather small (13-15 employees), with on average some 6-7 disadvantaged workers per co-operative. The average percentage of disadvantaged workers in the total workforce is lower than 50%.

If co-operatives are distributed according to the percentage of disadvantaged workers in the total workforce, one notes in 1996[9] a distinct prevalence (63.7%) of co-operatives with percentages between 31% and 60%. If one classifies as providers of supported employment those co-operatives with percentages of disadvantaged workers higher than 70% (which can be defined as sheltered shops), one finds that in both 1993 and 1996 they were in the distinct minority (respectively 11.7% and 16.4%).

---

[8] According to the Ministry of Labour's register of co-operatives, at the end of 1996 there were around one thousand work integration co-operatives. The INPS figure, however, is more reliable, since the Ministry of Labour surveys constituted co-operatives even if they are not operational, and cancels those that have ceased operations only after some delay.

[9] The fact that, in 1993, 34.4% of co-operatives had workforces comprising less than 30% of disadvantaged workers confirms that in that year the regularisation process was still under way and that it had practically ceased in 1996.

In France, these organisations have developed as associations. Since 1985, they have been recognised as 'enterprises intermédiares', and since 1988 as 'enterprises d'insertion' (see Demonstier, 1998). In 1995, there were at least 750 such organisations, with an average of 12 jobs each reserved for disadvantaged workers (6,500 in total). In 1994, they concluded about 20,000 employment contracts, 15,000 of which were for disadvantaged workers.

In Belgium (see Defourny, Nyssens and Simon, 1998), there are 150 'ateliers protegés' (sheltered employment centres) providing stable and paid work for about 20,000 handicapped people. Ten work integration social enterprises aimed at integrating disadvantaged workers into the open labour market are still in the experimental stage, but they already provide 2,000 jobs for disadvantaged workers. Some of them have already begun highly innovative projects.

Other more qualitative information is available for Spain (see Vidal, 1998), where some associations for the work integration of the disabled have developed complex organisational systems which enable them to provide their associates with complete work entry services ranging from formal education to on-the-job training and placement in open labour market.

First attempts at evaluation

Since social enterprises are a new and almost unknown phenomenon, there are still very few studies that seek to evaluate their economic and social outcomes and to compare their costs and benefits with those of alternative policies.

The general opinion among researchers, supported by the results of numerous case-studies, is that when a social enterprise has the characteristics described in this paper, the benefits of public support are greater than the costs, partly because some of the latter are unpaid, and therefore the net benefits are higher than those resulting from other policies. However, specific studies are required to confirm this opinion, especially because of the above-mentioned 'fragility' of the model, if work integration social enterprises, and especially 'open' ones, are be used systematically as a tool of active labour market policies.

In some countries, a number of first attempts have been made to assess the efficacy of the services supplied by work integration social enterprises. The results of two Italian evaluations are discussed below.

The first is a survey conducted in 1994 on a sample of 33 social co-operatives operating in four regions of northern Italy (see Borzaga, 1996). Predominant in the sample are co-operatives engaged in a single activity (64% of cases) performed largely in the following areas: maintenance of public and private green spaces, cleaning services, assembly activities, carpentry, farming, construction and refuse collection.

Earnings by the surveyed co-operatives are therefore rather differentiated. Averaged over the three years examined, the volume of sales can be broken down as follows: 53.6% from contracts with local administrations, 39.0% from contracts with private bodies, and 8.4% from public subsidies to work integration initiatives. None of the co-operatives examined depended solely on income from the public administration.

On 31 December 1993, the number of people working in the co-operatives surveyed amounted to 751, of whom 375 were ordinary workers, 255 were disadvantaged workers and 121 were volunteers.

Analysis of the data relative to the characteristics of the disadvantaged persons who entered the co-operatives between 1993 and 1996 (466) shows that there was a markedly larger percentage of men (76%) than women (24%). Just over half (54%) were younger than 30, and more than 80% had either elementary or compulsory school-leaving certificates. Their provenance was mainly from non-labour-force area (67% of cases). The ex-employed and/or unemployed accounted respectively for 12% and 20% of the entire sample. In terms of disadvantage, the largest group consisted of the handicapped (119) - mainly the mentally handicapped (60% of cases) - followed by drug addicts (106).

Of the 466 disadvantaged employed by the co-operatives surveyed, on 31 December 1993, 32% were still undergoing work integration while the remainder, having completed the process, had either joined the co-operative on a stable basis (26%) or had left it (42%).

The predominant cause of exit - which occurred in the majority of cases (55%) after a period of slightly more than twelve months in the co-operative - was abandonment of the integration schedule; slightly more than 44% instead left the co-operative because they had completed the schedule. Of those who left the co-operative on completion of the integration schedule, 66% were present in the labour market: in 79% of cases they were in employment and in 21% of cases in search of work. There were very few cases of subjects returning to the non-labour force (15%).

This analysis provides a first measure of the success of the work integration process. If, in fact, as well as the number of subjects integrated into the co-operative itself in a stable manner (120) one also takes account of those entering employment elsewhere (46), and if one excludes from the calculation those still undergoing integration, one may conclude that the work integration process has had a positive outcome in 52% of cases.

Only 24 workers (20%) remained in the co-operative even though external work integration had been envisaged for them. The failure to achieve the objective was in this case mainly due to either lack of opportunity (50% of cases) or to refusal by potential employers (12% of cases).

As instead regards calculation of the average amount of time taken by the disadvantaged workers to complete the integration process and to find stable employment in the co-operative, figures are available for around 38% of those finding stable employment: 18 months on average elapse from the beginning of the scheme to hiring by the co-operative.

The second study, flanked by detailed cost-benefit analysis, was carried out in the province of Trento (northern Italy) by the local *Agenzia del Lavoro*.[10] It examined 115 disadvantaged persons involved between 1992 and 1995 in ten work integration co-operatives. This survey is interesting because it assesses an experiment where the *Agenzia del Lavoro* met the expenses accruing to co-operatives in training disadvantaged workers and, specifically, part of the labour cost of both disadvantaged and ordinary workers who received on-the-job training, and the costs of hiring training consultants.

Of the 115 disadvantaged workers examined, 87 had completed the work integration programme. Of these 43 (53%) found steady work, 32 in enterprises other than the co-operative, and the rest in the co-operative itself. Two-thirds of those who found permanent employment had been in work for at least two years. The work integration programme lasted between 1.6 years for those who found work in ordinary firms and 2.4 years for those who were hired on a permanent basis by the co-operative.

The cost-benefit analysis yielded distinctly positive results, even with very restrictive hypotheses. Even taking account of only monetary benefits, and using diverse discount rates and hypotheses on the duration of the working lives of the work-integrated subjects, the cost-benefit analysis confirmed that the costs sustained by the *Agenzia* were entirely repaid in the form of higher taxes and social contributions, and that the disadvantaged workers and their families obtained greater benefits. Much more limited, indeed almost nil, were the benefits obtained by the co-operatives. This, though, is in line with their nature

---

[10] See Agenzia del Lavoro della Provincia Autonoma di Trento (1997).

as non-profit organisations whose principal goal is not the accumulation of capital but maximisation of the number of people integrated into work.

Social enterprises, job creation and employment policies

Both the supporters and critics of social enterprises pay close attention to their ability to create jobs. The analysis presented in this chapter permits a discussion of this aspect taking into account the various types of social enterprise.

It is evident that social enterprises providing social and community care services are able to create new jobs in a sector where demand is expanding. They certainly create new jobs when they activate new private demand (directly from consumers or indirectly from donors), but also when they activate a mix of private and public demand.

One may therefore conclude that social enterprises create new employment even when they depend wholly or partly on public funding: it is not certain, in fact, that in the absence of enterprises willing to engage in these activities, perhaps even with limited financing, the same public resources would in any case be committed to the production of services. It should be pointed out, in fact, that a good proportion of the social services today provided by social enterprises have been 'invented' by the latter, and that they exist thanks to their ability to innovate productive processes and/or products. Only subsequently have these services been activated and sustained by means of public funds.

These social enterprises, however, do not necessarily employ disadvantaged workers. Indeed, social enterprises providing social and community care services tend to employ medium-to-high skilled workers, according to the type of service produced. The experience of several countries shows that attempts to employ certain categories of disadvantaged workers (the adult long term unemployed, in particular) in the production of social services have failed because the skills of the majority of these workers have been incompatible with those required to ensure services of an adequate quality. Nevertheless, it is possible to think of policies which would foster employment in social enterprises providing social and community care services by providing temporary employment subsidies, as long as the enterprises are allowed to choose workers on the basis of their skills and their ability to modify these skills.[11]

As for the quality of the jobs created by social enterprises, and in particular as regards the fear that they would help to expand the secondary labour market, one notes that the few and still experimental surveys conducted to date confirm for the European countries the findings forthcoming in the United States on workers in the non-profit sector: although wage levels are generally lower than those paid by for-profit firms and the public sector, the level of satisfaction of these workers is not lower.[12]

Employment of disadvantaged workers is instead the prime objective of work integration social enterprises. Yet these do not necessarily create new and stable jobs: in several cases they produce services designed to increase the employability of these workers and to overcome failures of the labour market. Only the subgroup of organisations which this paper has called 'closed' work integration social enterprises create new jobs, whereas all the others instead create stable jobs for the non-disadvantaged persons employed in the production of employment services.

From the economic point of view, the correct way to interpret the role of work integration social enterprises is to consider them as active labour market policy instruments. They in fact assist in the selection and on-the-job training of subjects who require investments in selection and training higher, and riskier, than those which for-profit firms regard as economically convenient, given that they exceed the benefits expected even when taking the subsidies available into account.

---

[11] An interesting scheme in this regard has recently been undertaken in Italy. In 1997 an agreement was signed between 'Italia Lavoro' and the 'Consorzio Nazionale delle Cooperative Sociali' whereby the co-operatives belonging to the consortium would hire 700 workers taking part in the 'socially useful work' programme. These workers were taken on for one year, with a work schedule of 20 hours per week, while they continued to receive unemployment benefit. The Consortium undertook to guarantee permanent employment for 50% of these workers. At the end of the project (September 1998) the percentage of workers who had found stable employment (within or without the co-operative) was 65%. It should be pointed out that Consorzio delle Cooperative Sociali has been the only organisation to reach an agreement of this kind with Italia Lavoro.

[12] The first result from a survey conducted in 12 Italian provinces, comparing the worker satisfaction in public units and in social enterprises, confirm that the level of satisfaction is about the same in the two kinds of organisations.

Given these considerations, which derive from the theoretical analysis conducted in previous sections, it is possible to argue that policies regarding work integration social enterprises require profound revision. To date, the countries that have supported the development of these enterprises have relied on two main instruments:

a) the assignation to social enterprises of publicly-financed 'works of public usefulness';

b) the granting of subsidies, usually fixed-term, calculated on the basis of the unemployment benefits to which the workers hired were entitled.

These policies were based on the conviction that work integration social enterprises were social policy instruments with which to combat the social exclusion of hard-to-place persons.

A policy more coherent with the characteristics of these enterprises and able to exploit their potential instead requires that:

a) work integration social enterprises should be recognised as labour policy instruments and therefore included in the network of institutional relations centred on these policies;

b) the contribution by work integration social enterprises to the employability of disadvantaged people should be contractually defined: the subsidy should be commensurate with the expenditure made to recover disadvantaged workers for work and to train them, and therefore with the degree of employability of these workers and the expected duration of the recovery process. However, no particular constraints should be placed on enterprises as regards extension of these workers' employment (though without subsidies) and discounting a certain failure rate;

c) work integration social enterprises should be required to use instruments which increase the employability of disadvantaged workers, for example personalised work-entry projects, periodic assessment of results, etc.;

d) linkages should be encouraged between social enterprises and traditional firms, which should hire disadvantaged workers once they have completed the selection and training process in the social enterprises (through reduction of compulsory quotas or through specific grants).

The systematic linking of work integration social enterprises and active labour market policies would be particularly beneficial to welfare-to-work programmes such as the New Deal for welfare-to-work now being implemented in the United Kingdom. They have in fact similar objectives and common forms of intervention. Thus the aim of the New Deal is to act on the employability of unemployed workers by using not only employment subsidies but also counselling and guidance services, job-search support, general and specific training both scholastic and on-the-job. Work integration social enterprises are able to provide several of these services, especially for the more hard-to-place.

The New Deal and similar welfare-to-work programmes would therefore benefit from systematic connection to and support for work integration social enterprises. This would make it possible:

a) to recover for the programme those persons, mainly young, who are not followed by the Employment Offices because they cannot or are unwilling to apply for unemployment benefit;

b) to cushion the effects of the discriminatory policies still adopted by firms in order to select more productive workers or ones whose training requires less investment;

c) to recover resources from the local community and to target the schemes on the largest hard-to-place categories in the community.

In other words the assessment of work integration social enterprises (by law, as in Italy, or by agreements with the voluntary sector) and their systematic involvement into a specific policy aimed at encouraging their growth would give more efficacy to welfare-to-work programmes than the generic temporary placement of more difficult workers in voluntary organisations.[13]

Conclusions

If analysis of the evolution and characteristics of social enterprises goes beyond the superficiality with which they have often been considered, it is clear that

---

[13] As pointed out by Training & Employment Network (1998), until June 1998 'there has been limited progress in engaging the social economy sector of co-operatives and community business.' The reason seems to be found in the 'generic approach by Government towards non-profit organisations.' To overcome this difficulty it could be useful to promote the development of work integration social enterprises within the non-profit sector.

they can in no way take the place of labour policies. Nor can they solve the problem of unemployment on their own. However, they can be used as a specific instrument of such policies, giving a major contribution to the efficacy of policies designed to increase the employability of the hardest-to-place groups of workers, as long as they are clearly defined and systematically included among and co-ordinated with active labour market policy instruments.

Enough experiments have been conducted in different countries that can be used to assess innovative policies, both at European and national level, for the development of work integration social enterprises.

References

Agenzia del Lavoro della Provincia Autonoma di Trento (1997)
'Monitoraggio e valutazione dell'attività del progetto per il supporto delle cooperative sociali di tipo b', mimeo, Trento.

Amin ,A., Cameron, A. and Hudson, R. (1998)
'Welfare to Work or Welfare as Work? Combating Social Exclusion in the UK', working paper.

Arulampalam ,W., et al. (1996)
Modelling Work-Related Training and Training Effects Using Count Data Techniques', ESCR Research Centre on Micro-Social Change, University of Essex.

Ashenfelter, O. C. and LaLonde , R. J. (Eds.) (1996)
The Economics of Training, Elgar, Cheltenham.

Ballet, J. (1996)
'Les Entreprises de Solidarité', mimeo, Université de Versailles St. Quentin en Yvelines.

Berkowitz, M. and Berkowitz, E. (1990)
'Labor Force Participation among Disabled Persons', *Research in Labour Economics,* 11, pp. 181-200.

Ben-Ner, A. (1994)
'Who Benefits from the Non-Profit Sector? Reforming Law and Public Policy Towards Non-Profit Organisations', *The Yale Law Journal,* 104, (3), pp. 731-762.

Ben-Ner, A. and Van Hoomissen,T. (1991)
'Non-Profit Organisations in the Mixed Economy: a Demand and Supply Analysis', *Annales de l'Economie Publique Sociale et Cooperative*, 62 (4).

Booth, A. L. and Snower, D. J. (Eds.) (1996)
Acquiring Skills. Market Failures, their Symptoms, and Policy Responses, CEPR, Cambridge.

Borzaga, C. (1998)
'Italie. L'impressionnant développement des coopératives sociales', in Defourny J., Favreau L. and Laville J.L. (Eds.), *Insertion et nouvelle économie sociale. Un bilan international*, pp. 99-126, de Brouwer, Paris.

Borzaga, C. (1996)
'Social Co-operatives and Work Integration in Italy', *Annals of Public and Co-operative Economics*, 67(2).

Borzaga, C., Gui, B. and Povinelli, F. (1998)
'Le rôle des enterprises d'insertion sur le marché du travail. L'éclairage d'une analyse économique', in Defourny J., Favreau L. and Laville J.L. (Eds.), *Insertion et nouvelle économie sociale. Un bilan international*, de Brouwer, Paris, pp. 267-291.

Borzaga, C. and Mittone, L. (1997)
'The Multi-Stakeholders versus the Non-Profit Organisation', Discussion Paper No. 7; Department of Economics, University of Trento, Trento.

Borzaga, C. and Santuari, A. (Eds.) (1998)
Social Enterprises and New Employment in Europe, Regione Autonoma Trentino-Alto Adige in co-operation with European Commission-DGV and CGM, Trento.

Coase, R. (1974)
'The Lighthouse in Economics', *Journal of Law and Economics*, 17.

Consorzio Gino Mattarelli (1994)
Primo Rapporto sulla Cooperazione Sociale, Edizioni CGM, Milano.

Consorzio Gino Mattarelli (1997)
Secondo Rapporto sulla Cooperazione Sociale, Edizioni CGM, Milano.

Defourny, J., Favreau L. and Laville, J.L. (Eds.) (1998)
    Insertion et nouvelle économie sociale. Un bilan international, de
    Brouwer, Paris.

Defourny, J., Nyssens, M., and Simon, M. (1998)
    'Belgique. De l'association sans but lucratif à la societé à finalité sociale',
    in Defourny J., Favreau L. and Laville J.L. (Eds.), *Insertion et nouvelle
    économie sociale. Un bilan international*, de Brouwer, Paris, pp. 73-98.

Demoustier, D. (1998)
    'France. Des structures diversifiées à la croisée des chemins', in
    Defourny J., Favreau L. and Laville J.L. (Eds.), *Insertion et nouvelle
    économie sociale. Un bilan international*, de Brouwer, Paris, pp. 41-71.

Dolton, P.J. (1993)
    'The Econometric Assessment of Training Schemes: A Critical Review',
    Paper presented at the International Meeting of Labour Economists,
    Maastricht.

Emerson, M. (1988)
    'Regulation or Deregulation of the Labour Market: Policy Regimes for
    the Recruitment and Dismissal of Employees in the Industrial Countries',
    European Economic Review, 32 (4), pp. 775-817.

Erhel, C., Gautié, J., Gazier, B. and Morel, S. (1996)
    Job Opportunities for the Hard-to-Place, in Schmid G. et al. (Eds.),
    International Handbook on Labour Market Policy and Policy Evaluation,
    Elgar.

Gautié, J., Gazier, B. and Silvera, R. (1993)
    'Couts salariaux et politique de l'emploi : perceptions, stratégies,
    indicateurs', Rapport pour le Ministère du Travail, Paris.

Grillo, M. (1995)
    Introduzione in Coase R., *Impresa, mercato e diritto*, Il Mulino, Bologna.

Gui, B. (1990)
    I sussidi marginali all'occupazione, Giuffrè, Milano.

Gui, B. (1991)
    The Economic Rationale for the 'Third Sector. Non-Profit and other
    Noncapitalistic Organisations', *Annales de l'Economie Publique, Sociale
    et Cooperative*, 62.

Hansmann, H. B. (1980)
'The Role of Non-Profit Enterprise', *The Yale Law Journal*, 89 (5), pp. 835-901.

Hansmann, H. B. (1987)
'Economic Theories of Non-Profit Organisation', in Powell W. (Ed.), *The Non-Profit Sector. A Research Handbook*, Yale University Press, New Haven.

Hansmann, H. B. (1996)
'Too many Non-Profit Organisations? Problems of Entry and Exit', *Osservatorio Giordano dell'Amore, Le organizzazioni senza fini di lucro*, Giuffrè, Milano.

Haveman, R. H., Halberstadt, V. and Burkhauser, R. V. (1984)
Public Policy Toward Disabled Workers, Cornell University Press, London.

Johnston, D. and Rudney, G. (1987)
'Characteristics of Workers in Non-Profit Organisations', *Monthly Labour Review*, July.

Kiernan B., and Stark, J. (1985)
Employment Options for Adults with Developmental Disabilities, Utah State University, Development Center, Logan, Utah.

Mayer, M. (1998)
'Changes in Politics and Political Action in the City', paper for the Panel 'Urban Movements and the City in Retrospect: Poor People's Movements and Urban Politics' at the ISA XIV World Congress of Sociology.

Mirvis, P. H. (1992)
The Quality of Employment in the Non-Profit Sector, *Non-Profit Management and Leadership,* 3 (1).

Mirvis, P. H. and Hackett, E. J. (1983)
'Work and Work Force Characteristics in the Non-Profit Sector', *Monthly Labour Review*, April.

OECD (1990)
Labour Market Policies for the 1990s, OECD publication, Paris.

OECD (1992)
'Employment Policies for People with Disabilities: Report by an Evaluation Panel', OECD Labour Market and Social Policy Occasional Papers, No. 8, Paris.

OECD (1994)
Disabled Youth and Employment, OECD publication, Paris.

Ortmann, A. (1996)
'Modern Economic Theory and the Study of Non-Profit Organisations : Why the Twain Shall Meet', working paper.

Ortmann, A. and Schlesinger, M. (1997)
'Trust, Repute and the Role of Non-Profit Enterprise', *Voluntas*, 8(2), pp. 97-119.

Pedersen, J. and Westergard-Nielsen, N. (1993)
'Unemployment: A Review of the Evidence from Panel Data', *OECD Economic Studies*, No 20.

Phelps, E. S. (1972)
The Statistical Theory of Racism and Sexism, *American Economic Review*, 4, pp. 659-661.

Preston, A. (1990)
'Changing Labour Market Patterns in the Non-Profit and For-Profit Sectors: Implications for Non-Profit Management', *Non-Profit Management and Leadership, 1*.

Preston, A. (1993)
'The Market for Human Resources: Comparing Professional Career in the Public, Private, and Non-Profit Sectors' in Hammack and Young, *Non-Profit Organisations in a Market Economy*.

Raam, O., Torp, H., Hernaes, E. and Goldestein, H. (1993)
'Evaluation of Labour Market Training Programmes. Some Experiences with an Experimental Design', paper presented at the International Meeting of Labour Economists, Maastricht.

Rudney, G. and Weitzman, M. (1983)
'Significance of Employment and Earnings in the Philantropic Sector 1972-1982', Working Paper No. 77, Yale University.

Schmid, G. and Semlinger, K. (1984)
Labour Market Policies for the Disabled. Experiences from the Federal Republic of Germany, Great Britain, Sweden and the U.S.A., Wissenschaftszentrum, Berlin.

Soraruf, F. (1996)
'Le caratteristiche dei lavoratori remunerati e volontari nelle co-operative sociali del Trentino', working paper ISSAN, University of Trento, Trento.

Spence, A. M. (1974)
Market Signaling: Informational Transfer in Hiring and Related Screening Process, Harvard University Press, Cambridge.

Stern, D. and Ritzen, J. M. M. (Eds.) (1991)
Market Failure in Training? New Economic Analysis and Evidence on Training of Adult Employees, Springler-Verlag, Berlin.

Thornton, C. and Maynard, R. (1986)
'The Economics of Transitional Employment and Supported Employment' in Berkowitz M. and Hill M. A. (Eds.), *Disability and the Labour Market*, ILR Press, Cornell University, Ithaca, pp. 142-170.

Training and Employment Network (1998)
'The Next Stages of a New Deal', working paper, London.

Vidal, I. (1998)
'Social Enterprises in the Field of Integration', EMES working paper.

Weisbrod, B. A. (1977)
'Toward a Theory of the Voluntary Non-Profit Sector in a Three Sector Economy', in Weisbrod, B. A., *The Voluntary Non-Profit Sector*, Lexington Books, pp. 51-76.

World Health Organisation (1980)
'International Classification of Impairments, Disabilities and Handicaps'. A Manual Classification Relating to the Consequences of Disease, Geneva.

CHAPTER 11
NEW APPROACHES TO PUBLIC INCOME SUPPORT IN CANADA

By Professor Alice Nakamura, University of Alberta
Ging Wong, Human Resources Development Canada
Professor W. Erwin Diewert, University of British Columbia, Canada

INTRODUCTION

'The economy and society are two sides of the same coin -- and that coin is people. We are all part of our society. We are all part of our economy. We ignore the health of either at our peril.'

(The Honourable Pierre S. Pettigrew
Minister of Human Resources Development Canada
April 22, 1999)

Recent reforms of Canadian social programmes address national level objectives, but have important local dimensions. These reforms involve new forms of partnership between the national and sub-national levels of government for the purpose of achieving more cost effective and responsive programme delivery. These are scientific reforms. In addition to building on lessons learned in other countries, the new Canadian reforms are motivated by and being evaluated and modified on the basis of empirical evidence about the operation of Canadian social programmes. This evidence has been produced by researchers at universities and in businesses, non-profit organisations and provincial governments across Canada working together with their federal counterparts.[14] These are proactive reform measures that use new and improved

---

[14] One important part of this largely informal research network is the Canadian Employment Research Forum (CERF) that was founded and has continued to operate with core funding from Human Resources Development Canada (HRDC). Ging Wong is the current government co-chair and Alice Nakamura is the current academic co-chair of CERF.

data resources, new information technologies, and the expertise and programme experiences of a nation rather than just the federal bureaucracy in a campaign to maintain effective social programmes in the face of budgetary pressures and globalisation.

This chapter outlines five sets of reform initiatives that are interrelated in their objectives and that were all undertaken or fostered by the Department of Human Resources Development Canada (HRDC). Statistics Canada and Industry Canada have also been important partners in some of these initiatives. All of the initiatives are of potential value for keeping Canadians at work rather than on welfare, though they are not welfare reform measures.

'Welfare' is the term used in many countries for needs-based income support programmes. Welfare benefits usually increase with the number of dependent children. The approval process involves family means testing (making the verification of family composition an issue). Usually, the support can continue over substantial periods. In addition, welfare programmes are usually funded out of general tax revenues rather than through user fees or payroll taxes.

Most of the developed countries also have mandatory 'unemployment insurance' to provide financial assistance for labour force participants who are temporarily out of work. Support levels are usually based on insured earnings, without regard for need factors such as the number of dependent children. Nor is poverty a criterion for qualifying to receive benefits. Like homeowner's or automobile accident insurance, unemployment insurance benefits can be collected by all those who have paid the premiums for the insurance and have suffered the insured risk – in this case, the risk of becoming unemployed. The programmes are typically paid for through payroll tax premiums levied on employers or workers or both.

Lessening the welfare trap is one of the stated objectives of several of the reform initiatives we discuss. The term 'welfare trap' refers to the dilemma faced by parents with dependent children and whose job prospects are so poor that they cannot earn as much from even full-time, full-year work as they would receive by staying on public income support. The welfare trap term came to be used because the main programme providing public income support in the United States is welfare. However, in Canada, many of those who would be on welfare in the United States are on unemployment insurance. Thus in Canada, a more appropriate term might be the 'public income support trap.'[15]

---

[15] Barrett, Doiron, Green and Riddell (1994) use matched administrative files for UI and for welfare in five provinces to trace the increasing overlap of the caseloads for

The reform measures we discuss build in a constructive way on the complementarities between the welfare and unemployment insurance programmes in Canada. These initiatives also reflect a new imperative to design social programmes that, as a package, promote, or at least do not undermine, the economic health of the nation. This has been of special concern in Canada because of the persistence of higher unemployment rates and lower productivity growth compared with the United States.[16] If effective social security programmes can be provided at lower cost, this will help keep Canadians in jobs by lessening the tax drag on the economy.[17] These initiatives should be of interest in other countries also struggling to control spending on income transfer programmes while still maintaining an effective social safety net.

The Initiatives Discussed

Five sets of initiatives are discussed:

1. Innovative features of Canada's Employment Insurance (EI) programme.

The EI reforms were brought in with the passage of Bill C-12 in 1996. These include a change in the unit of account for qualifying for benefits from weeks of employment in covered jobs to hours of work. Two complementary types of worker side experience rating were also introduced.

---

welfare (referred to by a variety of names including income assistance and social assistance) and the unemployment insurance programmes, and the increasing movement of individuals back and forth between the programmes. See also Blank and Hanratty (1993), Browing, Jones and Kuhn (1995), Christofides and McKenna (1995), Osberg (1995), Bruce, Bailey, Warburton, Cragg and Nakamura (1996), Kahn and Lang (1995, 1996), and Phipps (1991, 1993) for empirical evidence on the caseload overlap between the Canadian unemployment insurance and welfare programmes and the impacts on the labour supply of workers of inadequate employment opportunities.

[16] For background and different evidence and prominent views on some of these issues having to do with social programmes and the state of the Canadian economy see Davies (1998), Diewert and Fox (1999), Diewert, Nakamura and Sharpe (1999), Foot (1998), Fortin (1994), Fortin and Fortin (1999), Mintz and Wilson (1994), Osberg and Lin (1999), Picot and Heisz (1999), Scarth (1997), and the 'Introduction and Overview' by Sharpe and Grignon (1999).

[17] On the concept and the measurement of indirect 'dead weight' costs of taxation see Diewert (1981, 1984, 1987, 1988), Diewert and Lawrence (1996), and Diewert, Lawrence and Thompson (1998).

2. The Canadian Out of Employment Panel (COEP) surveys.

The Department of Human Resources Development Canada in collaboration with Statistics Canada initiated the COEP data surveys. These are surveys of workers who had a recent job separation. These surveys were designed to support research on job search and the evaluation of unemployment insurance and other programmes for the unemployed.

3. The National Child Benefit (NCB) programme.

The NCB programme helps reduce the income support trap by providing financial assistance for children in low-income families where the parents are employed.

4. The Self-Sufficiency Project (SSP).

The fourth initiative considered – the SSP -- is still at an information collection stage. This is an experimental investigation of the effectiveness of using earnings supplements as an inducement for long term welfare recipients to leave that programme for full-time work, and of the efficacy of full-time work as a means of achieving wage growth over time. This experiment is a shared undertaking of the federal government through HRDC and the provinces of British Columbia and New Brunswick. SSP also has a sophisticated data collection and research component that was implemented in partnership with Statistics Canada.

5. New publicly accessible Internet recruiting information (IRI) services.

On-line recruitment information services are the last of the five categories of initiatives discussed. New information technologies have the potential to reduce the costs and improve the effectiveness of labour market information exchange.

The concluding section discusses how national economic imperatives and the Canadian societal imperative of maintaining a strong social safety net can be fulfilled while drawing on the advantages of local administration and delivery for many social services. The initiatives discussed reflect a vision of an alternative to laissez faire capitalism at the one extreme with minimal social services, and at the other extreme, of public services that meet real needs but also undermine the health of the national economy over time.

The Importance of Economic Incentives

All programmes that take money from some through taxation and give it to others as transfer benefits require controls to deal with programme abuse. Both economic and surveillance control mechanisms can be utilised.

The *economic mechanisms* rely on impersonal price incentives. These have the advantage of operationally transforming a central control problem into decentralised, day-to-day personal choices. In contrast, *surveillance mechanisms* rely on investigation of programme participants to check on whether the stated rules and regulations are being obeyed, with penalties being imposed on the violators.[18]

Surveillance mechanisms have been the main means for controlling inappropriate use of provincial welfare programmes. Surveillance mechanisms have also been part of the unemployment insurance programme in Canada (both the old UI and the new EI) (see Wong, Roy, Laurendeau, Routhier, Guest, and Kardas, 1992; Burgess, 1992; Roy and Wong, 1997; and Wong and Roy, 1997). For example, to qualify for programme benefits, an applicant must establish that he or she is truly out of work.

Price incentive mechanisms have not been utilised for expenditure control in either the welfare or the unemployment insurance programmes in Canada. In fact, the price incentives inherent in the old UI programme inadvertently encouraged inappropriate programme use. Three of the initiatives discussed in this chapter -- the EI reforms, the NCB programme, and the SSP -- attempt to better align the economic incentives created by Canada's income support programmes.[19] The challenge of using economic incentives to control public safety net expenditures is to find methods that do not conflict with the basic reasons for having the programmes in the first place.

---

[18] These issues are further developed as they pertain to EI in Nakamura (1995) and in Nakamura, Cragg and Sayers (1994). There is a long history of attempts at reforming welfare systems through the reform of the economic price incentives. See, for example, the early proposals of Guy H. Orcutt and Alice Orcutt (1968) that were a foundation for the U.S. and Canadian negative income tax experiments.

[19] See Nakamura and Wong (1997) and Nakamura and Diewert (1997) for further discussion of direct versus indirect programme costs and benefits, and the importance of allowing for both. In our view, too many more sophisticated economic evaluations and analyses of social programmes only pay attention to the indirect labour supply incentive effects, thereby failing to connect well with the stated objectives and requirements of the enabling legislation.

With this background, we now proceed to discuss the five sets of social policy initiatives listed above. We begin with changes to the Canadian unemployment insurance programme. In particular, we outline some of the main changes that were made in moving from the old Unemployment Insurance (UI) to the new Employment Insurance (EI) with the passage of Bill C-12 (the EI Act).

Bill C-12 and the Switch from Unemployment Insurance (UI) to Employment Insurance (EI)[20]

The original purpose of Canada's UI programme was to help committed workers with their household expenses while they searched for new jobs, and to guard against downward macroeconomic spirals due to the expenditure cutbacks of the unemployed. The way the rules were prior to the early 1970s, a person who normally worked for only part of the year and who became unemployed could only collect UI benefits for the remainder of that person's *usual* work year.

However, over time in Canada, unemployment insurance increasingly came to be used as a source of income supplementation for individuals who habitually did not have full year work. The programme also came to be relied on as a payroll supplement by some firms, and as a regional economic equalisation mechanism and a source of regional development assistance. A series of revisions of the UI rules in the early 1970s made habitual use more likely. Back then, the rules were changed so that those qualifying for benefits could continue to receive support without consideration of how long the job they had lost would *normally* have lasted. Also, variable regional entrance requirements and extended benefit provisions were enacted. Those changes made it so that workers in high unemployment regions needed fewer weeks of work to qualify for programme benefits than those in lower unemployment regions, and could continue to receive these benefits for longer.

The variable regional entrance provisions and extended benefits introduced a *reverse experience rating* into the UI programme: the greater the risk of the insured hazard, the *more* (rather than the less) coverage a participant was given for the same premium rates. The empirical record demonstrates that, over time, individuals, employers and governments alike responded to these economic incentives in much the way that the theories of economists would predict (see

---

[20] This section draws heavily on Nakamura (1995), Nakamura and Diewert (1997), and Nakamura and Wong (1997).

the House Report, Newfoundland and Labrador, 1986; Richards and Watson, 1994; Corak, 1994; Corak and Pyper, 1995; and May and Hollett ,1995).

One reason that the reverse experience rating features of the post-1974 Canadian unemployment insurance programme gained initial acceptance was that, back then, there was tripartite funding for the programme from worker taxes, from employer taxes, and from federal level general tax revenues. However, since 1990, the funding has been solely from the worker and employer payroll taxes, making it less reasonable for the programme to provide pure income transfers. Moreover, this programme never was well designed for use as a delivery mechanism for income transfers (see Kesselman, 1983, 1986).

The Axworthy Social Security Reform Initiative

In October 1994, after an extensive public consultation, HRDC released *Improving Social Security in Canada: a Discussion Paper.* That document, which we refer to hereafter as simply the *'Discussion Paper'*, outlined a menu of possible reforms of the UI programme and explained why reform was needed.[21] The *Discussion Paper* highlighted five areas of concern, some of which parallel concerns often mentioned in welfare-to-work discussions.

There was concern about the growth over time of repeat use of UI:

> 'Almost 40 per cent of the people on Unemployment Insurance in 1993 had claimed UI benefits at least three times in the previous five years - and the number is rising. The number of such 'frequent claimants' has almost doubled between 1980 and the early 1990s.' (*Discussion Paper*, p. 18)

The *Discussion Paper* noted that the UI caseload and expenditures had grown in recessions and had failed to drop back to pre-recession levels during good times, resulting in a persistent upward drift.

---

[21] One group that was used to generate ideas for the reform was the Axworthy Social Security Reform Task Force. That advisory body, which Alice Nakamura was part of, was set up by Lloyd Axworthy, the Minister then of Human Resources Development. The Axworthy Task Force made extensive use of a group of 22 UI evaluation studies that had been commissioned by HRDC prior to the start of the Axworthy reform effort. The Task Force also drew on other relevant research including the massive research reports of the earlier Royal Commission on the Economic Union and Development Prospects for Canada (see Canada 1985), often referred to as the Macdonald Commission.

Secondly, there was concern that the intent of the UI programme rules was increasingly being abused. The *Discussion Paper* (p. 42) pointed out that: 'The UI programme allows some employers and industries to organise their work schedules around the weeks required to qualify for UI.' There was evidence of a developing UI culture, with some individuals and families treating reliance on public income support as a way of life. This was undermining political support for the UI programme.

A third concern was that the UI payroll tax was contributing to the underlying problem of too little employment. The *Discussion Paper* stated that:

> 'Unemployment insurance premiums are a form of payroll tax. Currently, they represent 42 per cent of federal and provincial payroll taxes and are the largest source of federal revenue next to personal income taxes. It is widely agreed that, at least in the short run, payroll taxes discourage job creation.'
>
> (*Discussion Paper*, p. 50)

A fourth *Discussion Paper* concern was that the UI programme was having unintended distortionary effects on the nature of the available employment. Under the programme rules in effect in 1994, an employer did not have to pay UI premiums for those hired for under 15 hours per week. The proportion of workers in jobs of under 15 hours per week and in other forms of non-standard employment not covered by the UI programme had been growing. There was concern, though no direct proof, that this was happening *because* these sorts of employment were exempt from UI taxation.

For an unemployment insurance programme to be effective as a macroeconomic stabiliser, there must be broad participation. A fifth *Discussion Paper* concern was the erosion of worker participation in the UI programme. Important causes of this erosion included the growth of part time and other forms of non-standard employment that were excluded from UI coverage. There was concern that this was weakening the automatic stabilisation capacity of the programme.

The EI reforms we discuss were motivated by these problems.[22]

---

[22] We only discuss a subset of the Bill C-12 reforms.

Reform of the Active Training and Job Search Component

The old UI programme included insurance side income support and also a range of so-called 'active' education, training and job finding services intended to improve the employability of UI recipients. Both the income support and the active employment services components of the old UI programme were administered by HRDC. Bill C-12, the EI Act, brought about a transfer of administrative responsibility for the employment services from the federal to the provincial and territorial levels of governments. This was done in the hopes of better harnessing the advantages of local knowledge and flexibility. These reforms also opened the way for better integration of the employment services being provided to EI beneficiaries with those being provided to the participants in the provincial welfare programmes -- a pressing need given the large and growing overlap of the EI and welfare caseloads.

Several of the provinces including Quebec opted for full devolution to the provincial level of the administrative control of the active employment services. Others chose co-management with the federal government. Pierre Pettigrew, the Minister of Human Resources Development who was responsible for overseeing the implementation of the EI reforms, points to the varying ways in which this devolution took place with the different provinces as 'yet another illustration of ... federalism that responds in different ways to different needs' (1999, p. 102).

HRDC does retain certain oversight responsibility for all EI programme expenditures and responsibility for reporting to Parliament on the use of funds collected through the EI payroll taxes. The devolution of administrative control for active employment services to lower levels of government, and the push for greater co-ordination of all social services regardless of the level of government responsible, mirror similar changes that Finn (Chapter 6) reports have been taking place in the United States, the United Kingdom and the Netherlands.

Reform of the Insurance Side Income Support Component

Under EI, the income support component of the unemployment insurance programme continues to be administered by HRDC, but changes were made in this part of the programme too. We focus here on the changes in the thresholds for qualifying for benefits and the new worker side experience rating features.[23] In particular, we cover the following three EI innovations:

1. The criteria for determining eligibility for benefit coverage were changed from numbers of *weeks* of work at jobs offering at least 15 hours of work per week, they are now specified in terms of threshold values for *hours* of employment at all jobs held.

2. An 'intensity rule' was introduced that reduces the rate at which earnings are replaced for regular workers who have collected EI benefits for more than 20 weeks over the previous five years.

3. Experience rating was introduced in the benefit clawback provisions of EI. This experience rating results in the repayment of greater amounts of the benefits collected by higher-income individuals who had received benefits for more than 20 weeks over the previous five years, with the repayment rate rising with increased use of the programme.

Though operationally distinct, these three reform measures have linked objectives.

The first of these -- the re-specification of the thresholds for qualifying for benefits in terms of hours rather than weeks of work -- prevents employers from minimising their EI tax payments by increasing the share of jobs they provide that are for less than 15 hours per week. Under EI, employers must pay this tax on all hours of work, up to the insurable maximum on earnings for each worker.[24] The potential pool of beneficiaries was broadened by these changes,[25] which should help to strengthen the macroeconomic stabilisation benefits of the programme. These changes have also improved the inter-worker equity. Under

---

[23] There were also a number of other important insurance side innovations introduced in Bill C-12 that space prohibits us from discussing here.

[24] The old UI thresholds for qualifying for benefits were 12 to 20 weeks of work, depending on the regional unemployment rate, at a job providing at least 15 hours of work per week. The new EI thresholds were set at 420 to 700 hours for regular workers, depending on the local unemployment rate. 420 hours of work would result from 12 weeks of work for 35 hours per week, and 700 hours of work would result from 20 weeks of work for 35 hours of work per week. These new thresholds were set so that all those working 35 hours a week or more at *all* jobs would qualify for benefits just as before, or would qualify sooner because of being able to count hours of work at auxiliary jobs of under 15 hours per week.

[25] Workers must pay this tax on all hours of work, though those who earn less than $2,000 in the year have their premiums refunded to them.

the old UI, someone who had worked 15 hours per week for 12 weeks, for a total of only 180 hours that year, could qualify for benefits while another person who had worked 50 hours for 11 weeks, for a total of 550 hours, before being laid off could not receive benefits. Under the new EI eligibility rules, it is the second of these workers rather than the first who could qualify.[26]

The second and third EI insurance side measures introduce worker side experience rating. It is important to understand what is meant by experience rating, and by *worker side* versus *employer side* experience rating. Insurance coverage consists of a <u>level of coverage</u>, defined by the amounts and conditions of benefit entitlement, and a <u>premium rate</u>. 'Experience rating' in insurance programmes means that the premium rate for a given coverage level rises, or else that the level of coverage provided for a given premium rate falls, as the risk of the insured hazard rises.[27] With automobile accident coverage, the premium rate typically rises for a given coverage level the greater the amount of accident claims the person seeking coverage has made recently. If this person is unwilling to pay more in premiums, then he or she must be satisfied with less insurance coverage as a consequence of the increase in the price of automobile insurance for any given level of coverage for this person.

In the United States, unemployment insurance premiums are paid entirely by employers on behalf of their workers. Employer side experience rating is a long established feature of unemployment insurance in the United States. With U.S. style employer side experience rating, the insurance tax rates for employers rise the more their workers use the insurance programme.[28]

---

[26] However, the hours of the first worker would count toward qualifying if that person found more weeks of work subsequently or had worked previously.

[27] Working with price indexes that involve decompositions of value into price and quantity components and the Product Rule of index number theory (see Nakamura and Diewert, 1997, for a definition and explanations of this rule and its use) was what led to the recognition that experience rating could be accomplished through the adjustment of insurance coverage levels while keeping the premium rates constant. Those who exhaust their unemployment insurance benefits are eligible to apply for welfare supplements. This includes men and women without dependent children.

[28] Of course, there are practical limitations on how high the employer tax premiums can be raised. Once an employer already faces the maximum premium rate, there will be no further rate increases even if the employer lays off more workers who apply for and take up UI benefits. Perhaps because of this, the U.S. employer side experience rating has not succeeded in stopping regular repeat use or the resulting cross-subsidisation from stable employers and workers to those with intermittent, part-year jobs.

In Canada, the unemployment programme did not involve any experience rating prior to the enactment of Bill C-12. Instituting experience rating on the employer side had seemed unfeasible since, in Canada, both the workers and the employers pay premiums for unemployment insurance. It had seemed wrong to raise the payroll tax rates for workers who had suffered a recent bout of unemployment. In addition, Canada has more employment that is intrinsically seasonal than the U.S. does. It was feared that raising the UI premium rates for employers in seasonal industries whose workers draw heavily on unemployment insurance benefits could put many of these employers out of business. Nevertheless, the growing repeat use of UI benefits was expensive. Also, seasonal repeat use of unemployment insurance does *not* serve a business cycle stabilisation function. In addition, this sort of programme use was undermining public support for the programme. It seemed unfair for some persons to draw unemployment insurance benefits year after year, particularly since some of those doing this were in families that were better off than many of those who paid the costs of this programme through the worker payroll taxes.

The variable regional entrance and extended benefit provisions of UI are retained under EI. However, under EI these provisions are counteracted by 'worker side experience rating' of two types.

The first is the new *intensity rule*. This rule reduces the benefit replacement rate for all regular workers by one percentage point with each added 20 weeks of benefits collected over the previous five years, from 55 percent down to a minimum of 50 percent.[29] The rationale for the intensity rule is that those who have collected benefits for more weeks in the recent past are at greater risk of making future claims. This form of experience rating does not raise the immediate out-of-pocket costs of workers. However, it does make it less attractive for workers to collude with their employers on planned work interruptions financed via the unemployment insurance programme. It is only possible for employers to shift their labour costs onto an unemployment relief programme to the extent that their workers are eligible to collect.

The EI programme couples the mild experience rating of the intensity rule with *clawback rules* that involve more severe worker side experience rating.

Clawbacks were also a feature of the old UI programme. UI benefits were taxable as regular income. In addition, anyone who received UI benefits and then ended up with a taxable income for the year of more than 1.5 times the

---

[29] Workers in poor families are exempt from this rule and may qualify for higher replacement rates.

maximum insurable earnings was subject to a flat 30 percent clawback. Unfortunately, however, this old UI clawback rate was not an effective deterrent to intentional repeat use of the programme by some workers in high marginal income tax brackets.[30]

Under the new EI, those who have collected *less* than 20 weeks of benefits in the previous five years face essentially the same mild clawback provisions as they did before under UI. The main change for them is that the multiple that is used to determine the level of earnings beyond which the clawback provisions apply was reduced from 1.5 to 1.25. However, for those who also have collected *more* than 20 weeks of benefits over the previous year and who have taxable incomes greater than the maximum yearly insurable earnings, the EI clawback rate is steeply experience rated, rising to 100 percent for those who have claimed 120 weeks of benefits in the previous five years.[31]

Evaluation studies to-date of the EI programme suggest that the innovations it introduced are mostly, though not all, functioning as hoped.[32] Programme expenditures have declined[33] while, at the same time, substantial numbers of those holding part-time jobs have become eligible for benefits. The EI worker side experience rating protects the generosity of the programme for occasional

---

[30] The clawback rate was applied to the total benefits received in the taxation year, or the amount by which his or her income for the tax year exceeded 1.5 times the maximum insurable earnings, whichever was less.

[31] For those who collected 21 to 40 weeks of benefits in the previous five years, the EI clawback rate is 50 per cent; for those who collected benefits for 41 to 60 weeks, the EI clawback rate is 60 per cent; and so on up to 100 per cent for anyone with more than 120 weeks of benefits. The clawback only applies to those who end up with an annual taxable income greater than 1.5 times the maximum insurable earnings.

[32] Ging Wong is currently overseeing an empirical evaluation of the outcomes of the Bill C-12 reforms.

[33] The rate at which some groups – new and re-entering workers, in particular – have qualified for EI may have fallen below what is desirable. Under EI, new and re-entering workers must meet a threshold of 900 hours in order to qualify for benefits, regardless of the unemployment conditions in the region where they are. This higher threshold is probably not needed now that the programme involves experience rating based on programme use over the previous five years. Nakamura and Diewert (1997) argue that it would be preferable if new and re-entering workers faced the same eligibility rules as all other workers.

users -- the sort the programme is well suited to help -- while reducing the benefits provided to better off repeat users.[34]

The Canadian Out of Employment Panel Surveys (COEP)

'What was perhaps unique about the current UI reform is the extent to which evaluation results helped shape and support the policy process.... The significance of these evaluations lay in the ability to counter social policy mythology with the closest thing to hard facts that anyone could find. In areas as emotional and opinion-laden as the bread and butter issues which lie at the heart of social policy, the ability to lay a fact on the table can go a long way....'

(Norine Smith 1996,
on her HRDC experiences
with the drafting of the EI Bill C-12)

Federal leadership has included the active development of data resources that are needed for meaningful programme development and evaluation. Statistics Canada has played an essential role in this regard. Other federal departments have also come forward with important data development initiatives. In the context of this chapter, some of the survey and also the administrative data initiatives of HRDC are of special importance. Without access to the appropriate administrative and survey data, proponents favouring different approaches to social policy problems are left arguing about the credibility and prevalence of the anecdotes each have amassed. Good data resources help foster better interactions among the different levels of government and among governments and different public interest groups.

EI, like the old UI programme, provides income support and employment services for labour force participants who have had a job termination. The Canadian Out of Employment Panel (COEP) surveys were instituted by HRDC in collaboration with Statistics Canada to enable better research on the activities of labour force participants following job loss and better evaluations of the effectiveness of programmes intended to help the unemployed get back into the workforce.[35] The 1993 and 1995 COEP surveys were carried out following the

---

[34] It is important to note that the direct reductions of the benefits to repeat users via the intensity rule and the clawback provisions of EI do not depend on behavioural changes, though additional savings may result if behavioural changes occur.

[35] Ging Wong of HRDC initiated and has continued to actively shape and develop the HRDC-Statistics Canada COEP survey project.

passage of two previous UI reform bills, and the 1996 COEP survey was designed to permit a better evaluation of the specific reforms enacted with the passage of Bill C-12, the EI Act.

The 1996 COEP involves 10 cohorts of individuals who experienced at least one job separation between July 1995 and December 1997. The first four cohorts of the 1996 COEP represent individuals who had a job separation before the implementation of the new EI regime. Cohorts 5 and 6 had separation dates corresponding to the six-month phase-in period for the EI programme, and the remaining four cohorts had separation dates that are after the new EI programme rules were fully implemented. A large number of studies have been completed or are in progress now that use the COEP96 data to learn more about the labour market behaviour and outcomes for different demographic groups, and to evaluate what does and does not work well about the new EI programme.

Participants in the COEP surveys were chosen using HRDC's administrative files. More specifically, they were chosen using the Records of Employment (ROE) files. Workers are issued a ROE when they leave a job for any reason.

The COEP data include employment histories of individuals as well as a wide range of other information. There is information on the reasons for, and the behaviour of workers following, job loss. Information is collected on job search activity, job search outcomes, volunteering, and the training and education undertaken. There is also financial information on debt and the receipt of asset income, transfer payments, and public income support benefits from UI/EI, and there is information on household composition and consumption. In addition to providing the basis for evaluation of the unique provisions of the EI programme reforms, the COEP data have made possible far reaching basic research on job search behaviour and the determinants of successful job search.

The National Child Benefit (NCB)

'Among the most serious evidence that the system is misfiring is the high and persistent level of children's poverty.'
(Human Resources Development Canada 1994,
The Discussion Paper, p. 69 and p. 71)

'Better income support for low-income families with children could be provided through a strengthened federal Child Tax Benefit.... As part of this approach, the federal government would need to work with the provinces to ensure that families on social assistance get the full benefit from this reform.... [I]t would give low-income families a secure source of income support for their children, and put parents in a stronger position to leave social assistance for the job market.'

(Human Resources Development Canada 1994,
The Discussion Paper, p. 77)

'The National Child Benefit is the most important social programme to be brought forward in the last thirty years.'

(Pierre S. Pettigrew 1999, p. 101)

The 1997 Budget Papers explain the purpose of the National Child Benefit programme (NCB) as follows:

'Right now, the combined effect of federal and provincial programmes is to reduce the child benefits of parents who leave welfare to enter the workforce. Parents should not be put in the position of penalising their children in order to take a job. The [NCB] benefit would be directed to working families, who would see their incomes rise.'

The NCB combines two significant trends of the last 20 years: the trend toward delivery of social programmes through tax credits or benefits and the trend away from unilateral federal control of social programmes towards an approach negotiated with sub-national levels of government.[36] The programme involves no new law, but rather an increased federal tax credit of about C\$1.7 billion to low income families. The provinces, territories, First Nations and Ontario municipalities (the sub-national NCB partners) have made a corresponding commitment to 'reinvest' the savings they realise from being able to reduce welfare payments to families who receive the NCB. These reinvestments are to be used to finance provincial and other sub-national government benefits and services reflective of each jurisdiction's special needs and priorities and consistent with the central goals of the NCB: to reduce the depth of child poverty and help low income families find and keep work.

---

[36] Similar programmes were already in existence in Canada and elsewhere when this new benefit was announced. In particular, the NCB has many similarities to a successful Quebec programme and to a British Columbia child benefit programme. See the *Discussion Paper*, pp. 71-79 for a brief review of related Canadian programmes. Nakamura and E.M. Diewert (1994) explain the motivations for this programme. Their paper helped pave the way for the BC programme and then for the NCB.

Suitable sub-national government reinvestments under the NCB include income support programmes and tax measures for low-income families with children, as well as the extension of child-care or other in-kind benefits to these families. They also include educational initiatives aimed at preventing or lessening the consequences of child poverty such as nutrition and teen parent programmes. The NCB should help to offset possible EI induced additions to the welfare rolls as well as freeing up provincial resources for local initiatives to help the children of the working poor. The NCB is funded out of general federal tax revenues.

Only low-income working families are eligible to benefit from the new NCB monies. For the first phase of the NCB beginning in July 1998, families with net incomes for the previous year of less than C$22,922 were eligible for the full benefit. There was an increase of C$605 for the first child bringing the amount to $1625; an additional increase of $405 for the second child, bringing the amount to C$3050; and a further increase of C$305 for each additional child, bringing the amount up to C$4475 for three children.[37] In the 1998 Budget, the Federal Government announced that it would contribute an additional C$850 million to the NCB programme over 1999 and 2000.

The greater work effort of poor parents stimulated by the NCB should contribute not only to less child poverty but also, in the longer run, to improved living standards for the parents as they grow older. Parents who rely on welfare and do not work when their children are small typically get little or no training on the job. The wage rates they can command when they go back to work tend to decline rather than rise with the passing years, leaving them poorly suited to support themselves once they no longer have dependent children. This is a more serious problem for women than men since they tend to live longer, have lower wage rates on average when they do work, and work less partly because they typically assume more responsibility for raising children. The NCB should help some parents of dependent children formerly caught in the public income support trap to work, or work more, leading to more accumulated on-the-job experience, more secure employment, and higher earnings in years to come.

In the debate leading up to the announcement of the NCB, the implications for parents receiving welfare benefits were clearly recognised. We believe that the NCB also lessens the unemployment insurance related component of the public income support trap. The NCB raises the monetary return from work for

---

[37] Families with incomes over $25,921 were ineligible to receive an increased NCB benefit. Those in between with incomes of $22,922 to $25,921 were eligible for some increase, but less than the full amounts that those with lower incomes were eligible to receive.

parents who qualify -- making low wage work more attractive compared with collecting unemployment insurance benefits while staying home. This effect of the NCB complements the effects of the EI experience rating reforms which reduce the possibilities for habitual reliance on unemployment insurance benefits for those with sufficient earnings to be affected by the intensity rule and the clawback experience rating provisions.

The Self Sufficiency Project (SSP)

> 'The Self Sufficiency Project (SSP) is a large, innovative social demonstration and research project in Canada that … makes work pay by offering a generous earnings supplement to long term, single-parent welfare recipients who find full-time jobs and leave the Income Assistance (IA) welfare system. SSP seeks to answer this question: If work paid better than welfare, would welfare-dependent single parents take jobs and leave the welfare rolls?'
>
> (Berlin, Bancroft, Card, Lin, and Robins, March 1998, p. vi)

The SSP Programme

The Self-Sufficiency Project (SSP) is a joint initiative of HRDC and the provincial governments of British Columbia and New Brunswick. This programme represents yet another attempt to lessen the pull of the welfare trap.

SSP is a rigorous demonstration project designed to test the functioning and effectiveness of an earnings supplementation programme for long term single parent welfare recipients. Based on a random assignment evaluation design, the programme provides temporary earnings supplements to selected single-parent welfare families in British Columbia and New Brunswick. To collect the supplements, those chosen must leave the welfare rolls and take a job providing at least 30 hours of work per week (referred to as 'full-time work' in the SSP context). One reason for the full-time work provision is to try to steer programme participants toward job situations offering experience and on-the-job training that might make it possible, over time, for them to command higher wages.[38] The SSP supplement was offered to participants on a time-limited basis. They had to find a job within one year of being offered the supplement

---

[38] Blank, Card and Robins (1999) explain other reasons for this requirement having to do with how persons who had not been on welfare might react to an SSP-type programme.

314

and can then receive the SSP supplement payments for up to three years thereafter.

Many single parent welfare recipients have low levels of education and limited work experience. Because of this, the wages they can command in the workplace are often little more than the legal minimum. In fact, many can only find types of work that pay less than the minimum wage. When these single parents apply for and are approved to receive welfare, the benefits awarded rise with the number of dependent children and are often substantially more than what they could earn from work. This economic incentive to stay on welfare is part of the same dilemma that the National Child Benefit (NCB) programme seeks to address by providing supplemental child benefits to working parents. The SSP approach is complementary to the NCB. The SSP seeks to move participants who cannot earn enough to raise their families above a welfare level of support into types of employment that will result in wage growth. The objective is to help these parents achieve work based self-sufficiency.

The SSP Research Design

In developing this initiative, HRDC recognised the importance of testing the effectiveness of an SSP-type programme prior to nation-wide implementation. This is a relatively expensive programme. A random assignment design for those offered the SSP supplements was used to generate a data base that would allow researchers to determine the *incremental effects* of the programme on the propensity to leave -- and remain off of-- welfare, and the incremental effects on the wages received and other employment outcomes over time. As with the COEP data described above, the SSP initiative seeks to harness the power of modern data analysis in the service of research for improving our social programmes.

Between November 1992 and March 1995, more than 6,000 single parents who were long term welfare recipients were invited to join the main SSP study. In British Columbia, SSP operates in the lower mainland, which includes the Vancouver metropolitan area as well as neighbouring areas to the north, south, and east. In New Brunswick, the programme operates in a region covering roughly the lower third of the province, including the cities of Saint John, Moncton, and Fredericton.

Sample members were recruited for SSP's main study and randomly assigned between November 1992 and March 1995 in New Brunswick and between January 1993 and November 1995 in British Columbia. Each of those who accepted this initial invitation was assigned at random to a supplement programme or a control group. Members of the supplement programme group were given the opportunity to try to qualify for the SSP earnings supplements by taking up full-time work and leaving welfare, while members of the control group were not. Because the two groups were chosen to be similar in all respects except whether they were allowed to participate in the earnings supplement programme, the incremental impact of the SSP supplement programme can be measured by the differences between the outcomes for the supplement programme group and the control group.

Each participant's supplement is calculated as half the difference between gross earnings from employment and an 'earnings benchmark' set by SSP. The benchmark was C$37,000 in British Columbia and C$30,000 in New Brunswick when the programme began, and has been raised modestly over time to adjust for inflation. The supplement approximately doubles the earnings of many low wage workers before taxes and their work related expenses. After taxes and tax credits are considered, SSP makes most families C$3,000 to C$7,000 per year better off than they would be if they worked full time and remained on welfare. Unlike welfare or the NCB, supplement payments do not vary with family size, so the programme is less attractive for those with larger families.

A person selected into the SSP supplement programme and who took up the supplement within the 12 months after assignment could then continue to collect the supplement for up to three years. Participants were permitted at any time to return to welfare so long as they gave up the supplement while on welfare again and so long as they still met the welfare eligibility requirements. They could also renew their supplement receipt at any time over the three-year period by going back to work full time and going off welfare again. Unlike the NCB, this is a programme designed primarily to change the *future* earnings possibilities of participants through growth in wage rates.

Wage growth with increased work experience is also a hope of the NCB, but that programme aims to make work more attractive than welfare even for parents whose wages do not rise. The intent of the NCB is to help insure, on a continuing basis, an adequate standard of living for the children of low wage parents. Those parents can continue to collect NCB assistance for as long as they have dependent children and work. In contrast, a three-year time limit for receiving the SSP supplement was established to avoid the possibility of long term programme dependence.

Because the SSP supplements are generous (much more generous than the NCB is now), without wage growth over time, those on the programme will experience a large drop in their standard of living at the end of the three year supplement period. In fact, without wage growth, at the termination of the programme many of the participants still will face lower after-tax earnings than what they could get from welfare.

The SSP Research Questions

The SSP has the goal of answering a series of questions that are important for deciding whether an actual programme along the lines of the SSP should be enacted in Canada, and how much should be spent on this versus other programme options including enhancing the NCB assistance to working parents. Evaluation results for the first 18 months of SSP operation are available by now for the 5,288 of the original 6,000 single parents invited to join the main SSP study who completed a follow-up survey.[39] The results are based on data from four sources: a baseline survey administered at the time of random assignment, a follow-up survey administered approximately 18 months after random assignment, provincial welfare administrative records, and records from SSP's Programme Management Information System which tracks programme activities and supplement payments. Some of the questions that the SSP project is designed to answer are:

- Will welfare recipients want to participate in such a programme if given this option?

- Will they be able to find the full-time jobs they need to be able to take up the supplement?

- Will participants achieve high enough employment earnings over the three-year supplement period so that they will find it in their best interests to continue working when the supplements end?

- Will the public benefits of the programme be sufficient to justify the costs? How much should be spent on this sort of programme versus other types such as the NCB?

---

[39] More specifically, results are available for the first 18 months after each sample member was randomly assigned, including the month of the random assignment. Thus, for the earliest sample members randomly assigned, the period studied is November 1992 to April 1994. For those who were randomly assigned last, the period studied is March 1995 to August 1996. For SSP findings, see Card and Robins (1998), and Lin, Robins, Card, Harknett, Lui-Gurr and others (1998). See also Quet, Robins, Pan, Michalopoulos and Card (1999).

A full evaluation of the programme is underway. However, the evidence so far already suggests a tentative positive answer to the first two questions above. If the SSP programme succeeds for some who would otherwise have such low wages that they could not earn as much as they would get from welfare, this intervention may mean that these persons will leave welfare for good. This would be important, since examinations of welfare data reveal that a high proportion of those leaving welfare soon return. If those who participate in an SSP-type programme enjoy substantial wage gains as their labour market experience increases, these wage gains would be expected to go together with improvements in the security of their employment situations.

Internet Recruiting Information (IRI) Services

'The support mechanisms for shopping for machines are better developed than those available to employers and employees seeking job matches....This problem might be surmounted by developing electronic hiring halls ... for posting job seeker qualifications and job vacancies that could be accessed from any computer with a modem, anywhere within Canada or through established international e-mail computer network linkages. From junior high on, students could be familiarised with how to use these networks.... Active job seekers could search the electronic bulletin boards by key words to find jobs of interest, jobs in a specific location, and so on.'

(Alice Nakamura and Peter Lawrence, 1993)

'The Internet makes it possible to disseminate a vast amount of information to a great many individuals or groups for the cost of a telephone call.'

(Pierre S. Pettigrew 1999, p. 20)

'On-line recruitment systems, such as Campus WorkLink which is jointly operated by Industry Canada and the Canadian Association of Career Educators and Employers, are radically changing the availability of labour market information and hiring practices.'

(John Manley, Minister of Industry, August, 1999)

Infrastructure services have been the traditional purview of governments: the roadways, the rail lines, the ports and airports, the schools, and so on. Internet recruiting information (IRI) services for job seekers and for employers are a relatively new and expanding part of the portfolio of infrastructure services that governments are providing and are encouraging private sector businesses and non-profit organisations to provide more of as well.

The Need for Expanded IRI Services

These services did not exist prior to the development of the electronic information highways, and their potential uses are still being discovered. The initial usage was primarily for recruiting in software development and other specialised technical areas where employers were forced to conduct wide searches because of labour shortages. However, usage soon spread to other occupations. It now includes many areas where it is the job seekers rather than the employers who are led by specialisation or by scarcity of opportunity to search widely. For many employers and job seekers, IRI services are rapidly becoming a major means of search and first contact. They are a valuable complement to - not a substitute for - the traditional means of job search.

Searching for work in new places

Print materials about employment opportunities, such as help wanted ads in newspapers, usually carry only small amounts of information about the job openings and the desired qualifications of the applicants. Those looking for work from a distance need more specific and extensive information to make better choices about which openings they should follow up on. It can be hard for job seekers to find out-of-town print materials. Most libraries do not have all of the relevant out-of-town newspapers, newsletters and so on. Moreover, out-of-town publications tend to arrive with delay.

A further problem is that a large portion of jobs are never openly advertised. Candidates for these jobs are found through informal contacts. Because of this, a person coming into a new locality without prearranged employment or personal connections faces greater difficulty finding work than local labour force participants.

Local area job search

Most people prefer to work in, or near to, the localities where they have been living. Those who find a local job are able to maintain their networks of family, friends and business associates. Also, living costs during the search period will usually be lower this way, and there are no moving costs to pay. If most people prefer to find work locally and if local area job searches tend to be more successful and cost effective, it is important for these searches to be thorough. By now, it is recognised that IRI services can be helpful for local area as well as distance job searches.

On the job seeker side, there are a number of problems impeding local area searches that effective IRI services can mitigate. These pertain to the initial stages of job search:

- locating employers with suitable openings,

- submitting an initial application,

- submitting follow-up materials, and

- arranging for employment interviews.

Many workers begin their search for work while still employed. It can be difficult for employed job seekers to receive and respond to messages from recruiters during their regular working hours. The dollar and time costs of responding to job postings in hard copy form are a second impediment.[40] Another problem is the psychological discomfort that job seekers build up as a consequence of repeat in-person rejection experiences. Rejections are common in the initial stages of job search.

With IRI services, worker-recruiter contact and communications are facilitated by the substitution of confidential electronic messaging for telephone contacts. These services enable low or zero marginal cost transmissions of employment credentials such as work histories and transcripts. In addition, electronic messaging is a medium of communication that may make it easier for job candidates to deal emotionally with rejections during the initial stages of job search, so that they can keep on applying.

Employer needs

Employers also have IRI service needs. Many are poorly connected to local area networks for the exchange of employment information. This is particularly

---

[40] These costs include typing and word processing, photo copying, postage, and courier and fax charges. With electronic information exchanges at the initial stages of job search, an applicant will only need to provide hard copies of certificates and other evidence of job qualifications to those employers interested in proceeding to the interview stage of the recruitment process.

common for businesses that are small or new or that hire infrequently. Employers face problems getting the word out about job openings they are unable to fill from within. Help wanted ads in newspapers are widely used, but the expense can be prohibitive for many small businesses. Also, most public methods for the exchange of employment information expose employers to the possibility of getting too many applications from job seekers who do not have the needed qualifications. Private employment services are useful for screening applicants, but charge fees that are substantial for small and newer businesses and that are high enough that larger businesses are typically unwilling to use these services when hiring for jobs below the executive or highly skilled categories.

In a 1993 paper and associated memos and talks, Nakamura and Lawrence made a number of specific suggestions for ways in which the power of new information technologies could be used to help employers as well as job seekers with their recruitment activities. Their recommendations first found their way onto the Canadian public policy agenda through a 1994 HRDC *Discussion Paper*:

> '[E]mployers and employees could feed information about their respective requirements and skills into a computerised system, and get back a list of either potential jobs or applicants for immediate action. Such an 'electronic hiring hall' could be accessed from a Canada Employment Centre, or a provincial or municipal office, or a home or business computer terminal.'
>
> (Human Resources Development Canada,
> *The Discussion Paper*, p. 34)

IRI Services Developed and Implemented by HRDC and Industry Canada

By now, HRDC and Industry Canada have developed a portfolio of IRI services. The IRI initiatives have focused on job seeker needs, and particularly on the needs of participants in large government programmes. Attention was directed toward areas where the private sector was not providing the needed services and where non-government, non-profit organisations had not come forward to fill the gap. The federal government sought to provide IRI services in areas of market failure, with the objective of improving the outcomes and reducing costs for other government programmes.

Services for the unemployed

The initial HRDC investments in this area were directed toward the unemployed and especially toward those receiving unemployment insurance benefits. HRDC created the National Job Bank and the Electronic Labour Exchange (ELE).

The National Job Bank began as a mainframe computer support system (NESS) for the paper-based job posting bulletin boards in the front offices of the Canada Employment Centres across the country. This NESS system evolved into a mainframe system linked into kiosks across Canada. The system could be accessed by unemployed job seekers and others as well through the regional Canada Employment Centre offices. Eventually, it became possible to use the system through provincial government offices, and at some public locations such as libraries and shopping centres. The Internet version of the National Job Bank was built about three years ago and now interfaces seamlessly with the older mainframe/kiosk version of the system.[41]

The National Job Bank only handles job postings. In contrast, the ELE is a skills-matching system designed to help employers and workers connect on-line. A job seeker using the ELE first chooses a job category, and then fills out a checklist on his or her skills and other qualifications. Once this step is finished, the ELE system tries to match the job seeker's qualifications with an employer who has a position that requires those qualifications. If there are no suitable job openings on the system, the job seeker can choose to advertise his or her qualifications to employers visiting the ELE site.[42]

IRI services for post-secondary level recruitment

Post secondary education is another expenditure area for the federal government, though it is the provinces that have most of the administrative responsibility in this area. Many of those finishing post- secondary education programmes need job finding help. HRDC and Industry Canada have collaborated to produce a range of IRI services to aid the school-to-work transition process.[43] Helping graduates of post-secondary education

---

[41] The National Job Bank can be found at jb-ge.hrdc.gc.ca.

[42] The Electronic Labour Exchange can be found at www.ele-spe.org.

[43] HRDC in collaboration with other federal departments, and provincial and community partners, has developed the Youth Resource Network of Canada (see www.youth.gc.ca).

programmes find work that makes use of their training helps Canada get a better return on public expenditures in this area. Also, it makes it less likely that these graduates will eventually require unemployment insurance or other income support and more likely that they will be ongoing tax paying participants in the Canadian economy.

Many post-secondary graduates must conduct geographically wide searches if they are to find positions that will make use of their specialised educations. On graduation, many post-secondary graduates also have work experience from jobs they held prior to, or while, pursuing their post-secondary education programmes. This further specialises the positions where these graduates can fully utilise their skills. Post-secondary job seekers and the employers who need their talents and skills have greater needs for searching beyond their immediate localities than is the norm for the labour market as a whole.

Campus WorkLink:NGR

> 'Campus WorkLink connects more than 130,000 students and recent graduates to a pool of over 30,000 potential employers who can post job notices or search résumés when filling job vacancies. One of the benefits of on-line recruitment is that human resources managers can quickly sift through large quantities of information to select the individuals whom they want to interview.'
>
> (John Manley, Minister of Industry, August, 1999)

In Canada, the post-secondary sector is heavily subsidised from general provincial and federal tax revenues. The justification for the federal contribution to these institutions is that they are building the human capital stock of the *nation*; not just for the specific localities in which these institutions are located. It is appropriate, therefore, that employers throughout Canada should be able to conveniently and cheaply find and communicate with the students or graduates of these institutions who might be interested in working for these employers. The campus career placement centres, each acting in isolation, cannot provide nation-wide connectivity, though their offices serve many other valuable purposes and will continue to be needed.

In 1995, Industry Canada took an important step toward meeting this need for some form of nation-wide one-stop career placement services for new and recent post-secondary graduates. With the encouragement of a number of the university presidents, Industry Canada developed and implemented what is now called Campus WorkLink:NGR. Industry Canada administers this system in partnership with the Canadian Association of Career Educators and Employers (CACEE) and continues to receive financial assistance from Industry Canada. Most of the directors of the campus career placement offices belong to CACEE.

Campus WorkLink:NGR specialises in entry level jobs for those with post-secondary credentials, and is available to all students and new graduates of accredited universities and colleges in Canada. In addition to employer profiles and national recruitment campaigns, Campus WorkLink:NGR allows employers to target job postings to the students and recent graduates of the public and private post-secondary institutions that are Campus WorkLink:NGR partners.

By now, almost 600 of the Canadian post-secondary institutions have signed partnership agreements through their campus career placement offices. This number includes all but about 5 percent of the public post-secondary institutions. However, a few of the campus career placement offices that have declined to partner with this national service are on the campuses of publicly funded universities that have very large student bodies. Because of this, there are still tens of thousands of Canadian students and new graduates who cannot access all of Campus WorkLink:NGR's features -- namely the thousands of job postings that employers specifically target to students and graduates of post-secondary institutions that are Campus WorkLink:NGR partners.

For this and other reasons, it is still the case that the vast majority of the students and graduates of Canadian post-secondary institutions are not registered with or using Campus WorkLink:NGR. This has become a source of concern to some because of developments in the United States.

A Potential Brain Drain Problem

Internet recruiting information services have evolved more quickly in the United States than in Canada.

Large numbers of Canadian post-secondary students and alumni are now signing up with and posting their resumes on U.S.-based IRI services. Of course, long before the advent of Internet recruiting, some of the most accomplished graduates of Canadian post-secondary institutions were being hired away by U.S. and international firms. However, there is concern now that this selective brain drain problem could be exacerbated by the growing dominance of U.S.-based IRI services.

The concern is that U.S. and international employers who control and use these services will succeed in locating and making early offers to Canadian post-secondary graduates with scarce skills before Canadian employers can locate and make contact with them. Graduating students are most vulnerable to accepting U.S. offers when they have not yet been contacted by any Canadian employers. This is particularly the case for graduates who have large student loans that they must begin paying off soon after graduation. Many are also worried that they may have no Canadian opportunities for working in their chosen fields. However, faculty members know from direct contact with their students that many of them would strongly prefer to stay in Canada, near to their friends and families, if they could find suitable employment.

All of the open web IRI services are free for job seekers. This includes the many U.S. based and commercial ones. It is the employers who pay. Of course, Canadian employers can pay to post on the U.S. based IRI services but they will receive less good value than their U.S. counterparts. This is not because of discrimination by the IRI service providers. Canada is a smaller country. It is inevitable that the Canadian proportion of job seekers using IRI services that operate North America-wide will be much smaller than the U.S. proportion. Also, U.S. employers are more likely to be in a position to offer compensation packages that are attractive to job seekers both sides of the U.S.-Canada border.

Canadian employers would have a better chance of attracting needed talent produced by Canadian post-secondary institutions if these employers could quickly, easily and cheaply find and communicate with the relevant students and graduates of these institutions who have the needed skills and who might be interested in working for Canadian employers. Campus WorkLink:NGR by itself can only partially fill this need. Actually, this would be so even if all the campus career placement offices became Campus WorkLink:NGR partners since the graduates can only continue to use this service for three years following graduation.

CareerOwl: A Non-Profit Complement to the Government IRI Services

'In facilitating rapid and appropriate job placement for our most outstanding graduates, CareerOwl helps to maximise the effectiveness of our investment in higher education and to keep our most productive workers here in Canada.'

(Paul Davenport, President, University of Western Ontario,
Roderick Fraser, President, University of Alberta,
Martha Piper, President, University of British Columbia)

As noted, large numbers of students and alumni of Canadian universities, colleges and technical schools are using Campus WorkLink:NGR, but even larger numbers are not.[44] There is a need for IRI services to complement the post-secondary coverage of Campus WorkLink:NGR. This is especially true in the light of the general trend toward more job changing over the working lifetime. Increasing numbers of those who finished their post-secondary educational programmes more than three years ago will need to search for new jobs. This is after these workers are no longer eligible to use Campus WorkLink:NGR and when that service would no longer be suitable even if they were eligible because it specialises in entry level jobs for students and new graduates.

CareerOwl is a technologically advanced IRI service built with the private donations of money and expertise of Canadian university faculty members and students[45] and intended to function as a complement to Campus WorkLink:NGR. It is an open web-based service that allows job seekers to search over job postings and to post their own resumes for employers to search over. On the employer side, information about jobs can be posted or targeted to employer-specified groups of students and alumni without any requirement for membership with CareerOwl on the part of the campus career placement offices of the educational institutions that these job seekers attended.

While available to all, CareerOwl has special features to facilitate career-long post-secondary level recruitment. The reason most commonly given by employers for *not* using IRI services for upper end recruitment is that open postings on large systems for positions of this sort can attract far too many applicants, including many who do not have the needed qualifications. Peter Lawrence -- a professor of electrical engineering at the University of British Columbia and a specialist in tele-robotics -- was the one who recognised that an open web software system could be designed that would permit employers, at their discretion, to make job postings that could be seen by, or sent out to, only those job seekers with the required qualifications. The CareerOwl software

---

[44] There are those who are not eligible at all (mainly those more than three years beyond completion of their post-secondary studies). There are those who are not interested due to being from institutions where the campus career placement offices have declined to partner with Campus WorkLink:NGR. And there are those who are not interested for other reasons. Survey research is underway to determine the breakdown of non-users by these categories.

[45] The CareerOwl system is managed by the CareerOwl Institute which is a non-profit, but also a *non-charitable*, organisation incorporated for Canada-wide operation. The significance of this being a non-charitable organisation is that no tax write-offs were claimed for the start-up funds that were donated to create CareerOwl.

permits employers to determine the sorts of job seekers who will receive or be able to view their job postings. For instance, employers can pre-screen job seekers by their levels of education, the institutions where they obtained this education, their years of work experience, the languages they know, and where they are willing to work.[46]

In addition to pre-screening options, CareerOwl offers busy job seekers advanced virtual agent technology. Job seekers can give information about their employment needs and can request their virtual agents to watch for posting meeting these needs. When the virtual agent finds such a posting, the user is notified of this by e-mail.

Another valuable feature for both employers and job seekers is CareerOwl's specially tailored messaging system that facilitates the direct, one-on-one exchange of information between employers and job seekers while allowing them the choice of remaining anonymous until whenever they choose to disclose contact information. It is believed that these features will be of special value for the recruitment of more experienced workers, many of whom are interested in carrying out their job searches while still employed. Soon after the CareerOwl service first went on-line, Jennifer Lewington wrote in the Globe and Mail:

> 'CareerOwl (www.CareerOwl.ca) is one of a new breed of Internet job sites. What makes CareerOwl special is its communication technology -- essentially an application software which runs over the Internet.'

Since CareerOwl is an open web system, all those using other co-operating Canadian IRI services (including students and alumni using co-operating campus internet systems) can also come over onto the CareerOwl system and

---

[46] From 1993 on, Nakamura and Lawrence recommended that an IRI service with the capacity for job-by-job prescreening and targeting should be built and made available for use by Canadian employers as part of the infrastructure of the nation. In the winter of 1998/99, David Bates, a New Zealand software developer and economist, was employed for a year to design and build the CareerOwl software system and web site, working together with a team of students and alumni. The other members of the team that worked under David Bates to turn the Lawrence-Nakamura vision into a functioning internet recruiting information system were Kiyotsugu Adachi, Jason Carter, Paul Chow, and Erik Diewert at the Vancouver development site for the project and, in Edmonton, Susan Budge, Aileen Hooda, Nathan Morcos, Mike Stansberry, and Richard Watson. The development operations took place in off campus space made available to the project without charge by faculty members.

check job postings there that employers have enabled job seekers with their qualifications to see. The use of CareerOwl in this way by those who have signed up on other Canadian systems can be facilitated automatically by any Canadian system with compatible objectives and that contacts CareerOwl to enable this. CareerOwl strongly supports inter-system linkages of this sort. These linkages can enable different sorts of worker and industry groups to have systems of their own, supported by different sorts of software systems and with special features for their own members, while nevertheless furthering the connectivity of the Canadian labour market.

With linkages between co-operating Canadian IRI services, employers need only post on one of the inter-linked systems in order for their job postings to be found by job seekers on all of them. This is important in the post-secondary labour market where some of the campus career placement offices and many of the industry groups that hire at the post-secondary level already have highly developed internet systems of their own. Linkages among co-operating systems are the key to avoiding the impractical necessity of having all potential users agree on just one sort of system. CareerOwl supports the use of the internet to facilitate job seeker and employer choice while at the same time providing nation-wide connectivity.[47]

The CareerOwl initiative is important for the new concepts in IRI system functionality that it introduces and for the important ways in which this faculty and student volunteer effort interfaces with the campuses (the faculty being the main point of contact with the students) as well as with the IRI infrastructure initiatives of Industry Canada and HRDC. CareerOwl is an initiative that grows out of considerations and insights that are potentially important as well for other countries that are spending public funds to provide high quality post-secondary education services, and are finding that they are losing significant numbers of those trained to foreign recruiters.

An Important Investment in Canadian Productivity

The HRDC, Industry Canada and CareerOwl initiatives to expand the availability and improve the usage of IRI services in Canada are an important and proactive step toward expanding employment hours, reducing public

---

[47] We are greatly indebted to Kelly Meechan, the Director of Co-operative Education, Engineering at the University of British Columbia for repeatedly stressing the importance of this while CareerOwl was being developed. Her advice in this regard became the guiding spirit of the CareerOwl initiative.

income support costs, and improving the productivity of the Canadian economy.[48]

High quality, low cost IRI services can help Canadian students and workers be more aware of the evolving skill needs of Canadian employers. This, in turn, can aid them in making better choices about the areas in which to take courses and invest their study time, and may help them to be more realistic in their job search expectations. Better human capital investment decisions by individuals can help Canada achieve a higher rate of return on public investments in education.

Locating appropriate candidates for available job openings is an important and often costly step in the hiring process. IRI services can lower these recruitment costs. These services can also enable businesses to search more widely for needed talent and skills.

A business or other productive unit that has a job opening is usually an organisation that will function better as soon as the position can be filled, and that would begin paying the new person as soon as he or she can be hired. If IRI services can shorten up the periods of search for employers with openings by even a few hours on average, this will raise productivity and will also increase the hours of employment and employment income (though not necessarily the number of jobs). This will boost government tax revenues as well, thereby increasing the funds available to pay for public services.

Finally, by reducing the costs of recruitment and improving the outcomes, IRI services have the potential to lower the costs of domestic labour relative to other input factors including capital equipment and labour purchased from outside of Canada. This too should help raise employment and employment earnings.

Concluding Remarks

This chapter outlines five interconnected initiatives fostered by Human Resources Development Canada in collaboration with other federal and provincial partners:

---

[48] Productivity improvement means that there has been a reduction of input costs for the same output, or enhanced output with the same input.

1. The *EI reforms* of the Canadian unemployment insurance system that were brought in with the enactment of Bill C-12.

2. The COEP panel data surveys instituted to enable scientific, information-based monitoring and evaluation of the EI and earlier unemployment insurance reforms, and to enable research on job finding processes.

3. The National Child Benefit (NCB) programme of support for children in low income families with at least one working parent.

4. The Self Sufficiency Project (SSP) that makes it financially desirable for low income single parents to take full time jobs that may facilitate wage growth over time.

5. The array of on-line recruitment information (IRI) services that HRDC and Industry Canada have been encouraging, and the non-profit, non-government CareerOwl service started as a volunteer project by staff, students and alumni of the universities of Alberta, British Columbia and Western Ontario.

Together, these initiatives have laid the foundation for the development of a new approach to Canadian social policy.

All of these initiatives have federal government roots, but important local dimensions. They take account of the fact that people live in specific localities and that jobs too are in specific places. They involve new partnership arrangements with sub-national levels of government. These initiatives also reflect a government sector choice to become more proactive in dealing with problems of unemployment. Government departments that provide assistance for those having difficulty meeting their own needs have typically been *reactive* in their offerings:

- Reactive in responding directly to the *immediate needs* of clients already in difficulty.

- Reactive to the *sources* of the difficulties that their clients face such as the failures of large businesses and plant closings, shifts in the patterns of trade, and technological changes that produce regional or industry-specific shortages of jobs.

–   Reactive to the *chronic problems* of special needs clients, such as those with little education or training, or who are illiterate, or who lack proficiency in an official language, or who have health conditions or family responsibilities that limit where and when they can work.

The social programme initiatives discussed in this paper can help in all of these reactive ways.   However, these new reforms have important *proactive* components as well.

Consider the EI reform measures.   A central objective is to preserve a valued safety net programme while protecting the Canadian economy which is the long run source of jobs and prosperity for the people of this nation.

Consider the NCB and the SSP programmes.   Both programmes are forward looking in that they seek to improve the situation of children in poor families in ways that research suggests will improve their chances of growing up to be economically self-sufficient.   The NCB and SSP programmes are forward looking as well in trying to improve the *future* labour market prospects of parents so it will be easier for them to be self-supporting once they no longer have dependent children to care for.   Both the NCB and the SSP programmes make it easier for poor parents to work and still provide their children with an economic standard of living that is as good or better than they would have by relying on public income support instead.

Consider the data development initiatives that are being carried forward in collaboration with Statistics Canada.   These are helping to insure the availability of the raw information that is an essential input into scientific programme evaluation and policy formation exercises.

Finally, consider the initiatives to expand the availability and quality of Internet recruiting information (IRI) services.   By helping to make these services available cheaply as part of the nation's infrastructure, the federal government is acting not only to help those who have been unemployed find work -- a reactive service -- but also to help Canadians *avoid* spells of unemployment.   Publicly available IRI services can reduce employment search costs and improve the outcomes for both employers and job seekers.   This will enhance labour productivity in Canada, enhance the competitiveness of Canadian firms, help raise the incomes of Canadian families and help reduce the requirements for public income support.

References

Banting, Keith G. and Beach, Charles M. (1994)
Reforming Our Public Income Support Programs: A Focus on Children,
School of Policy Studies, Queen's University.

Barrett, Garry, Doiron, Denise, Green ,David and Riddell, Craig (1994)
The Interaction of Unemployment Insurance and Social Assistance,
Employment and Immigration Canada, Ottawa.

Berlin, G., Bancroft, W., Card, D., Lin, W. and Robins, P.K. (1998).
*Do Work Incentives Have Unintended Consequences? Measuring 'Entry
Effects' in the Self-Sufficiency Project*, Social Research and
Demonstration Corporation, Ottawa.

Blank, Rebecca M., Card, David and Robins, Philip K. (1999)
'Financial Incentives for Increasing Work and Income Among Low-
Income Families,' Working Paper 6998, National Bureau of Economic
Research.

Blank, Rebecca M. and Hanratty, Maria (1993)
'Responding to Need: A Comparison of Social Safety Nets in Canada
and the United States', in David Card and Richard B. Freeman (Eds.),
*Small Differences that Matter: Labor Markets and Income Maintenance
in Canada and the United States*, University of Chicago Press.

Browning, M. Jones, S.R.G. and Kuhn, P. (1995)
'Studies of the Interaction of UI and Welfare Using the COEP Dataset', a
paper in the series UI, Income Distribution and Living Standards,
sponsored by Human Resources Development Canada.

Bruce, R., Bailey, N. Cragg, J. Nakamura, A. and Warburton, B. (1996)
'Those Returning to Income Assistance,' *Canadian Journal of
Economics*, Vol. 29, Special Issue, April 1996, pp. S33-S38.

Burgess, P.L. (1992)
'Compliance with Unemployment Insurance Job-Search Regulations,'
Journal of Law and Economics, 35, pp. 371-396.

Canada (1985)
*Royal Commission on the Economic Union and Development Prospects
for Canada [Macdonald Commission] Report*, Supply and Services
Canada, Ottawa.

Card, David and Robins, Philip K. (1998)
'Do Financial Incentives Encourage Welfare Recipients to Work? Initial Findings from the Self-Sufficiency Project,' *Research in Labor Economics*, Vol. 17, Solomon Polachek (Ed.), Greenwich, CN: JAI Press.

Christofides, L.N. and McKenna, C. J. (1995)
'Employment Patterns and Unemployment Insurance', a paper in the series *UI Impacts on Worker Behavior*, sponsored by Human Resources Development Canada.

Corak, Miles, (1994)
'Unemployment Insurance, Work Disincentives, and the Canadian Labor Market: An Overview' in Richards and Watson (1994), pp. 86-159.

Corak, Miles and Pyper, Wendy (1995)
'Firms, Industries and Cross-Subsidies: Patterns in the Distribution of UI Benefits and Taxes', a Human Resources Development Canada Evaluation Report, Ottawa.

Davies, James B. (1998)
'Marginal Tax Rates in Canada: High and Getting Higher,' *Commentary*, C.D. Howe Institute.

Diewert, W. Erwin (1981)
'The Measurement of Deadweight Loss Revisited', *Econometrica*, 49:5, pp. 1225-1244.

Diewert, W. Erwin, (1984)
'The Measurement of Deadweight Loss in an Open Economy' *Economica*, 51:1, pp. 23-42.

Diewert, W. Erwin (1988)
'On Tax Reform', *The Canadian Journal of Economics*, 21, pp. 1-40.

Diewert, W. Erwin and Lawrence, D.A. (1996)
'The Deadweight Costs of Taxation in New Zealand', *Canadian Journal of Economics*, 29, pp. S658-S673.

Diewert, W. Erwin, Lawrence, D.A. and Thompson, F. (1998)
'The Marginal Costs of Taxation and Regulation', in *Handbook of Public Finance*, Thompson F. and Green, M.T. (Eds.), New York, Marcel Dekker, pp. 135-171.

Diewert, W. Erwin and Fox, Kevin J. (1999)
'Can Measurement Error Explain the Productivity Paradox?', *Canadian Journal of Economics*, 32(2), pp. 251-280.

Diewert, W. Erwin, Nakamura, Alice O. and Sharpe, Andrew (1999)
'Introduction and Overview,' v-xxviii.

Foot, David K. (1998)
Boom, Bust and Echo 2000, Macfarlane Walter and Ross, Toronto.

Fortin, Pierre (1994)
'A Strategy for Deficit Control through Faster Growth', *Canadian Business Economics*, 3(1), pp. 3-26.

Fortin, Mario and Fortin, Pierre (1999)
'The Changing Labour Force Participation of Canadians, 1969-96', *Canadian Business Economics*, 7(2), pp. 12-24.

Human Resources Development Canada (1994)
Improving Social Security in Canada: A Discussion Paper.

Kahn, S. and Lang, K. (1996)
'Hours Constraints and the Wage / Hours Locus', *Canadian Journal of Economics,* 29 (Special Issue, Part 1), pp. S71-S75.

Kahn, S. and Lang, K. (1995)
'The Causes of Hours Constraints: Evidence from Canada', *Canadian Journal of Economics,* 28, pp. 914-928.

Kesselman, Jonathan R., (1983)
Financing Canadian Unemployment Insurance, Canadian Tax Foundation, Toronto.

Kesselman, Jonathan R., (1986)
'The Royal Commission's Proposals for Income Security Reform', *Canadian Public Policy*, 12, Supplement 101-11.

Lin, Winston, Robins, Philip K., Card, David, Harknett, Kristen, Lui-Gurr, Susanna et al (1998)
When Financial Incentives Encourage Work: Complete 18-Month Findings from the Self-Sufficiency Project, Social Research and Demonstration Corporation, Ottawa, Ontario.

May, Doug and Hollett, Alton (Eds.) (1995)
   The Rock in a Hard Place: Atlantic Canada and the UI Trap, C.D. Howe
   Institute, Toronto.

Mintz, Jack M. and Wilson, Thomas A. (1994)
   'Options for the Goods and Services Tax', *Canadian Business
   Economics*, 3(1), pp. 27-36.

Nakamura, Alice O. (1995)
   'New Directions for UI, Social Assistance, and Vocational Education and
   Training', presidential address delivered to the annual meeting of the
   Canadian Economics Association, University of Quebec at Montreal, 3
   June 1995, and published in the November 1995 issue of the *Canadian
   Journal of Economics*.

Nakamura, Alice O., Cragg, John G. and Sayers, Kathleen (1994)
   'The Case for Disentangling the Insurance and Income Assistance Roles
   of Unemployment Insurance', *Canadian Business Economics*, 3(1, Fall),
   pp. 46-53.

Nakamura, Alice O. and Diewert, Erik M. (1994)
   'Reforming Our Public Income Support Programs: A Focus on
   Children'; in Banting and Beach (1994), pp. 177-198.

Nakamura, Alice O. and Diewert, W. Erwin (1997)
   'Unemployment Insurance in Canada: Problems and Recent Reforms',
   forthcoming in an Upjohn Institute volume edited by William Alpert and
   Stephen Woodbury. This paper builds on an earlier 1994 paper, 'The
   Canadian UI Programme: Problems and Suggested Reforms', prepared
   as part of the materials for the Conference on Employee Benefits, Labor
   Costs, and Labor Markets in Canada and the U.S., jointly sponsored by
   the U.S. Donner Foundation and the W.E. Upjohn Institute.

Nakamura, Alice and Lawrence, P. (1993)
   'Education, Training and Prosperity', presented at the Stabilisation,
   Growth and Prosperity Conference, Queen's University, 15-16 October
   1993 and published in revised form in T.J. Courchene (Ed.), *Stabilisation,
   Growth and Distribution: Linkages in the Knowledge Era*, The John
   Deutsch Institute for the Study of Economic Policy, Queen's University,
   1994, pp. 235-279.

Nakamura, Alice and Wong, Ging (1997)
Canada's Social Security Programs and Payroll Taxes, forthcoming in a volume edited by Albert Berry.

Newfoundland and Labrador (1986)
Royal Commission on Employment and Unemployment: Building on Our Strengths. Chaired by Doug House, Queen's Printer, St. John's.

Orcutt, Guy H. and Orcutt, Alice [now Alice Nakamura] (1968)
'Incentive and Disincentive Experimentation for Income Maintenance and Policy', *American Economic Review*, 58, pp. 754-772.

Osberg, Lars (1995)
'Is Unemployment or Unemployment Insurance the Problem in Atlantic Canada?', in May and Hollett (1995), pp. 215-228.

Pettigrew, Pierre S. (1999)
The Politics of Confidence (translated into English by Phyllis Aronoff and Howard Scott from the French version titled *Pour une politique de la confiance*, published in 1998), Stoddard Publishing Company, Toronto.

Osberg, Lars and Lin, Zhengxi (1999)
'How Much of Canada's Unemployment Is Structural?', presented at the CSLS Conference on the Structural Aspects of Unemployment in Canada, April 22-23, Ottawa.

Phipps, Shelley (1993)
'Does Unemployment Insurance Increase Unemployment?', *Canadian Business Economics*, 1 (Spring), pp. 37-50.

Phipps, Shelley (1991)
'Behavioural Response to UI Reform in Constrained and Unconstrained Models of Labour Supply', *Canadian Journal of Economics,* 14 (1), pp. 35-54.

Picot, Garnett and Heisz, Andrew (1999)
'Canadian Labour Market Performance in Historical Context', presented at the CSLS Conference on the Structural Aspects of Unemployment in Canada, April 22-23, Ottawa.

Quet, Gail, Robins, Philip K., Pan, Elsie, Michalopoulos, Charles and Card, David (1999)
  Adding Employment Services to the Self-Sufficiency Project's Financial Incentives: Implementation and 18-Month Results of the SSP Plus Study, Social Research and Demonstration Corporation, Ottawa, Ontario

Richards, John and Watson, William G. (Eds.) (1994)
  Unemployment Insurance: How to Make It Work, C.D. Howe Institute, Toronto.

Roy, A.S. and Wong, G. (1997)
  'Incidence of Non-Compliance with UI Regulations and Associated Claimant Characteristics', forthcoming in *Evaluation Review*.

Scarth, William (1997)
  'A Job-Creation Strategy for Governments with No Money,' *Commentary*, C.D. Howe Institute.

Sharpe, Andrew and Grignon, Louis (1999)
  'Symposium on Labour Force Participation in Canada in the 1990s: An Introduction and Overview,' *Canadian Business Economics*, 7(2), pp. 12-24.

Wong, Ging and Roy, Arun S. (1997)
  'Effectiveness of UI Non-Compliance Detection', *The Canadian Journal of Program Evaluation*, 12(2), pp. 21-34.

Wong, G., Roy, A, Laurendeau, M., Routhier, A., Guest, C. and Kardas, W. (1992)
  Evaluation of UI Claimant Abuse, Insurance Programs Directorate, Employment and Immigration Canada, Ottawa.

THE CONFERENCE PROGRAMME AND SPEAKERS

**International conference on
the Local Dimension of Welfare-to-Work**

18-19 November 1998, Sheffield, United Kingdom

**Organised jointly by the Organisation for Economic Co-operation
and Development (OECD) and the Department for Education and
Employment (DfEE), UK, with support from the
German Marshall Fund of the United States**

Rationale

High levels of unemployment and social exclusion in many OECD countries
have led governments to experiment with new labour market policies involving
a common shift from passive income support to more active approaches, which
act on employability and skills in order to help the excluded to find
employment. This type of approach, often termed welfare-to-work, relies
increasingly on local organisations and partnerships to design, develop and run
appropriate programmes.

The purpose of this conference is to examine the local dimension to welfare-to-
work policies in OECD countries and to spread international experience on
effective approaches and tools. Recent innovations in the United Kingdom will
be presented - the New Deal and Employment Zones - and compared with
initiatives in other OECD countries that share this local delivery dimension.

Conference Themes

The following questions will be asked:

- To what extent is policy design at a local level pursued in OECD countries, what are the strengths and weaknesses of this approach, and what is the appropriate balance between local and central agencies?

- How effective are local partnership mechanisms in stimulating policy innovation, adapting policies to local conditions and mobilising social partners?

- What locally based policy tools work well in promoting the employability of unemployed and inactive people, and in reducing welfare dependence?

CONFERENCE PROGRAMME

Wednesday 18 November - Site visits

Accompanied site visits in and around Sheffield. The visits took into account local experience of the welfare-to-work programme in helping combat unemployment and social exclusion. Delegates also had the opportunity to speak to individuals on each site.

Thursday 19 November - Conference

Chair of morning session - Kenneth Kerr, LEED Bureau member, Canada

8.45	Registration	
	Session 1 The importance of the local dimension in welfare-to-work	
9.15	An overview of the international trends and issues	*Herwig Schlögl, Deputy Secretary-General, OECD*
	Session 2 Recent policy innovations in the UK	
9.30	The local aspects of the New Deal: methods of achieving local innovation and first results	*Roger Lasko, Regional Director, Yorkshire and Humber Employment Service, UK*
9.45	Local partnerships: a key element of the New Deal	
	Lessons from local partnerships in the UK	*Professor Mike Campbell, Director, Policy Research Institute, Leeds Metropolitan University, UK*

	Co-operation with partners: advantages and trade-offs for the Employment Service	*Diane Headley, District Manager, Wearside Employment Service, City of Sunderland, UK*
	The point of view of the private sector: motives, obstacles	*John Deighan, Area Director and General Manager of Swallow Hotels, an employer member of a New Deal local partnership, UK*
	General Discussion	
10.45	Break	
11.10	The impact of greater flexibility: the Employment Zone experience	
	Aims, instruments and impacts of Employment Zone policy	*Mark Bilsborough, Department for Education and Employment, UK*
	Local innovations, success factors and barriers	*Dave Simmonds, Centre for Social Inclusion, UK*
	General discussion	
12.10	Developments and issues in welfare-to-work in the UK	*The Rt. Hon. Andrew Smith, Minister for Employment, Welfare-to-Work and Equal Opportunities, UK*
12.30	Lunch	

Chair of afternoon session - Paavo Saikkonen, LEED Bureau member, Finland

Session 3   The policy context in other OECD countries

13.30   A different approach to welfare-to-work

Introductory presentation: A comparative overview of selected OECD countries

Dr. Dan Finn, Portsmouth University, UK

Panel discussion, facilitated by *Paul Cullen, Chairman of the LEED Committee*, on lessons that can be drawn from the different approaches taken in different OECD countries

Lyn Hogan, Vice President for Policy and Planning, Welfare-to-Work Partnership, Washington, USA

Ging Wong, Human Resources Development, Canada

Matelda Grassi, President, ItaliaLavoro, Italy

Paul Plunkett, Director, Work for the Dole, Department of Employment, Education, Training and Youth Affairs, Australia

Mark Greenberg, Centre for Law and Social Policy, Washington, USA

General discussion

15.00   Break

15.25   **Session 4   Social enterprises: a tool for re-integration in the labour market**

A brief summary of Intermediate Labour Market experiments in the UK

Alistair Grimes, Manager, Community Enterprise, Glasgow, UK

Lessons from social enterprises in Europe and their potential as a local development tool to promote integration into the labour market

Professor Carlo Borzaga, Trento University, Italy

The case of France, which has developed a considerable expertise in social enterprises for the re-integration of the long-term unemployed

Vincent Delpey, Ministry for Employment and Solidarity, France

General discussion

16.40   **Session 5   Assessing innovations: perspectives for the future**

Panel discussion, chaired by *Dr Robert Butcher, Department for Education and Employment, UK*

John Greenwood, Executive Director, Social Research and Demonstration Corporation, Canada

Norman Bowers, Head of Division, Directorate for Education, Employment, Labour and Social Affairs, OECD

Mike Allen, General Secretary, Irish National Organisation of the Unemployed, Ireland

*Hugh Tollyfield, Head of Job
Seeker Advice and Adjudication,
Employment Service, UK*

*Robert Straits, W. E. Upjohn
Institute for Employment
Research, USA*

General discussion

17.50   Session 6   Closing comments

*Sergio Arzeni, Head of the LEED
Programme, OECD*

**19.45   Reception hosted by the Rt Hon David Blunkett, MP, Secretary of
State for Education and Employment**

OECD PUBLICATIONS, 2, rue André-Pascal, 75775 PARIS CEDEX 16
PRINTED IN FRANCE
(04 1999 06 1 P) ISBN 92-64-17065-0 – No. 50925 1999